Debrett's
Kings and Queens
of Britain

A portrait of Queen Elizabeth I by or after George Gower, Serjeant Painter to the Queen. The painting was probably made to commemorate the defeat of the Spanish Armada in 1588, and a naval battle scene can be discerned in the background.

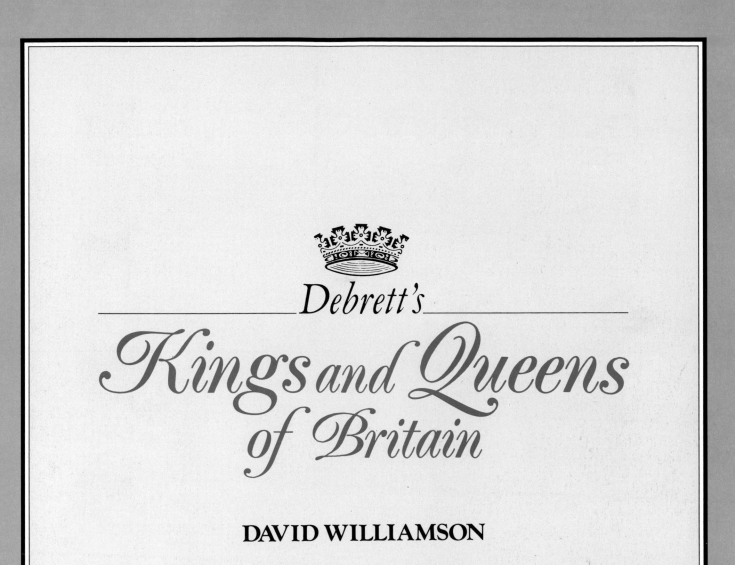

Debrett's
Kings and Queens
of Britain

DAVID WILLIAMSON

Webb & Bower

MICHAEL JOSEPH

First published in Great Britain 1986 by
Webb & Bower (Publishers) Limited
9 Colleton Crescent, Exeter, Devon EX2 4BY

in association with Michael Joseph Limited
27 Wright's Lane, London W8 5SL

Designed by Vic Giolitto

Production by Nick Facer

Picture research by Anne-Marie Ehrlich

Tables by Malcolm Couch

Copyright © David Williamson

British Library Cataloguing in Publication Data

Williamson, David
    Debrett's Kings & Queens of Britain.
    1. Great Britain—Kings and rulers
    I. Title
    941'.009'92   DA28.1

ISBN 0-86350-101-X

Typeset in Great Britain by P&M Typesetting Ltd, Exeter, Devon

Printed and bound in Hong Kong by Mandarin Offset International Ltd.

CONTENTS

To
The Memory
of
My Father
Geoffrey Williamson

INTRODUCTION

This book is not a history of England; neither is it a biographical dictionary, though the elements of history and biography are both to be found here. It is an attempt to set the characters of the very varied men and women, who as sovereigns or consorts have reigned over this country, against the background of their times and to show how they were affected by heredity, family connections, environment, illness and politics to act as they did. Above all, it is an attempt to show them as ordinary human beings with the same feelings, passions and failings as any other man or woman. If I seem to have dwelt over long on medical details and deathbeds, it is because these were matters of absorbing interest to our ancestors who recorded them more minutely than things we might consider more important today. More often than not, however, such details do give us an insight into the characters of the individuals concerned which cannot be gleaned elsewhere.

For obvious reasons, it is very hard to put flesh on the bare bones of many of those early kings and queens for whose lives we have to rely on bare statements of fact, and for this reason a detailed treatment of each individual only commences with the Conquest. What we do know of earlier sovereigns, from the ancient Britons onwards, has been dealt with in the first three sections. The sketches of the individual sovereigns are preceded by what might be termed their 'vital statistics'

and every effort has been made to ensure the accuracy of the dates and other details. All proper names have been given in their English forms or in the forms by which they are most familiar to English readers. For example, in the case of French kings, 'Louis' is preferred to 'Lewis', but 'Philip' to 'Philippe'; in the case of Spanish kings, 'Pedro' is preferred to 'Peter', but 'Ferdinand' to 'Fernando' and 'Philip' to 'Felipe'. I make no apology for such seeming inconsistencies.

It is almost essential for a work of this nature to include some genealogical tables and these have been set out as clearly and succinctly as possible in Appendix B. They have been designed to show the connecting links of each house or dynasty and complement the main text by demonstrating how the blood lines of Saxons, Normans, Danes, Irish, Scottish and Welsh rulers have converged into one channel.

I would like to thank all those who have helped me with their comments and suggestions in the writing of this book, especially Charles Kidd, the late Patrick Montague-Smith, Robert Golden, Morris Bierbrier, Arthur Addington and Christopher Quaile, and a very special thanks to Anne Brennan, who deciphered my scrawl and produced a typescript in a third of the time it would have taken me.

DAVID WILLIAMSON

KINGSHIP IN ANCIENT BRITAIN

Geoffrey of Monmouth, writing in the first half of the twelfth century, sought to tell the story of Britain from its mythical foundation by Brutus the Trojan until the coming of the Saxons. The vast scope of his narrative may be compared to that of James Michener's *Hawaii*, a work equally fictitious which was written for similar reasons, namely to explain the growth of a nation and to entertain at the same time.

Geoffrey claimed that his *History of the Kings of Britain* was translated from 'a certain very ancient book written in the British language' which had been given to him by Walter, Archdeacon of Oxford. It was dedicated to two of the leading noblemen of the day, Robert, Earl of Gloucester (*d.* 1147), an illegitimate son of King Henry I, and Waleran, Count of Mellent (*d.* 1166). In it he tells of the wanderings of Brutus, the great-grandson of Aeneas, forced to leave Italy after accidentally killing his father and eventually, after many adventures, coming to Albion, which he renamed Britain from his own name,

after driving out the aboriginal giants. The story continues with the fabulous deeds of Brutus's descendants and successors from about 1100 BC until the coming of the Romans, when fact begins to blend with fiction. The list of Geoffrey's fabulous kings will be found in Appendix A.

Lewis Thorpe's introduction to his translation of Geoffrey's *History* points out that it might 'be said to bear the same relationship to the story of the early British inhabitants of our own island as do the seventeen historical books in the Old Testament, from Genesis to Esther, to the early history of the Israelites in Palestine'. What, then, was the true story? Of the original inhabitants of Britain we know nothing. It was probably

Stonehenge. This view gives some idea of the majesty of the brooding stone monument set on Salisbury Plain. The stones were quarried in the Wiltshire Downs and brought by water on rafts and overland on rollers to their present site, a remarkable piece of engineering for a primitive people to accomplish.

peopled by nomadic tribes seeking new hunting fields and moving northwards and westwards during the time when Britain was still joined to Continental Europe by land. These people, whoever they were, were eventually displaced and superseded by the Celts.

Herodotus (484-407 BC) calls the British Isles the *Cassiteriades*, or Tin Islands, from whence tin was imported to the Mediterranean. A century or so later the Greek traveller Pytheas visited Britain and described its rich agriculture of cattle and sheep farming, its metal workers, pottery makers, wool spinners and weavers. The Britons of whom he wrote were Celts, those ancient people who migrated westwards from their original home in eastern Europe until they were spread across most of the Continent. They were a mixture of several races which had come to form a linguistic group, eventually dividing into the Brythonic or 'P Celtic' and the Goidelic or 'Q Celtic'. The Welsh, Breton and Cornish languages derived from the first; the Irish, Manx and Gaelic from the second. To give an example of the two, the word for son was *map* in 'P Celtic' and *mac* in 'Q Celtic'.

Scholars now believe that the Celts may have reached Britain as early as 2000 BC and that further waves of immigration from the Continent took place over the succeeding centuries. If so, it has been argued, they were the people responsible for the building of Stonehenge, that ancient, brooding monument on Salisbury Plain, whose origin and purpose have been matters of speculation and theorizing for over two millennia and will doubtless remain so till the end of time.

When Julius Caesar arrived in Britain in the late August of 55 BC, he found a land divided into several kingdoms enjoying a high standard of civilization with an organized society, a pantheon of Celtic gods and goddesses, and a plentiful coinage in gold, silver and bronze. The tribes were ruled by kings (and in some cases queens) and dynasties had been established, some holding sway in both Britain and Gaul.

To deal with the threat from Rome, several tribes had banded together in a loose confederation headed by Caswallon (whom Caesar called Cassivellaunus), the King of the Catuvellauni, a tribe whose territory lay north of the Thames. Their tribal capital was at what we now call Wheathampstead, near St Albans. The Catuvellauni (also known as the Cassi) had migrated from Gaul in the second or third century BC. Caswallon had fought with neighbouring tribes and came to be regarded as high king of Britain. He commanded a chariot force and joined with other tribes such as the Atrebates, the Cantii and the Trinovantes in operating a 'scorched earth' policy in the face of Caesar's advancing army and was so successful that Caesar felt Britain was not worth the battle and withdrew in September 54 BC. Caswallon continued to reign peacefully for several years

A sculptured head of Julius Caesar in the Museo Barracco at Rome.

and moved his capital to Verulamium. He was succeeded by Androco, perhaps his son, whose reign seems to have been short and who was succeeded by Tasciovanus, perhaps also a son of Caswallon. He enjoyed the same prestige as Caswallon and died about AD 10, when he was succeeded by his son Cunobelinus, Shakespeare's Cymbeline, whose name in Celtic signifies 'The Hound of Bel', Bel being an important Celtic god. He again moved the capital to Camulodunum (the fort of Camulos, the patron god of the Catuvellauni), the modern Colchester, and issued a plentiful coinage in gold and silver. His fame was such that it was known in Rome and it was only after his death in AD 43 that Claudius felt the time was ripe to begin the conquest of Britain.

Opposition to the Romans was led by Cunobelin's son Caradoc (Caractacus to the Romans), who, after a resistance of nine years, was forced to take refuge with the Brigantes of Yorkshire, only to be betrayed by their Queen Cartimandua, who delivered him in chains to the Romans. Caradoc was taken with his wife and children to grace a Roman triumph. On seeing the marvels of

A group of Celtic coins: (a) reverse of a gold stater of Cunobelinus, King of the Catuvellauni; (b) obverse of a silver coin of Epatticus, son of Tasciovanus and brother of Cunobelinus; (c) reverse of a gold stater of Commius; King of the Atrebates; (d) reverse of a coin of Tincommius, son of Commius. These coins date from the first century BC and the first century AD and are based on Greek and Roman coin types.

Rome he is said to have remarked: 'It is strange, indeed, that a people who have so many and such rich possessions of their own should envy me and mine. It is strange that the owners of these palaces should desire to drive us from our poor hovels.' Rome treated Caradoc with magnanimity, but it is not known if he was ever allowed to return to Britain.

The Brigantes were another Celtic tribe who emigrated to Britain from the Continent and established themselves in a large area of Yorkshire. Ptolemy lists nine Brigantian towns, one of which was Eboracum (now York). The Brigantian gold coinage reveals the names of several rulers – Volisios, Dumnocoveros and Cartimandua, believed to have been father, son and granddaughter. Cartimandua was reigning at the time of the Roman conquest and is the queen who betrayed Caradoc. As some accounts refer to her as his stepmother, it would seem that she had at one time been married to Cunobelin. By AD 51, however, she was the wife of one Venutius, a native Brigantian, whose military prowess in fighting the Romans is mentioned by Tacitus. Cartimandua's inclination to favour the conquerors led to discord between her and her husband and their divorce or separation. Cartimandua joined the Roman camp and acquired another husband in the person of Vellocatus, her standard-bearer. Thereafter, she disappears from history.

The rulers of several other Celtic tribes must be mentioned. Commius, King of the Atrebates in Gaul, was conquered by Caesar in 57 BC. He crossed to Britain and established his tribe in the south central region. On his death his dominions were divided between his three sons, Eppillus, who received north-east Kent, Tincommius, who received Sussex, and Verica, who received the main tribal lands in Hampshire. All three struck coins. A later Verica, who ruled Surrey and Sussex, was deposed in the time of Claudius and went to Rome to beg the Emperor to help restore him to his kingdom.

In accordance with their usual policy, the Romans allowed the rulers who submitted to them to enjoy a certain amount of autonomy as 'client kings', their position being anomalous to that of an African 'paramount chief' in colonial days. One such was Cogidubnus, King of the Regni, perhaps a grandson of the older Verica, whose subservience brought him, or enabled him to build, the vast and magnificent palace at Fishbourne, near Chichester, which has been excavated comparatively recently. He proudly styled himself 'Tiberius Claudius Cogidubnus, Legate of the Emperor in Britain'.

Another 'client king' was Prasutagus, King of the Iceni in Suffolk and Norfolk. On his death in AD 60 he appointed Rome joint heir of his kingdom with his two daughters. The unfortunate girls were raped by some

Boadicea haranging her troops. A somewhat fanciful 18th century print in which the warrior Queen looks more like a figure from the French Revolution. Note her weeping daughters, the white haired and bearded druid and the fierce and stalwart warriors.

Boadicea in her chariot. A sihouette of the statue on the embankment at Westminster.

Roman officers and their mother, on violently protesting at this outrage, was jeered at and flogged. This goaded her into gathering her tribesmen together and heading an armed rebellion against the newly established Roman rule. She has gone down in history as 'Queen Boadicea', but the Celtic form of her name was probably something like Boudicca. Tacitus describes her fierce, ruddy countenance, her flowing red hair, her harsh voice and her red cloak so that we can picture her as she stands in her chariot, flanked by her daughters, urging on her forces. The Roman governor, Suetonius Paulinus, was absent in Anglesey, and Boadicea was able to capture Camulodunum and Londinium, killing, it is said, 80,000 Romans and their allies in the process. Only the return of Suetonius turned the tide. The Britons were defeated with great slaughter and Boadicea ended her life by taking poison in AD 62. Her revolt was the last against Roman rule in Britain which had been firmly established in the course of nineteen years and was to last for over three hundred.

ROMAN BRITAIN AND THE ENGLISH SETTLEMENT

It must not be supposed that kingship entirely disappeared from Britain during the period of Roman occupation. In the early days there were the 'client kings' who submitted to Rome and received suitable rewards for their subservience. This had become a common practice throughout the Roman Empire and enabled the Roman governors to exercise their power more easily by giving a semblance of continuity in government. One such king is mentioned by Bede, in his *History of the English Church and People*, as Lucius, who wrote to Pope Eleutherius (174–189) asking to become a Christian. The request was granted 'and the Britons received the Faith and held it peacefully in all its purity and fullness until the time of the Emperor Diocletian.' Geoffrey of Monmouth has 'lifted' Lucius from Bede and added the detail that he died without issue and an interregnum of about 150 years followed.

Several Roman emperors visited Britain, including Septimius Severus, who spent the last three years of his life here and died at York on 4 February 211. The persecutions of Diocletian (284–305) put a temporary end to Christianity throughout the Empire, but it revived again under Constantine the Great, whose mother Helena was allegedly the finder of the True Cross. She was long fondly claimed to be a British princess, the daughter of 'Old King Cole', no less.

The Romans occupied the whole of England and Wales but were unable to penetrate very far into Scotland. The terrain and the fierce tribesmen persuaded them it was not worth the battle and the great engineering feats of Antonine's Wall and Hadrian's Wall were erected to maintain and guard the northern border from the raids of the Picts and Caledonii. Ireland was left alone. After the Roman withdrawal from Britain the walls were unguarded and, incursions from the north becoming more frequent, the Britons vainly petitioned Rome for help in repelling invaders.

Kingship reappeared in Britain after the Romans left and in the first half of the fifth century southern Britain was ruled by a king known as Vortigern (not a personal name, but a title probably signifying 'overlord'). Unable to protect his borders, he sought the aid of mercenaries from the Continent. The traditional date for the arrival of the brothers Hengest and Horsa and their three long-ships is 449, but it is now believed to have been

some years earlier. They landed at Ebbsfleet in Kent and received a grant of land from Vortigern in return for their services against the Picts. In a few years they had fallen out with Vortigern and, in a battle fought at Aylesford, wrested Kent from the Britons. Horsa was killed in the battle, but Hengest was joined by his son Æsc and in the following year they drove the Britons out of Kent altogether in a battle fought at Crayford.

Later in the century, other Angles, Saxons and Jutes arrived: Ælle with his three sons Cymen, Wlencing and Cissa to settle in Sussex; Cerdic and his son Cynric to establish the Kingdom of Wessex; and other settlers to

Hadrian. The head and right hand of a statue of the Emperor Hadrian found in the Thames at London.

The obverse of a silver sestertius of the Emperor Hadrian. Roman coins attained a high standard of portraiture which only became debased towards the end of the Empire.

A section of Hadrian's Wall at Cuddy's Crag, Northumberland. The wall was constructed to repel marauding parties of Picts and Scots from making incursions into Roman occupied Britain.

establish kingdoms throughout England. The kingdoms so established are known in history as the heptarchy (i.e. the seven kingdoms, although the number varied and there were sometimes more and sometimes less). Although the kingdoms were quite independent of each other they formed a loosely knit confederation under the leadership of one king, usually the most powerful among them, who was elected as a sort of head king with the title of Bretwalda. The seven Bretwaldas listed by Bede were:

Ælla, King of the South Saxons (Sussex)
Ceawlin, King of the West Saxons (Wessex)
Ethelbert I, King of Kent
Redwald, King of the East Angles
Edwin, King of Northumbria
Oswald, King of Northumbria
Oswy, King of Northumbria

The founders of the Anglo-Saxon kingdoms all claimed descent from Woden, a semi-mythical god-king, who, if a real person, must have lived in the second or third century AD. Their royal pedigrees have been critically examined by Mr Kenneth Sisam and his conclusions can be found in *The Proceedings of the British Academy*, Volume XXXIX (1953).

British resistance to the Saxons in the fifth and early

sixth centuries was led by the legendary hero King Arthur, whose deeds form the central theme of Geoffrey of Monmouth's *History* and whose existence and exact status have provoked speculation and controversy to the present day.

THE KINGDOM OF KENT

The first Anglo-Saxon kingdom to be founded was also the first to receive Christianity. King Ethelbert I, Hengest's great-great-grandson (see Table II in Appendix B), married a Frankish princess, Bertha, daughter of the Merovingian King of Paris, Caribert 1. She was a Christian and was allowed to bring her chaplain to Kent with her and practise her religion.

Meanwhile, we are told, Pope Gregory the Great had seen some fair haired, blue-eyed children for sale in the slave market at Rome and enquiring whence they came was told that they were Angli. 'Non Angli, sed Angeli' (not Angles, but Angels), said the impressionable Pope

and resolved forthwith that the nation of the beautiful children should receive the light of the Gospel. One hopes that he opened his purse and bought them, too. This story is not told by Bede and is probably apocryphal but, be that as it may, Gregory despatched the monk Augustine to England. King Ethelbert already knew something of Christianity from his wife and agreed to receive Augustine and his party and hear what they had to say. He was an easy convert, being half-way there already, and granted Augustine a residence in the Royal City of Canterbury, of which Augustine became the first Archbishop after visiting France for consecration by the Archbishop of Arles.

King Ethelbert died on 24 February 616. Bertha had predeceased him and he had married again. His son and successor Eadbald (supposedly Bertha's son, too, but possibly the offspring of an earlier wife of Ethelbert) lapsed into paganism and took his stepmother to wife. He was eventually brought to repentance by Augustine's successor Laurence and put away his stepmother, restored Christianity and, like his father before him, married a Frankish princess. Thereafter he led an

Septimius Severus, the Roman Emperor who died at York in 211. This very fine portrait head is in the Vatican Museum.

An interesting French print of Carausius, a Roman Admiral of lowly origin, who seized power and proclaimed himself Emperor in Britain in 287. He reigned until 293, when he was overthrown and murdered by the equally obscure Allectus, Prefect of the Guards. The coins of Carausius are very numerous.

CARAUSIUS EMPEREUR DE LA GRANDE BRETAGNE.

De l'Hercule Romain je domptay la fierté,
Je rendis aux Bretons leur chere liberté,
Je fis par ma valeur trembler la Terre et l'onde,
Si le traitre Allectus, envieux de mon sort,
Pour prix de mes bienfaits n'eut avancé ma mort,
J'aurois pû parvenir a l'Empire du Monde.

exemplary life and the kings of Kent became renowned for their piety and the number of saintly abbesses to be found among their princesses. The blood of the Oiscings, as the Royal House of Kent became known from its second head, probably flows today in the veins of our present sovereign (see Appendix B).

THE KINGDOM OF NORTHUMBRIA

The powerful northern Kingdom of Northumbria alternated in the rule of two royal houses, those of Deira and Bernicia. One of the greatest early English rulers and the fifth Bretwalda was Edwin (616–633), who in 625 married as his second wife Princess Ethelburga of Kent, the daughter of Ethelbert and Bertha. Under her influence he was converted to Christianity and was baptized at York by St Paulinus on 12 April 627. Six years later he was killed in battle with Cadwallon, King of Gwynedd, and Penda, King of Mercia, on 14 October 633. Queen Ethelburga returned to Kent where she became Abbess of Lyminge and died in 647. The Kingdom of Deira, which was Edwin's patrimony, was finally united with Bernicia in 654.

The next great King of Northumbria and sixth Bretwalda was Edwin's nephew Oswald, of the Bernician line, who was defeated and killed by King Penda of

Mercia at Oswestry in August 641. He was succeeded by his brother (or half-brother) Oswy as King of Northumbria and seventh Bretwalda. Oswy annexed the neighbouring Kingdom of Mercia and also conquered the Britons of Strathclyde, the Scots of Dalriada and a large part of the Pictish Kingdom. His second wife was Edwin and Ethelburga's daughter Eanflaed, and she became the mother of his successor Egfrith. Oswy died on 15 February 670. The Northumbrian Kingdom existed another two hundred years, but very little is known of the later kings beyond their names.

THE KINGDOM OF MERCIA

The Kingdom of Mercia, which seems to have been established about 585, first became prominent under the great pagan warrior King Penda, who was defeated and killed by Oswy of Northumbria at *Winwidfeld* on 15 November 654. His sons became Christians and it was his second son Wulfhere who was to restore Mercian independence in 657 and greatly enlarge his kingdom before his death in 675. His brother and successor, Ethelred, abdicated and became a monk in 704 and was followed by a succession of comparatively unremarkable kings (with the exception of Ethelbald) until Offa ascended the throne in 757. He brought practically the whole of England under his sway and was addressed as 'King of the English' by Pope Adrian I. Among his achievements were the construction of Offa's Dyke, an

A medieval manuscript in the British Library showing King Offa of Mercia in battle.

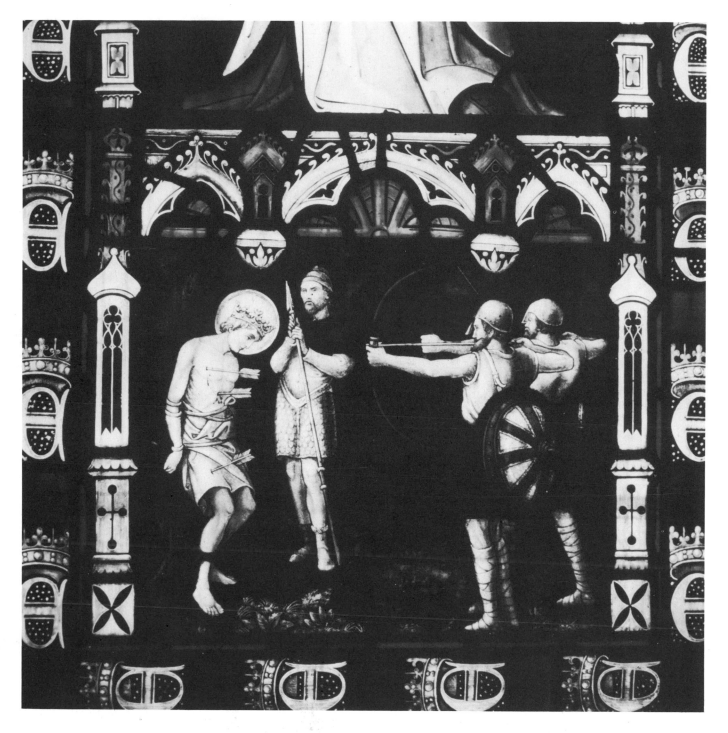

The martyrdom of St Edmund, last King of East Anglia, depicted in a stained glass window at Greensted Church, Essex.

earthwork stretching from the Wye to the Dee to withhold the incursions of Welsh marauders, and the compilation of a code of laws which were later adapted by Alfred the Great. Offa struck a handsome coinage and the head of his Queen Cynethryth also appears on some of his coins. This is unique in England and doubtless emphasizes Offa's imperial aspirations, as the Roman emperors had been in the habit of depicting their wives and other members of their families on the coinage. Offa also took the unprecedented step (for England) of having his only son Egfrith anointed king in his father's lifetime in 787. Offa died on 29 July 796 and Egfrith's reign sadly only lasted for 141 days. He died on 17 December 796 and was succeeded by a distant kinsman. Several more kings reigned in Mercia, but they were nonentities for the most part, and the last, Ceolwulf II, was deposed sometime before 883. The blood of the Mercian kings has probably passed into the veins of our later sovereigns through the wife of Alfred the Great, whose likely ancestry will be found in the tables in Appendix B.

Cynewulf, King of Wessex, from the Chronicle of Abingdon.

Queen Ethelswith, wife of Ine, whom she accompanied to Rome in 726, another imaginary portrait from the Chronicle of Abingdon.

THE KINGDOM OF EAST ANGLIA

The East Anglian kings were known as the Wuffings from Wuffa, whom Roger of Wendover reckoned as the first king (reigning *ca* 571–578). His grandson Redwald was the fourth Bretwalda and is almost certainly the king whose magnificent ship burial was excavated at Sutton Hoo in this century. He was a pagan but his immediate successors appear to have been Christians, although no details of the conversion of East Anglia have come down to us. The next memorable King of East Anglia was Anna, who bred a family of female saints and abbesses. He died in 654 and his brother and successor Æthelhere was killed by Oswy of Northumbria the same year. A series of shadowy kings continued to reign until East Anglia was conquered by the Danes in about 880. The last king, Edmund, was barbarously murdered for refusing to renounce Christianity, and later canonized. He is the saint of Bury St Edmunds.

THE KINGDOM OF SUSSEX

The genealogy of the kings of Sussex has not been preserved. Beyond the fact that Ælle, the founder of the kingdom, is reckoned as the first Bretwalda and was succeeded by his son Cissa in about 514, little is known apart from a few mentions of some subsequent kings.

THE KINGDOM OF ESSEX

The first King of Essex, according to Henry of Huntingdom, was Æscwine (reigned *ca* 527–587). His son and successor Sledda (to whom William of Malmesbury ascribes the founding of the kingdom) married Ricole, the sister of King Ethelbert I of Kent. Their son Saebert, the first King of Essex named as such by the Anglo-Saxon Chronicle and Bede, emulated his maternal uncle by converting to Christianity and being baptized by Mellitus, Bishop of London about 604. His

Ine, King of Wessex, an imaginary portrait from the Chronicle of Abingdon ca 1220. Note the serpentine arms of the throne on which the King is seated. This manuscript is in the British Library.

sons reverted to paganism, but Essex was reconverted to Christianity by St Cedd in the reign of King Sigeberht II in 653. The kings of Essex made no great mark on history and the kingdom was annexed to Wessex in 825.

THE KINGDOM OF WESSEX

The Kingdom of Wessex, which was eventually to absorb all the other Saxon kingdoms, was founded by Cerdic, who came to Britain with his son Cynric and five ships in 495 and in 519 'obtained the Kingdom of the West Saxons', in the words of the Anglo-Saxon Chronicle.

The Franks Casket, a whalebone ivory casket of Northumbrian workmanship dating from the early 8th century. The panels give some idea of the dress of the period.

Their descendants were much given to alliterative names beginning with the letter C. The third King of Wessex, Ceawlin (590–593), is listed by Bede as the second Bretwalda or acknowledged overlord of the southern English. The first Christian king was Cynegils, who was baptized by Birinus, Bishop of Dorchester in 635. The Kingdom of Wessex provides the only instance of a Saxon queen regnant in the person of Seaxburgh, who succeeded her husband Cenwalh in 672 and reigned for about two years. King Ine (reigned 688–726) founded the monastery of Glastonbury before abdicating and going to Rome, a not unusual practice for Saxon kings. He was followed by others of whom little is recorded beyond the fact that their ancestry went back to Cerdic. Beorhtric, who became king in 786, married Offa of Mercia's daughter Eadburh in 789 and was accidentally poisoned by her in 802. To expiate her inadvertent crime the Queen went on pilgrimage to Rome and died a beggar at Pavia *en route*. Her deed is said to have so horrified her countrymen that they decreed that no woman should again be honoured as *regina*, the king's wife merely to be known as consort or companion. The Saxon word for this was *cwen*, whence our 'queen'. Beorhtric was succeeded by another scion of the House of Cerdic, Egbert, with whom we commence another chapter.

The Kings of Wessex and All England

'King Beorhtric passed away . . . and Egbert succeeded to the Kingdom of Wessex', the Anglo-Saxon Chronicle tells us. As a young man, Egbert must have evinced some aspirations which led Offa, King of Mercia, and his son-in-law Beorhtric, King of Wessex, to expel him from England. He took refuge at the Frankish court of Charlemagne and it was there apparently that he met and married his wife, Raedburh (more euphoniously written as Redburga), who was alleged to be a close relation (perhaps a niece) of Charlemagne. Egbert returned to England and seems to have succeeded to the throne peacefully.

The Chronicle has nothing more to say of him for over twenty years, then in 825 he fought a battle at Ellendun, near Wroughton in Wiltshire, with Beornwulf, King of Mercia, in which he 'was victorious, and great slaughter was made there.' Following this victory, Egbert sent his son Ethelwulf into Kent 'with a great force, and they drove King Baldred north over Thames, and the Kentishmen submitted to him, and the men of Surrey and Sussex and Essex . . . And the same year the King of the East Angles and the court turned to King Egbert as their protector and guardian against the fear of Mercian aggression; and . . . the East Angles slew Beornwulf, King of the Mercians.' Two more shadowy kings reigned in Mercia in quick succession, then in 829 Egbert 'conquered Mercia and all that was south of the Humber', thereby becoming acknowledged as the eighth *Bretwalda* or 'Ruler of Britain'. He also made incursions into Northumbria and Wales, both of which submitted to him and paid tribute.

His final years were spent dealing with Danish invaders in the south and west, who allied themselves with the Cornish. The doughty old warrior put them to flight at Hingston Down. Egbert must have been well into his sixties when he died in the second half of 839 after a reign of 'thirty-seven years and seven months'. He was buried at Winchester.

Ethelwulf, who succeeded his father, had been sub-king in Kent, Essex, Sussex and Surrey since 825, so was well versed in government. On succeeding to the larger kingdom, the sub-kingship was taken over by Athelstan, who was either Ethelwulf's eldest son or, perhaps more likely, his younger brother. Ethelwulf spent the greater part of his reign dealing with the Danish marauders whose raids were made in increasing numbers.

His first wife was Osburh (Osburga), daughter of Ealdorman Oslac of Hampshire, the royal cup-bearer, a descendant of Cerdic's nephew Wihtgar, who had been settled in the Isle of Wight. She bore him at least four sons and one daughter, Ethelswith, who was married in 853 to her father's ally Burhed, King of Mercia. Osburga seems to have died soon after this event and the sorrowing Ethelwulf resigned his kingdom to his son Ethelbald and went on a pilgrimage to Rome, taking with him his youngest son Alfred, a boy of some eight years old, who had already been to Rome three years before we are told.

They were well received by Pope Leo IV who administered the rite of confirmation to Alfred, an act mistakenly taken by Asser, King Alfred's biographer, to be a consecration to future kingship, which was hardly foreseeable as Alfred had three elder brothers living. Ethelwulf and Alfred stayed in Rome for a year and on the return journey stopped at the court of Charles the Bald, King of the Franks and Charlemagne's grandson. Charles had a daughter Judith, who could not have been more than twelve or thirteen, and he gave her in marriage to Ethelwulf, the wedding being solemnized at Verberie-sur-Oise on 1 October 856. Ethelwulf returned home 'in good health' and died over a year later on 13 January 858. He was buried first at Steyning in Sussex, but was later removed to Winchester.

Ethelbald took over the Kingdom of Wessex on his father's resignation in 855, but only gained full control

Wimborne Minster, the burial place of King Ethelred I, whose tomb is marked by a late medieval brass.

on his father's death in 858. The only thing recorded of him is that he married his stepmother Judith, but was forced to put her away by the Church which frowned upon such 'incestuous' marriages. He died in the summer of 860 and was buried at Sherborne Abbey.

Judith returned to her father's court in France and later married Baldwin II, Count of Flanders, becoming an ancestor of William the Conqueror's queen, Matilda.

ETHELBERT   860–865

Ethelbert succeeded his brother, having been sub-king in Kent, Essex, Sussex and Surrey since 858. He died, apparently unmarried, in 865 and was buried at Sherborne Abbey.

ETHELRED 1   865–871

Ethelwulf's third son succeeded his brother Ethelbert and spent his whole reign fighting the Danish invaders, in which he was ably assisted by his youngest brother Alfred. Some time after Easter (15 April) 871, Ethelred was wounded at Merton and died of his injuries. He was buried in Wimborne Minster, where his grave is marked by a brass, made centuries later, representing a crowned king in ermine-trimmed robes.

Ethelred was married and had two sons, Ethelhelm and Ethelwold, but they were considered too young to reign and he was succeeded by his brother Alfred.

ALFRED THE GREAT   871–899

Alfred is the only English king (Canute was Danish) to

Alfred the Great's statue at Wantage, his birthplace. The statue was erected in 1901 to mark the supposed millenium of Alfred's death, then believed to have taken place in 901. It was later discovered that the Anglo-Saxon Chronicle had made an error in reckoning and the true date was 899.

have been designated 'the Great' and also the first to have a contemporary biographer in the person of Asser, the Welsh-born Bishop of Sherborne. Alfred was born at the royal manor of Wantage in Berkshire (now re-located in Oxfordshire) in 849, according to Asser, but elsewhere he is stated to have been twenty-three years old at his accession, implying a date of 847 or 848, which seems more likely in view of his early prowess against the Danes.

Alfred's great love of learning, which was to be manifested in later life, is said to have been inculcated by his mother who showed her sons a beautifully illuminated book of poetry and promised to give it to the first one to learn to read it. Alfred was the winner. While still in his teens, Alfred became the right hand of his brother King Ethelred and proved himself an able commander in the struggle against the Vikings. In 868 he married Ealhswith, the daughter of Ethelred Mucil, Ealdorman of the Gaini (a Mercian tribal group), and Eadburh (or Eadburga), a descendant of the Royal House of Mercia (see Appendix B, Table 8). She bore him a large family, of whom two sons and three daughters survived infancy.

When Alfred succeeded his brother Ethelwulf as king in April 871, the country was largely overrun by Danish invaders. A month after his accession he won a victory at Wilton and followed it up with a number of other successful skirmishes in the south of England, but within two years the Danes had most of Mercia and Northumbria in their grasp. Alfred's brother-in-law, King Burhed of Mercia, was driven out and went to Rome, where he died. After winning a sea battle in 875, Alfred concluded an uneasy and short-lived peace treaty with the invaders in 876. Further incursions into Devon soon followed and 'the host', as the Anglo-Saxon Chronicle terms the invaders, took refuge in Exeter where more peace negotiations took place. They withdrew to Mercia in the autumn of 877.

Alfred retired with his army into the island of Athelney, an inaccessible marshy area of Somerset. To this period belongs the story of Alfred disguising himself as a wandering harper and entering the Danish camp to gain vital knowledge of the enemy. Also attributed to this time is the story of the King taking refuge in a swineherd's hut and being soundly berated by the swineherd's wife for burning the cakes she had set him to watch.

Alfred left Athelney in May 878 and led his army into Wiltshire, being joined by large contingents from Somerset, Wiltshire and Hampshire. He met the Danes at *Ethandune* (Edington) and gained a resounding victory, driving the enemy back into their stronghold at Chippenham. The peace terms were settled a few weeks later, the Danes agreeing to withdraw from Wessex and return into East Anglia, Mercia and Northumbria, which were ceded to them and became known as the Danelaw. Their leader, Guthrum, accepted Christianity and Alfred stood sponsor at his baptism, giving him the name of Athelstan.

Over the next few years Alfred consolidated his kingdom, reorganizing the army, strengthening the defences, encouraging learning and religion and codifying laws. Alfred was a polymath and could turn his hand to most things, including the translation of classical texts and the invention of a candle-clock. For the better government of the realm he called together a great council of bishops, ealdormen and thanes to meet twice a year, the first embryo parliament.

Asser tells us that Alfred was afflicted with a mysterious illness which attacked him periodically causing great pain. The late Sir Iain Moncreiffe of that Ilk had suggested that this might be an early reference to the 'royal malady', porphyria, of which we shall hear more later. Alfred died on 26 October 899 and was buried at Winchester. His wife Ealhswith survived until 5 December 902.

EDWARD THE ELDER 899–925

Alfred was succeeded by his elder surviving son Edward, whose succession was at once contested by his cousin Ethelwold, a son of King Ethelred I, who seized Wimborne. Edward pursued him, but he escaped to the north and induced the Danelaw to receive him as king. He made harrying raids into Mercia until he was defeated and killed in 909.

Edward was crowned on 8 June 900 at Kingston-on-Thames, where the ancient coronation stone of the Saxon kings (which gave the town its name) may still be seen. In the course of his reign he annexed the Danelaw south of the Humber and was acknowledged as overlord by the Danish King of York, the King of Scots, the King of the Strathclyde Britons and others.

He was married three times and had a large family. His first wife, Ecgwynn (Egwina), is sometimes described as a concubine 'of humble origin', but there is no real reason to suppose this, even though her antecedents have not been recorded. At any rate, her son Athelstan was always regarded as Edward's heir and as a child was a great favourite of his grandfather Alfred. Edward's second wife was Elfleda, daughter of Ealdorman Ethelhelm. By her he had two sons, the elder of whom died very soon after his father, the younger being drowned in the English Channel in 933. There were also six daughters. Edward's third and last wife was Eadgifu, daughter of Ealdorman Sigehelm of Kent, who bore him two sons, successively kings, and two daughters. Edward's many daughters either made grand marriages with Continental royalty or became nuns (see Table 9 in Appendix B).

Edward the Elder died at Farndon-on-Dee in Mercia on 17 July 925, and was buried at Winchester. His widow, Queen Eadgifu, lived on for many years and died in the reign of her grandson King Edgar on 25 August 968.

ATHELSTAN 925–939

Athelstan, who succeeded his father, was crowned at

Kingston-on-Thames by Archbishop Wulfstan on 5 September 925. He approached his grandfather Alfred the Great in stature. He renewed hostilities with the Danes and won a great victory at Brunanburh in 937 and his rule or overlordship was acknowledged throughout Britain. Athelstan never married and died at Gloucester on 27 October 939. He was buried at Malmesbury Abbey.

EDMUND 1 THE MAGNIFICENT   939–946

Athelstan's eighteen-year-old half-brother Edmund succeeded him and was crowned at Kingston on 16 November 939. He was also a warrior king and captured many towns, including the five boroughs of Leicester, Lincoln, Nottingham, Derby and Stamford, from the Danes. He brought Northumbria into subjection and ravaged Strathclyde, which he ceded to Malcolm I, King of Scots, in order to secure him as an ally. His potentially great career was ended by his untimely death. On 26 May 946 he was dining with his thanes at Pucklechurch in Gloucestershire when an outlaw named Liofa was recognized in the hall. The King joined in the struggle to arrest him and was stabbed in the stomach, dying almost immediately. He was buried at Glastonbury Abbey.

Edmund's first wife was St Elfgifu (Elfgiva), who died in 944 and was buried at Shaftesbury, leaving two sons. His second wife was Ethelfleda of Damerham, daughter of Ealdorman Alfgar. She had no children by the King and remarried with Ealdorman Athelstan. She was still living in 975.

EDRED   946–955

Edmund's sons were considered too young to reign and so he was succeeded by his brother Edred, who was crowned at Kingston-on-Thames by Archbishop Oda on 16 August 946. He continued his brother's work in spite of being afflicted with some congenital defect (possibly porphyria), for which reason he never married. He died at Frome, Somerset, on 23 November 955 and was buried at Winchester, aged about thirty-two.

EDWY THE FAIR   955–959

Edwy, or Eadwig, the elder son of King Edmund, succeeded his uncle Edred at the age of fourteen or fifteen. He had fallen passionately in love with a young kinswoman, Elfgiva, and married her secretly, although she was within the prohibited degrees of kindred and affinity (the exact relationship is unknown; she may have been a niece of Edwy's mother). The coronation took place at Kingston-on-Thames in January 956 and it was noticed that the King absented himself from the banquet afterwards and retired to his quarters. Archbishop Oda sent Dunstan, Abbot of Glastonbury, a man who had risen to a position of great influence under Edred, to enquire after the King and request him to return to his duty. Dunstan found Edwy in the company of his young wife and her mother Ethelgiva. His horror and fury at this knew no bounds. He physically attacked the two women, dragging the King from their arms and forcing him to return to the banquet. Edwy made a valiant attempt to stand by his wife, but finally the marriage was annulled by Archbishop Oda in 958, the Anglo-Saxon Chronicle making a bare mention of the fact. In September 959 Elfgiva died at Gloucester in suspicious circumstances and Edwy followed her on 1 October.

Oda's hostility must be accounted largely responsible for these two untimely deaths. On his own death in 961 he was followed as Archbishop of Canterbury by Dunstan, whose influence reached its height in the next reign.

EDGAR THE PEACEFUL   959–975

Edwy's brother Edgar had been associated in the government since 957, Mercia and the Danelaw being under his special supervision. He was only fifteen or sixteen when his brother's death left him as sole ruler. He was to be the last great king of his dynasty. In all things he was guided by Dunstan, who virtually occupied the position of chief minister of the crown. All the other rulers of Britain submitted to Edgar's overlordship. The North Welsh princes agreed to pay a tribute of 300 wolves' heads for four years running, and the goodwill of Kenneth II, King of Scots, was secured by the cession of Lothian, while a limited autonomy was allowed to the Danes in the north.

Edgar's first marriage took place when he was about eighteen in 961. Ethelfleda was the daughter of Ealdorman Ordmaer and it seems logical to suppose that she died in childbirth the following year, leaving one son, Edward. Edgar then formed an attachment for a girl named Wulfthrith, said to have been a nun (probably a lay sister) at Wilton. She bore him a daughter at Kemsing, Kent. The girl, Eadgyth or Edith, eventually became Abbess of Wilton, where she died on 16 September 984, still in her early twenties. She is regarded as an Anglo-Saxon saint. Edgar's second

King Edgar, from the Edgar Bible in the British Library. This picture
shows Edgar, flanked by the Blessed Virgin and St Peter, adoring
Christ in Majesty.

marriage took place in 964. The lady of his choice was Elfthrith (Elfrida), the widow of his friend Ethelwold, Ealdorman of East Anglia, and the daughter of Ordgar, Ealdorman of Devon. She was an able woman and was destined to play a prominent part in future events.

Edgar is presumed to have been consecrated king at Kingston in the traditional manner soon after his accession, but in 937 Dunstan conceived the idea of a much grander ceremony based on the imperial coronations of the Holy Roman Emperors. A Coronation Order was carefully drawn up and it has formed the basis of all coronations since, not only in this country but in France and other Continental countries too. On Whit Sunday 11 May 973 Edgar was solemnly anointed and crowned at Bath Abbey by Dunstan and Oswald, Archbishop of York. His wife Elfrida was also anointed and crowned as no other Saxon queen had been, with the exception of King Ethelwulf's second wife Judith, who had been consecrated queen immediately after her marriage in France in 856. The coronation was followed by a great banquet at which the King and Queen presided over separate tables.

The celebrations over, Edgar proceeded to Chester, where he was to receive the homage of six (or eight, according to some accounts) subject kings from Wales, Scotland and the north, who, as a token of their submission, rowed him in state on the River Dee from his palace to the monastery of St John the Baptist and back in a great cavalcade of many boats.

Edgar lived only another two years, dying on 8 July 975 and being buried beside his father at Glastonbury Abbey. The Anglo-Saxon Chronicle is fulsome in its praise, but with typical English xenophobia adds that 'he loved evil foreign customs and brought too firmly heathen manners within this land, and attracted hither foreigners and enticed harmful people to this country.'

EDWARD THE MARTYR   975–979

Edgar was succeeded by Edward, the only child of his first marriage, and a boy of thirteen when he was crowned at Kingston by Dunstan in 975. His stepmother Queen Elfrida felt that her son Ethelred should have succeeded, as the son of parents who had both been crowned, and there was a certain amount of sympathy and support for this view throughout the country.

In March 979 Edward, who must have been an ingenuous young fellow, set out to visit his stepmother and half-brother at Corfe Castle, Dorset, where they resided. Elfrida, in the best tradition of wicked stepmothers, saw her chance. The young King was intercepted by her henchmen and was hacked to death on 18 March. He was buried at Wareham 'with no royal honours', but very soon miracles began to be attributed to his intercession and in 980 his body was re-interred 'with great ceremony' at Shaftesbury. It was not to remain undisturbed.

In 1931 an archaeological dig in the ruins of Shaftesbury Abbey unearthed bones believed to be those of Edmund. A medical examination made in 1970 found evidence to support the accounts of Edward's death which tell of his being knifed in the back and then dragged along the ground by his bolting horse with his foot caught in a stirrup. The Anglican and Roman Catholic Churches having both declined to accept the relics for reinterment, Mr John Wilson Claridge, the joint owner of the abbey site, offered them to the

Corfe Castle, now a picturesque ruin, having been blown up by the Parliamentarians in 1646.

Ethelred the Unready, from the Chronicle of Abingdon, looks ready enough with his outsize sword.

Russian Orthodox Church in Exile, who accepted with alacrity and determined to enshrine the remains in their chapel at Brookwood Cemetery, Surrey. This was done on 15 September 1984, but a High Court ruling on behalf of Colonel Geoffrey Claridge, the co-owner of the site, ordered the bones to be returned to the custody of the Midland Bank in Croydon immediately after the ceremony, and there they remain. Colonel Claridge, with the support of Shaftesbury town council and a large body of local public opinion, feels that the bones should be returned to Shaftesbury and it is to be hoped that they will, since the Orthodox arrangement seems particularly inappropriate for the final resting place of an English king. As a correspondent wrote in *The Times* of 27 September 1984: 'No Saxon can have deserved that fate.'

Queen Elfrida, after seeing her son safely established on the throne, ended her days peacefully as a nun at Wherwell, Hampshire, on 17 November 1000.

ETHELRED II THE UNREADY

979–1013 and 1014–1016

Ethelred was undoubtedly entirely innocent of any implication in the murder of his half-brother, being no more than ten or eleven years old at the time. Dunstan crowned him at Kingston on 14 April 979, and may have taken the opportunity of foretelling the calamities which were to fall upon the nation in expiation of the death of Edward, as he was to do many times before his death in 988.

Ethelred has gone down in history as 'the Unready' and it is an apt sobriquet (although an incorrect rendering of the original 'Redeless' which signified lacking in counsel). Coastal raids by pirates continued through most of the reign and in 986 the King himself laid waste the diocese of Rochester to gratify his own cupidity. A pestilence among cattle (possibly foot and mouth disease) made its first appearance in England in that year. In 994 the Norwegian King Olaf Tryggveson (called Anlaf by the Anglo-Saxon Chronicle) and King Sweyn of Denmark sailed up the Thames with ninety-four ships and besieged London until the King and his council bought them off for £16,000. Olaf visited Ethelred at Andover and there was an exchange of gifts and mutual assurances of non-aggression.

Sweyn of Denmark renewed his attack in 1004, sacking and burning Norwich, and the following year there was a great famine throughout the country which forced the Danish invaders to withdraw temporarily. They were back again very soon, however, and in the course of the next few years the whole of England came under their rule. In 1013 Sweyn was acknowledged as king and Ethelred fled, first to the Isle of Wight, then to Normandy. Sweyn's death early in 1014 brought about Ethelred's recall and he reigned uneasily until his death in London on St George's Day, 23 April 1016, 'after a life of much hardship and many difficulties', says the Chronicle. He was buried in St Paul's Cathedral.

Ethelred was first married about 985 to Elfgiva, daughter of Ealdorman Thored of Northumbria. She bore him a large family of sons and daughters, some of whom were to die before their father. After Elfgiva's death Ethelred married again, in the spring of 1002, this time choosing a bride from the Continent. She was Emma, the eldest daughter of Richard I, Duke of Normandy, and the marriage was to have very far-reaching repercussions. The new Queen assumed the popular English name of Elfgiva (the same as that of

Ethelred's first wife) and gave Ethelred two more sons and a daughter. After his death she married Canute.

Sweyn Forkbeard   1013–1014

Sweyn, who was acknowledged as king in the autumn of 1013, was the son of Harold *Bluetooth*, King of Denmark, whom he succeeded about 986. Harold in his turn was the son of Gorm the Old, the first generally accepted King of Denmark. Sweyn, as we have seen, successfully invaded England and wrested the kingdom from Ethelred.

His first wife, Gunhild, was the daughter of Mieszko I, Duke of Poland, and *his* first wife Dubravka, daughter of Boleslav I, Duke of Bohemia. Dubravka's brother Duke Boleslav II was a son-in-law of Edward the Elder if the identification of his wife based on numismatic evidence is a correct one. Gunhild was the mother of Harold, who reigned as King of Denmark from 1014 to 1019, and Canute, who accompanied his father to England and eventually came to rule a large Scandinavian empire.

Sweyn's second wife was Sigrid the Haughty. She had been divorced from King Eric the Victorious of Sweden and had also been courted by Sweyn's companion-in-arms Olaf Tryggvesson, who had attempted to woo her with the present of a brass bracelet plated with gold. The wily Queen detected the shoddiness of this at once and flung it back at him, whereupon he slapped her face and called her a 'heathen bitch'. He was a brave man, for only a little while before she had made some other prospective suitors drunk and then burned them alive in their lodging. This great lady bore Sweyn a daughter Estrith, or Astrid (later baptized as Margaret), who was to become the ancestor of the later sovereigns of Denmark.

Sweyn died at Gainsborough less than six months after gaining the kingdom on 3 February 1014. His body was taken back to Denmark and buried in Roskilde Cathedral.

Edmund II Ironside   April–November 1016

On Ethelred's death his eldest surviving son Edmund was chosen king by 'all the councillors who were in London and the citizens', and crowned at St Paul's Cathedral. From the start he had to contest the throne with Canute, Sweyn's son and heir. After Canute had won the fiercely fought battle of Ashingdon, the two kings met at Alney in Gloucestershire and agreed to divide the kingdom, Edmund taking Wessex and Canute Mercia. Edmund, however, did not live long to enjoy his share

for he died at Oxford on St Andrew's Day, 30 November 1016, and was buried with his grandfather King Edgar at Glastonbury. He had married in the summer of 1015 Ealdgith, widow of Sigeferth, son of Earngrim, an Anglo-Scandinavian thane, and left two infant sons, possibly twins, who were sent to far off Hungary for safe-keeping.

Canute the Great   1016-1035

As Alfred is remembered for burning the cakes, Canute is remembered for ordering the tide to turn when he

Canute and Elfgiva-Emma presenting an altar cross to the New Minster at Winchester, from the *Liber Vitae* of the New Minster in the British Library.

decided to give an object lesson to his flattering courtiers who had told him that even the sea would obey his commands. It did not, of course.

Canute was the younger son of King Sweyn and his first wife, the exotic Polish Princess Gunhild, and was born about 995. He accompanied his father on his later campaigns and was chosen king by the Danish fleet on Sweyn's death, but at first failed to establish his position. It was only after his victory at Ashingdon and the conclusion of peace with Edmund Ironside that he secured Mercia and the Danelaw. On Edmund's death he succeeded to the whole kingdom (being crowned at St Paul's Cathedral on 6 January 1017) and in 1019 the death of his elder brother made him King of Denmark also.

Canute had formed an alliance with Elfgiva, daughter of Elfhelm, Ealdorman of Northampton, and they had two sons. Soon after his accession he repudiated her (although she was a very able woman and was later to govern Norway with her son Sweyn) and on 2 July 1017 married Ethelred's widow, Emma of Normandy, whom he 'commanded . . . to be brought to him so that she might become his Queen'.

Emma was a willing bride, probably excited by the prospect of a vigorous young husband ten years her junior after her life with the prosaic Ethelred. She was to bear Canute a son, Hardicanute, later king, and a daughter Gunhild, who (renamed Kunigunde) became the first wife of the Emperor Henry III, and died in Italy on 18 July 1038. Canute's reign was a busy one and there was much coming and going between England, Denmark and Norway, which he conquered in 1030.

Canute was no more than thirty when he died at Shaftesbury on 12 November 1035. He was taken to Winchester for burial. The painted wooden chests which contain the mingled bones of the Saxon and Danish kings buried at Winchester may be seen on top of the choir screen in Winchester Cathedral.

Emma lived on through many vicissitudes to see two of her sons reign, but fell out of favour with her son Edward the Confessor, who confiscated her lands and goods 'because she had been too tight-fisted with him'. She died on 6 March 1052, aged about sixty-six or sixty-seven, and was buried at Winchester.

HAROLD I HAREFOOT   1035–1040

Canute had made his eldest son Sweyn governor of Norway with his mother Elfgiva of Northampton and it was his second son, Harold, who was elected by the Council to reign jointly with his half-brother Hardicanute, who was absent in Denmark (where he reigned as Canute II) when Canute died.

In 1037 Harold was acknowledged as sole king, as Hardicanute was still abroad, and crowned at Oxford. He banished Emma, who went to Bruges, where she was well received and given shelter by Count Baldwin V of Flanders, her niece's stepson. It is interesting to think that during her stay in Bruges she may well have met Baldwin's little daughter Matilda, who was later to become the wife of William the Conqueror.

Harold's reign was short and uneventful. He never married and died at Oxford aged about twenty-four, on 17 March 1040, being buried at St Clement Danes, London. Hardicanute had his body disinterred and flung into a marsh.

HARDICANUTE   1040–1042

Hardicanute, the son of Canute and Emma, was in Denmark when his father died. He was regarded as the legitimate heir to England, but tarried so long that the people got tired of waiting for him and elected his half-brother instead. In 1039 he joined his mother in Bruges and on Harold's death the following year set out for England with a fleet of sixty ships to claim his inheritance. He was crowned at Canterbury on 18 June 1040. He imposed crippling taxes which soon alienated those who had solicited his return and, in the words of the Anglo-Saxon Chronicle, 'never did anything worthy of a King while he reigned.' Hardicanute's reign was even shorter than his brother's. He died at a wedding feast at Lambeth 'as he stood at his drink and . . . suddenly fell to the ground with a horrible convulsion; and those who were near thereto took hold of him, but he never spoke again, and passed away on 8 June' 1042. He was buried with his father at Winchester.

EDWARD THE CONFESSOR   1042-1066

On Hardicanute's death 'the whole nation . . . received Edward as King, as was his right by birth.' Edward was the only surviving son of Ethelred the Unready and Emma and had been born at Islip, Oxfordshire about 1004. He was the half-brother of two of his predecessors, Edmund Ironside and Hardicanute, and his peaceful accession was largely engineered by Earl Godwin of Wessex, who had become the most powerful man in the land under Canute, a kinswoman of whom he had married. Edward had spent almost all his early life in exile in Normandy, but had latterly resided at the court of Hardicanute, of which he must heartily have disapproved, being a cold, sexless prude.

Edward was crowned in Winchester Cathedral on

Easter Sunday, 3 April 1043, probably with more ceremonial than had been seen since King Edgar's coronation at Bath in 973. On 23 January 1045 Edward was married to Earl Godwin's daughter Edith. Although he always treated her with the greatest consideration and respect (except for a short period when Godwin and his family were out of favour and he deprived her of her property and sent her to live with his sister in the convent at Wherwell), it was to be a marriage in name only, all Edward's inclinations being directed towards the religious life.

Edward's greatest achievement was the foundation of Westminster Abbey, which he built and endowed to expiate the breaking of a vow to make a pilgrimage to Rome. Matters of government were left in the hands of his brother-in-law Harold, Godwin's able son. Westminster Abbey was consecrated on Holy Innocents' Day, 28 December 1065. Edward, now over sixty, attended with all his court. It was the culmination of his life's work and he was now ready to die. The end came a few days later on 5 January 1066 and the King was buried the following day in his new foundation. He was canonized by Pope Alexander III in 1161 and his body was solemnly transferred to a new shrine on Henry III's rebuilding of the Abbey. It still rests there today.

Queen Edith lived on quietly at Winchester until 18 December 1075. William the Conqueror had her interred beside Edward at Westminster 'with great ceremony'.

HAROLD II   JANUARY–OCTOBER 1066

The hereditary heir to the throne on Edward's death was Edgar, the grandson of Edmund Ironside, but Harold,

Edward the Confessor, from the Westminster Psalter.

A silver penny of Edward the Confessor attributed to the moneyer Theodoric. The portrait, though barbarous, conforms to the accepted bearded type. The King appears to be wearing a closed crown with arches and two pendants and is holding a sceptre, or perhaps St Edward's Staff, which was to become part of the coronation regalia. The existing St Edward's Staff made for Charles II's coronation and reputed to contain a fragment of the true cross is now no longer used at coronations.

the son of Earl Godwin, had proved his ability, and was chosen king by the nobles immediately following Edward's death and was crowned in Westminster Abbey immediately after Edward's burial. Harold's father Godwin was the son of Wulfrith, whose pedigree has been cleverly deduced, on not altogether convincing evidence, from King Ethelred I, the brother and predecessor of Alfred the Great. If Harold's family was indeed of the male line of the House of Cerdic it seems very strange that no such claim was made during his lifetime to bolster up his right to the throne.

The threat of an invasion by William of Normandy was felt very early in the reign and Harold maintained an army in the Isle of Wight for four months. In the September, however, he received news that his brother Tostig, who had long been exiled, had landed in Yorkshire with Harold Hardrada, King of Norway. He

The following pages take us from the dawn of British History to the eve of the Norman Conquest. From mysterious, brooding Stonehenge and the eloquent loneliness of Maiden Castle, through the elaborately-wrought treasures of the Sutton Hoo ship burial and King Alfred's Jewel, to the Bayeux Tapestry's portrayal of Harold's coronation in January 1066.

The fine Norman nave of Waltham Abbey, Essex, the reputed burial place of Harold II, whose body is said to have been taken there secretly by his mistress Edith Swan-neck after the battle of Hastings.

Right, Stonehenge, on Salisbury Plain, one of the greatest and most mysterious structures of ancient Britain. Its origins probably go back to around 2000 BC and additions were made over several centuries. It was obviously the centre of a religious cult and may have served as a primitive type of calendar as well. Geoffrey of Monmouth called it the Giants' Ring and named it as the burial place of several of his mythical Kings, including Aurelius Ambrosius and Uther Pendragon, the uncle and father of Arthur respectively. One can well believe that the monument played an important role in the lives of Celtic kings.

Below, Maiden Castle, near Dorchester, Dorset, is the greatest Celtic hill-fort in Britain and was a stronghold of the Belgic tribes who resisted the Roman conquest. Geoffrey of Monmouth names its founder as King Ebraucus, otherwise noteworthy for his twenty wives, twenty sons and thirty daughters.

The ruins of Glastonbury Abbey **(above)**, the reputed burial place of King Arthur, whose supposed tomb, with that of his second wife Guinevere, was 'discovered' there in the twelfth century. Glastonbury was a sacred site from pre-Christian times and it was there that Joseph of Arimathaea was said to have hidden the Holy Grail and planted his staff which took root and became the famous 'Glastonbury Thorn' flowering on Old Christmas Day (6 January) each year. Flowers from the plant are traditionally presented to the reigning sovereign.

On the **right** and on the **facing** page are two of the treasures from the Sutton Hoo burial ship excavated near Woodbridge in Suffolk in 1939. It was almost certainly the sepulchre of King Redwald of East Anglia. The barbaric helmet is decorated with gilded bronze and silver and the ornaments from the King's body-harness are elaborately wrought and studded with jewels. The longboat in which the treasure lay was about 89 feet long and although its timbers had rotted away, their impression remained in the sand with the rusted iron rivets still in place. It has been estimated that it would take at least 38 men to row such a ship, which possessed no keel, mast or sail.

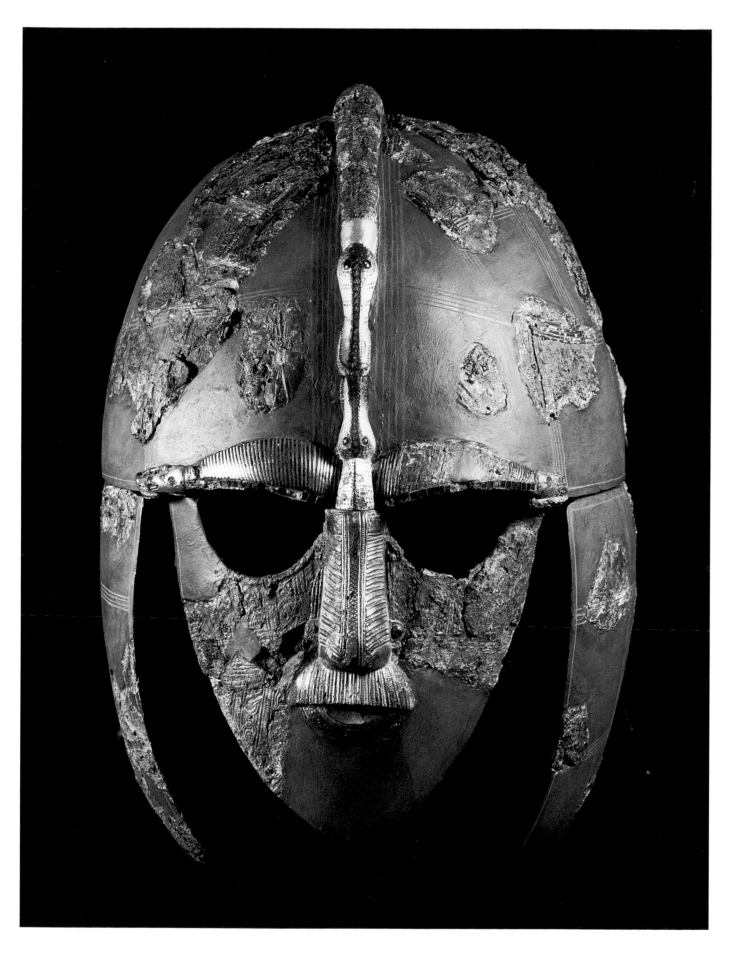

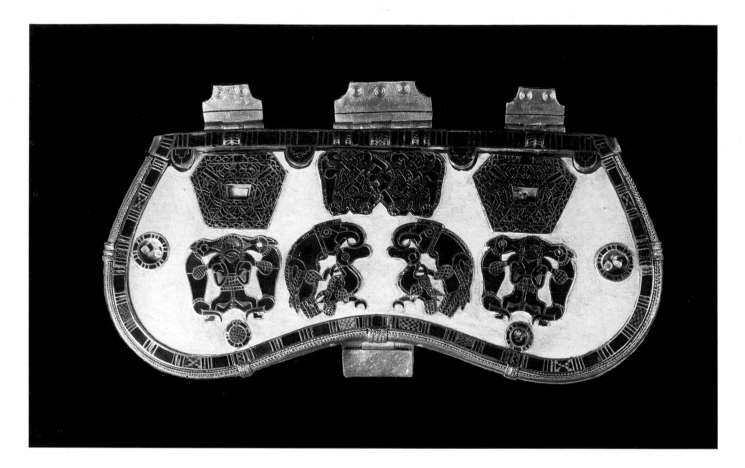

Two more of the treasures from the Sutton Hoo ship burial. **Above,** the King's solid gold purse lid, decorated with garnets and enamel in a design of weird fantasy figures of men, animals and birds. The three gold hinges would have attached the purse to the King's leather belt from which it depended like a Scotsman's sporran. Several gold coins of Merovingian origin were found with the purse. **Left,** the King's gold belt buckle, intricately wrought with typical Scandinavian designs similar to those on objects found in burial mounds in Sweden.

Opposite
Above, the painted ceiling of the central tower of Wimborne Minster, Dorset. King Ethelred I, brother and predecessor of Alfred the Great, was buried in the church in 871 and his tomb is marked by a floor slab of Purbeck marble with a copper plate bearing a (non-contemporary) likeness of the King and an inscription. A college of secular canons was founded here by Edward the Confessor in 1043. The central tower is supported by massive Norman piers and arches, the oldest portion of the existing church, which can be clearly seen in this picture.

Below, King Alfred's Jewel. This beautiful gold and enamel object was found buried at Newton Park, Somerset in 1693. It bears the inscription in Anglo-Saxon *Aelfred mec heht gewyrcan* (Alfred had me made). Newton Park is about four miles from the Isle of Athelney, where Alfred took refuge from the Danes. He founded a Benedictine monastery there and the 'jewel' may have been a pointer for following the lines in religious manuscripts. The figure holding two wands (reminiscent of the woven palm crosses distributed in churches on Palm Sunday at the present day) probably represents Christ and not Alfred himself.

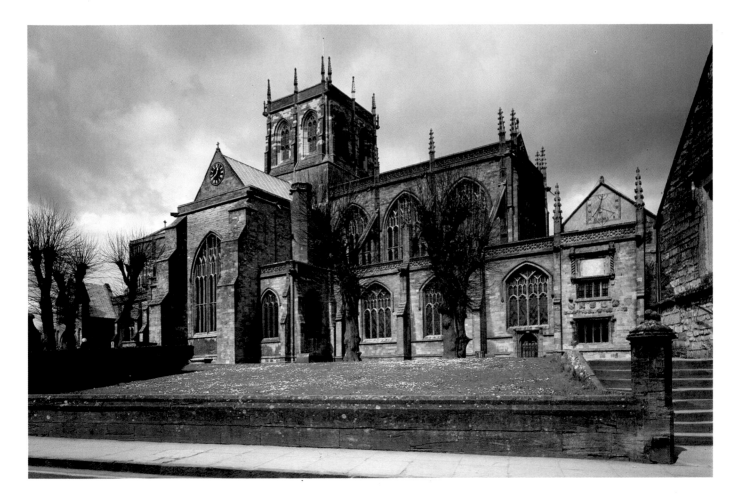

Sherborne Abbey **(above)** was the burial place of two Kings of Wessex, Ethelbald and Ethelbert, who are commemorated by a brass on the floor of the presbytery. Sherborne was originally an ecclesiastical see, but the bishopric was transferred to Old Sarum about 1075.

The choir of Winchester Cathedral **(left)**. On the top of the stone screens left and right may be seen the wooden coffers containing the indiscriminately jumbled remains of many Saxon Kings.

Corfe Castle **(opposite page)** was the scene of the murder of King Edward the Martyr at the instigation of his stepmother Queen Elfrida in 979. Later Edward II was imprisoned here before being removed to Berkeley Castle. It was blown up by the Parliamentarians in 1646 and is now a picturesque ruin.

Anglo-Saxon silver pennies (left) from the reigns of Ethelred the Unready, Canute and Harold Harefoot. Barbarous in style though they are, they make some attempt at individual portraiture which is lacking in the later medieval coinage, where a stylized crowned head of a king remained the pattern for hundreds of years and it was not until the reign of Henry VII that the monarch's head became a true portrait.

The section of the Bayeux Tapestry shown below shows Harold II being offered the crown on the left and seated enthroned after his coronation by Archbishop Stigand. The attendant nobles, one of whom bears the sword of state, are attired in short tunics and cloaks, but the King appears to be clad in coronation vestments similar to those still used. He wears an open crown and holds sceptre and orb. The Archbishop's vestments are more akin to those worn today in the Eastern Church rather than the Western.

THE KINGS OF WESSEX AND ALL ENGLAND 41

moved north with his army to inflict a crushing defeat on the Norwegians at Stamford Bridge on 25 September. News soon arrived that William of Normandy had landed at Hastings on 29 September and Harold and his army at once marched south again. His tired forces were no match for the Normans but the battle was hard fought and Harold fell on 14 October 1066. Traditionally his eye was pierced by an arrow, but this seems to have arisen through a misinterpretation of the battle scene depicted in the Bayeux Tapestry. If carefully examined it will be seen that the figure of Harold is being felled by a sword blow and it is a nearby figure who has the arrow in his eye. Harold was about forty-five years old at his death. William is said to have had his body buried on the sea shore, but there is a tradition that Harold's mistress Edith Swan-neck sought it out and took it to Waltham Abbey for burial.

Harold had lived happily with Edith for many years and she had borne him many children, including a daughter Gytha, named after Harold's mother, who was to seek refuge abroad after the Conquest and eventually to marry Vladimir Monomakh, Grand Duke of Kiev. Nearly three hundred years later Harold's blood was to return to the royal line of England via Gytha's descendants (see Appendix B, Table 14).

In 1065 Harold married Ealdgyth, the widow of Gruffydd ap Llywelyn, King of Gwynedd and Powys, and daughter of Alfgar, Earl of Mercia. She bore him at least one son, Harold, whose fate is unknown. There is much confusion between Ealdgyth and Edith Swan-neck.

THE HOUSE OF NORMANDY

The ducal House of Normandy, which acquired the English throne by conquest in 1066, owed its origin to Rolf or Rollo the Ganger, a Norse sea-rover who carried out a number of raids on the coast of northern France. He was finally granted the Duchy of Normandy as a fief of the crown from Charles the Simple, King of France, accepting Christian baptism at the same time. Rollo's ancestors can be traced with near certainty to the early Yngling kings in Sweden.

Rollo is credited with having contemptuously tipped the French monarch backwards off his throne when he came to do homage for his fief and he and his successors were well-nigh independent sovereigns, only paying lip-service to the French crown.

WILLIAM THE CONQUEROR	1066-1087

Born: Falaise, Normandy 1027 or 1028
Acceded: by conquest 14 October 1066
Crowned: Westminster Abbey 25 December 1066
Married: Eu 1053, Matilda, daughter of Baldwin V, Count of Flanders, and Adela of France
Children:
(1) Robert Curthose, Duke of Normandy: b. Normandy ca 1054; d. Cardiff Castle 10 February 1134; m. Apulia 1100, Sibylla of Conversano; two sons who both predeceased him
(2) Richard: b. Normandy ca 1055; d. (killed while hunting) New Forest ca 1081
(3) William, later King William II
(4) Cecilia, Abbess of Holy Trinity, Caen: d. Caen 30 July 1126
(5) Agatha, said to have been betrothed to Harold
(6) Adeliza, a nun
(7) Adela: b. Normandy ca 1062; d. Marcigny-sur-Loire 8 March 1138; m. Chartres ca 1081, Stephen, Count of Blois and Chartres; had issue, of whom Stephen later became King Stephen
(8) Matilda, mentioned in Domesday Book
(9) Constance: b. Normandy ca 1066; d. Brittany 13 August 1090; m. Caen 1086, as his 1st wife, Alan IV, Count of Brittany
(10) Henry, later King Henry I
Died: Priory of St Gervais, near Rouen, 9 September 1087
Buried: Abbey of St Stephen, Caen

William the Conqueror was the illegitimate son of Duke Robert the Devil, or the Magnificent. His father is said, in a romantically unlikely story, to have fallen in love with a young girl he saw washing clothes in a stream as he looked out from his castle at Falaise. He wooed her, installed her as his official mistress, and in due course she bore William and also probably a daughter. The girl's name was Herleve, and her father, Fulbert, a citizen of Falaise, is usually described as a tanner, although opinions differ as to the exact rendering of his occupation, ranging from what we would now call an undertaker to furrier. Unions such as that between Duke Robert and Herleve had been by no means uncommon in the ducal House of Normandy. Its founder, Rollo the Ganger (reckoned as Duke Robert I from the name he received in Christian baptism) was succeeded by the son of one Popa, or Papie, the pagan wife or concubine he repudiated in order to marry the daughter of the King of France. When she died childless, Rollo resumed his relationship with Papie. Their son, Duke William Longsword, was also succeeded by the son of a concubine, Duke Richard the Fearless, who married his mistress Gunnor, the mother of all his children, after the death of his first wife. One of Gunnor's daughters was Emma, who as we have seen was twice Queen of England. Gunnor's eldest son, Duke Richard the Good, was the first Duke of Normandy to be succeeded by undisputedly legitimate sons, first Duke Richard III, who reigned for just under a year, then Duke Robert II, William the Conqueror's father. The taint of bastardy, therefore, mattered very little where the ducal

succession was concerned and it can hardly have had any psychological effect on William, as some have claimed.

William was only seven or eight years old when he succeeded to the duchy on the death of his father in 1035. His mother married Herluin de Conteville, a Norman noble, after Duke Robert's death and bore him two sons, who later, as Robert, Count of Mortain, and Odo, Bishop of Bayeux and Earl of Kent, were to be among the staunchest supporters of their elder half-brother. William grew up under the protection of Alan, Count of Brittany, Gilbert, Count of Brionne, and Osborn the Seneschal. All three fell victim to an assassin. When William was still under twenty he defeated an attempt to wrest the duchy from his control by his cousin, Count Guy of Burgundy, and a faction of dissatisfied nobles.

In 1053 William made an advantageous marriage with Matilda, the daughter of his neighbour, Count Baldwin of Flanders. There was some ecclesiastical objection to the marriage which has never been satisfactorily unravelled and it was not until 1059 that the Pope gave his approval. The couple expiated their 'sin' by founding two abbeys – the Abbaye-aux-Hommes (St Stephen's) and the Abbaye-aux-Dames (Holy Trinity) – at Caen. William and Matilda became devoted to each other and, in an age when marital infidelity was the norm, we hear of no mistresses and the two bastards attributed to William can both be proved spurious.

William's marriage may well have been partly motivated by his growing ambition to gain the throne of England, for Matilda was a direct descendant of Alfred the Great. William had visited his first cousin once removed, Edward the Confessor, in 1051, when he had been well received and designated as Edward's successor. In 1064 fortune played into his hands when Harold, Earl of Wessex, was driven ashore on the coast of Ponthieu. He was received with great honour, but before sending him home William extracted an oath from him to uphold his claim to the English throne on the death of Edward.

Edward died at the end of 1065 and Harold was crowned king in January 1066. William at once began careful preparations for an invasion. He was not hurried and, when he was ready to set sail in the late summer, was delayed further by an adverse wind. Harold, meanwhile, was forced to march north to deal with the Norwegian invasion and while he was away the wind changed and William landed with his troops at Pevensey on 28 September. He stumbled on leaping ashore, but allayed the fears of those of his supporters who saw this as an ill omen by holding aloft a handful of sand and shouting that he had already taken possession of his kingdom. William bided his time at Hastings and began constructing a castle there while waiting for Harold to arrive from the north. He may have thought that Harold would surrender easily, exhausted by his action against the Norwegians and his march south, but the battle, when it took place on 14 October, was hard fought, and after a full day's fighting ended with Harold's death. William marched to London with his victorious army, laying the land waste around the city until local resistance collapsed and the English nobles led by Edgar Atheling submitted to the Conqueror.

On Christmas Day 1066 William was crowned at Westminster Abbey by Aldred, Archbishop of York. The shouts of acclamation – in English as well as French – from the congregation inside the abbey alarmed the Norman guards stationed outside. Mistaking the noise for signs of an insurrection, they began a massacre of the Saxons living nearby, burning and pillaging their houses until the King himself appeared at the doorway of the Abbey to quell the tumult.

Although the south and east of England quickly submitted to William's rule, over the next five years there were risings in various parts of the country. The south-west submitted in 1068 and the rebellion in the north of the Earls Edwin and Morcar was put down in person by William in 1069 and was followed by the 'harrowing of the north', a laying waste from York to Durham. A rising in the Isle of Ely led by Hereward the Wake was put down in 1071. During this period the Normans had to live like an army of occupation, building castles from which a few men could dominate the subject population.

Gradually during William's reign English lords were superseded by Norman and other French barons and the Continental system of feudal land tenure was introduced. In the Church too English bishops were replaced by Continental prelates and Lanfranc of Pavia, who was appointed Archbishop of Canterbury, reorganized the English Church on European lines. The Domesday Survey, commanded in 1086, gave the King, as chief lord of this feudal system, an exact account of his power and resources for administrative purposes.

After 1071 William felt secure enough in England to turn again to his Continental possessions which were more vulnerable to attack than his island kingdom. His borders were continually threatened by his neighbours, the King of France and the Count of Anjou, who enlisted the support of William's disaffected eldest son Robert. The rest of William's reign was taken up with a series of intrigues by these enemies.

The French King's facetious remarks about William's excessive corpulence prompted him to threaten to 'set all France ablaze'. In 1087 the French garrison at Mantes made a raid into Normandy and William retaliated by sacking Mantes. As he was urging on his men his horse stumbled on a hot cinder and he was flung violently against the high pommel of his saddle. He sustained grave internal injuries, probably a ruptured bladder, from which peritonitis ensued, and he died after much suffering on 8 September.

His burial in his foundation of St Stephen at Caen was fraught with incident. As the cortège neared the church a citizen barred the way, claiming that it had been built on land illegally seized from his family, and was only appeased by an on the spot payment of cash. On reaching the grave it was found that it had been made too small and the bearers, in attempting to force the already fast decomposing corpse into it, burst it open so that a vile stench filled the church, causing all but the hardiest to flee, and the burial was completed by a handful of faithful retainers.

The writer of the Anglo-Saxon Chronicle, who knew William and at one time lived in his court, summed him up as 'a man of great wisdom and power, and surpassed in honour and in strength all those who had gone before him. Though stern beyond measure to those who opposed his will, he was kind to those good men who loved God . . . He wore his royal crown three times a year as often as he was in England: at Easter at Winchester, at Whitsuntide at Westminster, at Christmas at Gloucester. On these occasions all the great men of England were assembled about him.' He was grasping and mendacious but a great ruler and far in advance of his times as a legislator.

William, who was about sixty at the time of his death, was a tall man of ruddy complexion, always inclined to corpulence and for most of his life probably clean shaven. The only contemporary likenesses of him are in the Bayeux Tapestry. Long popularly supposed to have

The Abbey of the Holy Trinity at Caen, founded by Matilda of Flanders and known as the Abbaye-aux-Dames. It was a twin foundation with William the Conqueror's Abbey of St Stephen (the Abbaye-aux-Hommes). The ducal pair founded these abbeys to expiate the unspecified sin they had incurred by their marriage.

been the work of Queen Matilda and her ladies, it is now believed to have been commissioned by William's half-brother, Odo, Bishop of Bayeux. The figures depicted in it are hardly portraits but do convey some idea of personality and appearance and, above all, costume.

Matilda of Flanders

Born:	Flanders *ca* 1031
Married:	Eu 1053
Crowned:	Winchester Cathedral 11 May 1068
Died:	Caen 2 November 1083
Buried:	Abbey of Holy Trinity, Caen

The Conqueror's queen was a lady of diminutive stature whose early life is surrounded by mystery. When he first sought her hand, she is said to have rejected him with the crushing retort that she would not have a bastard for her husband. In retaliation William burst into her apartment in her father's castle at Lille and, dragging her across the room by her hair, gave her a sound beating. His daring on this occasion, we are told, so impressed her that she at once changed her mind and accepted his hand.

There were, as we have seen, strong papal objections to the marriage, the reasons for which have never been clear. There are some indications that Matilda was not free to marry because she had already been betrothed to Brihtric Meaw, a young Saxon nobleman who visited her father's court as an emissary of Edward the Confessor. There is also the possibility that she had compromised herself with a Flemish commoner named Gherbod and given birth to two children – Gherbod, who later received the Earldom of Chester, and Gundred, who married William de Warrenne, Earl of Surrey. This has been the subject of controversy over several centuries and still continues to exercise the minds of historians and genealogists. Married to William at last in 1053, and with dispensation finally granted by Pope Nicholas II in 1059, Matilda became an exemplary wife and mother.

She was a woman of great capability and William had no hesitation in leaving her in charge as regent of Normandy during his absences in England. William first returned to Normandy after the conquest in March 1067 and remained until early December. It was during the last days of his stay that the future Henry I must have been conceived. Matilda, although pregnant, left Normandy to join him in England in the spring of 1068 and was crowned at Winchester on Whitsunday. Her coronation banquet is said to have been the first at which the King's Champion made his appearance to challenge any who might dispute the King's right to the throne. He was a Marmion, one of William's Norman followers, and the office was to become hereditary in his descendants, the Lords of Scrivelsby. It passed by marriage to the Dymokes, who still possess the proud title, although the full exercise of the ancient and honourable office ceased with the coronation banquet of George IV.

Matilda accompanied William to the north of England and gave birth to Henry at Selby, probably in September 1068. He was almost certainly her last child. She remained in England until the following year when she returned to Normandy for good and busied herself with the affairs of the duchy and her religious foundations at Caen and Rouen.

In 1083, Matilda, aged about fifty-two, fell ill, and William hastened from England to be at her side. She died at Caen on 2 November 1083 and was buried there in her foundation of the Holy Trinity. Her magnificent tomb was desecrated by the Calvinists in 1562 and later restored in simpler fashion only to be destroyed again during the French Revolution.

WILLIAM II *Rufus*   1087–1100

Born:	Normandy 1056–60
Acceded:	9 September 1087
Crowned:	Westminster Abbey 26 September 1087
Died:	New Forest 2 August 1100
Buried:	Winchester Cathedral

The accession of William II, the Conqueror's second surviving son, to the throne of England shows that the principle of the hereditary right of succession was not established at this time. His elder brother Robert, despite his rebellion against his father, inherited the Norman lands that his father had himself inherited, but William felt free to leave the land he had acquired by conquest to his favourite younger son.

Of the two, Rufus was probably the better choice for, despite his bad reputation, he did have some kingly qualities lacking in his elder brother. He was a good leader of men and a successful soldier. He resembled his father physically, his ruddy complexion and red hair earning him the sobriquet of 'Rufus', by which he is always known. However, whereas the Conqueror was always above reproach in his dealings, William Rufus exploited his position for his own benefit and the extravagance of his court was in marked contrast to that of his father.

William's reputation has suffered because the Church – which kept most of the records of the time – disapproved of his lifestyle and the way in which he delayed the appointment of bishops and abbots in order to help himself to Church revenues. Chroniclers write of William's debaucheries as being 'hateful to God and man', without being too specific. The inference is that he was a homosexual and William of Malmesbury states that it was the fashion in William's court for young men to 'rival women in delicacy of person, to mince their gate, to walk with loose gestures and half naked.' William was never married and there is no indication that he was ever interested in women.

For several years after his accession William campaigned in Normandy, alternately supporting his brother against the King of France and opposing him for the control of Normandy. This was one of William's primary concerns for, while England and Normandy were under separate rule, the barons who held land in both places found it well-nigh impossible to serve two lords. If they supported William, then his brother might deprive them of their Norman lands; if they supported Robert, then they were in danger of losing their English estates. The problem was temporarily solved when Robert decided to join the First Crusade and, in order to finance the expedition, pledged Normandy to William for 10,000 marks.

There is no doubt that William was unpopular, especially because of his treatment of the saintly Anselm, whom he had appointed Archbishop of Canterbury in a moment of panic in 1093 when he thought he was dying. William's opposition to the Archbishop's attempts to reform the Church forced Anselm to leave the country, whereupon the King took over the revenues of the archbishopric. 'He was very harsh and fierce in his rule over his realm,' records the Anglo-Saxon Chronicle, '. . . everything that was hateful to God and to righteous man was the daily practice in this land during his reign. Therefore he was hated by almost all his people and abhorrent to God.'

William's death in the New Forest has become the subject of much speculation, and there were certainly many mysterious and inexplicable circumstances surrounding it. On 2 August 1100 he rode out from Winchester on a hunting expedition accompanied by his younger brother Henry and several nobles and knights. According to most accounts the King went in pursuit of a stag followed by Walter Tirel, a knight. The King shot an arrow at the stag but missed and called out to Walter to shoot, which he did, accidentally killing the King. This was the generally accepted version and, if true, could only have been told by Tirel, who later denied that he was present. Nobody was ever held to blame, so unloved was Rufus.

William's body was left in the charge of a handful of peasants. They loaded it on to a farm cart and the next morning it arrived at Winchester Cathedral 'with blood dripping from it the whole way', according to William of Malmesbury. There it was interred with little ceremony (the clergy denying it religious rites) in the crossing under the tower, the collapse of which in the following year caused many heads to nod sagely, though the matter-of-fact William of Malmesbury adds 'it would have collapsed in any case . . . because it was badly built.'

William had started to rebuild the Palace of Westminster, and Westminster Hall was completed in his lifetime. When visitors exclaimed on its size he was wont to boast that it was 'but a bedchamber' to the palace he intended to build.

HENRY I BEAUCLERC 1100–1135

Born:	Selby, Yorkshire *ca* September 1068
Acceded:	2 August 1100
Crowned:	Westminster Abbey 6 August 1100
Married:	1st, Westminster Abbey 11 November 1100, Matilda (formerly called Edith), elder daughter of Malcolm III, King of Scots and his second wife (St) Margaret, daughter of Edward Atheling
Children:	(1) A son (?): *b.* prematurely *ca* July 1101; *d.* in infancy
	(2) William, Duke of Normandy: *b.* Winchester before 5 August 1103; *d.* (drowned in the wreck of the White Ship) off Barfleur 25 November 1120; *m.* Lisieux June 1119, Matilda (formerly called Alice), daughter of Fulk V, Count of Anjou
	(3) Matilda, declared heiress-presumptive 1126, disputed the throne with Stephen: *b.* Winchester *ca* 1103/4 (possibly twin with William); *d.* Rouen 10 September 1167; *m.* 1st, Mainz 7 January 1114, Henry V, Holy Roman Emperor and German King (*d.* Utrecht 23 May 1125); 2nd, Le Mans 22 May 1127, Geoffrey V (Plantagenet), Count of Anjou (*d.* Château-du-Loir 7 September 1151); three sons, of whom the eldest later became King Henry II
Married:	2nd, Windsor Castle 29 January 1122, Adeliza, daughter of Godfrey I (the Bearded), Duke of Lower Lorraine, Marquess of Antwerp and Count of Louvain
Died:	St Denis-le-Fermont, near Gisors 1 December 1135
Buried:	Reading Abbey

The Conqueror's youngest son, the only one of his children to be born in England, first saw the light of day at Selby in the autumn of 1068, his mother Queen

Matilda having accompanied William on his expedition to subjugate the north. Like many youngest sons, he became his mother's favourite and on her death in 1083 she left him her English estates, which, however, he was not allowed to hold during his father's lifetime. Meanwhile he is reputed to have acquired a good education, learning to read and write Latin and also studying English and English law. It might be surmised that this was undertaken with a view to his entering the Church, often the destiny of youngest sons. His learning was to earn him the sobriquet of 'Beauclerc' (fine scholar), of which he became very proud, and in later life he was to declare that 'an unlettered King was but a crowned ass.'

Henry was knighted by his father at Westminster on Whitsunday 1086 and after the King's death the following year he became one of those barons who suffered from the Conqueror's decision to leave Normandy to Robert and England to William. Until Robert resigned Normandy to William in 1096, Henry was constantly being forced to choose between his two overlords, and whichever side he came down on, he was likely to annoy the other.

Once England and Normandy were reunited under William Rufus, Henry was able to serve the King, and he was fortuitously on hand in the New Forest on the day his brother was killed on 2 August 1100. The following day, after William's burial at Winchester, such councillors as were at hand elected Henry king and, after securing the treasury, he immediately left for London, where on 6 August he was crowned in Westminster Abbey by Maurice, Bishop of London.

Henry's first act as king was to issue a charter promising a return to his father's ways, and to restore Anselm to the Archbishopric of Canterbury. His next was to seek a wife and his choice very expediently fell upon Edith (renamed Matilda in honour of his mother), the elder daughter of Malcolm Canmore, King of Scots, by St Margaret, who was the granddaughter of Edmund Ironside. He thus reinforced the strain of Saxon blood in the royal family.

The vexed question of lay investiture of ecclesiastical estates threatened relations between Church and State for several years. Anselm refused to do homage to the King for the archiepiscopal estates, claiming he held them from the Pope. The King would not give way and Anselm was deprived of his fiefs and again forced into exile. A compromise was reached in 1107 when the King's sister Adela, Countess of Blois, suggested that the bishops should pay homage for fiefs held of the King, who in his turn would allow clerical investiture.

Henry was a wise ruler, a good judge of men, and a skilled diplomat. The affairs of Normandy occupied the early years of his reign. Robert had returned from the Crusade but proved such an ineffective ruler that his barons revolted and invited Henry to come to their aid. Robert was taken prisoner at Tinchebrai and Normandy passed under Henry's rule. More troubles in Normandy and war with France continued to occupy the next few years. In 1109 Henry's foreign policy triumphed in the betrothal of his only legitimate daughter Matilda to the Emperor Henry V, the marriage taking place in 1114.

In 1120 Henry's only legitimate son, William, was tragically drowned with his entourage in the wreck of the White Ship when returning from Normandy. Henry, it is said, never smiled again. Queen Matilda had died in 1118, and in 1122 Henry took a second wife, Adeliza, daughter of Godfrey, Count of Louvain, but the marriage was to remain childless. At Christmas 1126 he designated his daughter, the widowed Empress Matilda, as his successor and the following May he chose a second husband for her in the person of the young and handsome Geoffrey, son of the Count of Anjou, who was ten years or more her junior.

Henry was continually travelling from England to Normandy and back throughout his reign. He left England for the last time on 1 August 1135. An eclipse the next day was seen as an evil portent and, in the words of the Anglo-Saxon Chronicle 'men ... said that some important event should follow upon this; and so it did, for in that very year the King died in Normandy.' At the end of November Henry was at his royal hunting-box at St Denis-le-Fermont, near Gisors, where, says Henry of Huntingdon, 'he devoured lampreys which always disagreed with him, though he was excessively fond of them, and when his physicians forbade him to eat them the King did not heed their advice.' A severe case of ptomaine poisoning followed and Henry died on 1 December. He was sixty-seven, a good age for those days, though far short of the eighty years attained by his eldest brother Robert who had ended his days in prison in Cardiff Castle a year earlier.

Henry's body was brought back to England and interred in Reading Abbey, which he had founded. No trace of his tomb remains today, the site being covered by a car park. 'He was', says the Anglo-Saxon Chronicle, 'a good man, and was held in great awe. In his days no man dared to wrong another. He made peace for man and beast.' The last reference calls to mind the Woodstock menagerie, which Henry brought together, the first English zoo. In his interest in natural history, as in many other things, he was a man far in advance of his time.

Henry's marriage to Matilda produced only two surviving children, that to Adeliza none, but a number of mistresses bore him a large illegitimate progeny, several of whom made a mark in the world, especially Robert, Earl of Gloucester, who was to play such an important part in the next reign.

The only contemporary depictions of Henry are his

An illustrated medieval manuscript showing William I, William II, Henry I and Stephen.

coins and his great seal. Neither can be said to be in any way a likeness, but they, and a lively imagination, helped to inspire the portrait of Henry engraved by George Vertue in the eighteenth century.

Matilda of Scotland

Born: Dunfermline 1079 or 1080
Married and
  Crowned: Westminster Abbey 11 November 1100
Died: Palace of Westminster 1 May 1118
Buried: Westminster Abbey

Henry's first queen was chosen for her descent from the Saxon kings rather than for any other consideration. She was born at Dunfermline in 1079 or 1080 and was consequently twenty years old when negotiations for her marriage commenced. Indeed, she had been expected to take the veil and was living under the protection of her aunt, the Abbess Christina, at Romsey, when Henry demanded her hand in marriage. The wedding was solemnized at Westminster on 11 November 1100 by Archbishop Anselm, who crowned her the same day. The following July she gave birth prematurely to an infant which did not survive and in the succeeding years her children William and Matilda were born at Winchester, possibly (though not certainly) twins.

Matilda, true to her convent upbringing and following the footsteps of her mother, St Margaret, was given to good works. She built a leper hospital at St Giles-in-the-Fields, London and founded the Augustinian Priory at Aldgate. On 1 May 1118 she died at Westminster and was buried in the Abbey. All trace of her tomb has disappeared.

Adeliza of Louvain

Born: Louvain ca 1105
Married: 1st, Windsor Castle 29 January 1122
Crowned: Westminster Abbey 3 February 1122
Married: 2nd, 1138, William d'Aubigny, 1st Earl of Arundel (d. 12 October 1176)
Died: Afflighem, Flanders 23 March or April 1151
Buried: Afflighem

In hopes of further legitimate issue Henry married again after the loss of his only son William. His bride, whose age is uncertain but who was certainly younger than his daughter Matilda, was Adeliza, the daughter of Godfrey the Bearded, Duke of Lower Lorraine, Marquess of Antwerp, and Count of Louvain. The marriage took place at Windsor on 29 January 1122.

The coronation of the new Queen at Westminster Abbey on 3 February 1122 gave rise to an amusing incident. The King, wearing his crown, had taken his seat on the throne to await his consort's crowning when the aged Archbishop Ralph d'Escures, verging on senility, entered. Seeing the King he flew into a rage, thinking that his right to place the crown on the sovereign's head had been infringed. He at once snatched the crown from the King's head (one version has it that he knocked it off with his pastoral staff) and insisted on reimposing it with his own hands. Henry's second marriage remained childless; the once potent sire of many illegitimate children was potent no longer.

In 1138 the young widowed Queen married William d'Aubigny, 1st Earl of Arundel, to whom she bore a large family before, wearied by married life, she retired to the convent of Afflighem in Flanders, where she died and was buried in March or April 1151.

STEPHEN 1135–1154

Born: Blois ca 1096
Acceded: 1 December 1135
Crowned: Westminster Abbey 26 December 1135
Married: Westminster (?) 1125, Matilda, only daughter and heiress of Eustace III, Count of Boulogne, and Mary of Scotland
Children: (1) Baldwin: b. ca 1126; d. London before 2 December 1135
  (2) Eustace, Count of Boulogne: b. 1130 or 1131; d. Bury St Edmunds 10 August 1153; m. Paris after February 1140, Constance of Toulouse; no issue
  (3) Matilda: b. ca 1133; d. ca 1135
  (4) William, Count of Boulogne: b. ca 1134; d. Toulouse 11 October 1159; m. ca 1149, Isabel de Warrenne; no issue
  (5) Mary, Countess of Boulogne: b. ca 1136; d. St Austrebert 1182; m. ca 1160 (annulled 1169), Matthew of Alsace, Count of Boulogne in right of his wife; two daughters
Died: Dover Castle 25 October 1154
Buried: Faversham Abbey

Henry I's nephew Stephen of Blois was such a weak and ineffective character that it is a wonder how he attained the crown. Born at Blois in 1096 or 1097, he was the third son of Stephen, Count of Blois and Chartres, and Adela, the strong-minded daughter of the Conqueror. Still a child when his father died while on the First Crusade in 1102, he was brought up by his energetic and capable mother and also became a favourite of his uncle

Henry, who endowed him with lands in England and with the counties of Mortain and Alençon. In 1125 a brilliant marriage was arranged for him with the niece of Henry's first queen, yet another Matilda, the only daughter and heiress of Eustace III, Count of Boulogne.

In 1126 Stephen was the first of the lay barons to swear to acknowledge his cousin, the Empress Matilda, as heiress to England and Normandy. He again swore fealty on the birth of her son Henry in 1133. In spite of these solemn oaths, on the death of his uncle Stephen left his county of Boulogne (but a day's journey from south-east England) and went straight to London where he secured the support of the citizens. He was crowned on St Stephen's Day 1135 by William de Corbeil, Archbishop of Canterbury.

Matilda protested against Stephen's succession but he was recognized by Pope Innocent II. Stephen secured the royal treasury with the aid of his brother Henry, Bishop of Winchester, and set about bribing many of his opponents, including his wife's uncle, David I, King of Scots. At the same time he gained popular support by promising to restore the laws of Edward the Confessor, a promise never to be fulfilled. Baronial insurrections and wars with the Scots (terminating in Stephen's victory at the Battle of the Standard) occupied the early years of the reign.

Matilda landed in England in the autumn of 1139, where she was ably supported by her half-brother Robert, Earl of Gloucester, and was joined by several powerful barons. In the course of the civil wars which ensued, Stephen was captured at Lincoln in February 1141 and imprisoned at Bristol. His brother, Bishop Henry, turned against him and a legatine council of the English Church held at Winchester declared Stephen deposed and proclaimed Matilda 'Lady of the English' on 7 April 1141.

Stephen's supporters continued the struggle and, having managed to capture Robert of Gloucester, exchanged him for Stephen, who had himself re-crowned on the anniversary of his first coronation. This was still not an end to the strife which ravaged the country, Stephen and Matilda alternately gaining the upper hand. In 1144 Stephen lost Normandy to Geoffrey of Anjou, Matilda's husband. A feud with the papacy led to an interdict in 1148, not raised until 1151. In 1152 Stephen sought to secure the succession in his own family by crowning his son Eustace, a practice in use in France, but the Pope refused to sanction it.

Matilda, by this time, had retired to Normandy, but her son Henry, now grown to manhood, took her place in 1153 and was joined by all her old supporters. This time the matter was settled without further bloodshed and by the Treaty of Westminster it was agreed that Stephen should retain the crown for life and that Henry should succeed him.

The following year Stephen, now fifty-seven or fifty-eight, was at Dover when he was seized with what in the light of modern knowledge appears to have been an acute attack of appendicitis aggravated by bleeding piles, and he died in great agony on 25 October. He was buried with his wife and son Eustace, who had both predeceased him, in Faversham Abbey, his own foundation. Stephen was a sad figure, but most of his troubles were of his own making or the result of his weakness of character. Although brave in battle, he was politically inept, completely lacking the deviousness of his uncle Henry I, an essential for survival in those days.

Stephen's coinage is of inferior quality to that of his predecessors but he is depicted in profile facing right and George Vertue based his engraving on this likeness.

Matilda of Boulogne

Born:	Boulogne (?) *ca* 1105
Married:	Westminster (?) 1125
Crowned:	Westminster Abbey 22 March 1136
Died:	Hedingham Castle, Essex 3 May 1152
Buried:	Faversham Abbey

Stephen's wife was to prove one of his most active and staunch supporters throughout his long struggles. A great heiress, she was the only daughter of Eustace III, Count of Boulogne and Mary of Scotland, the younger sister of Henry I's first queen. She was born between 1103 and 1105. On her father's death she succeeded to the county of Boulogne and in 1125 Henry I arranged her marriage to his nephew Stephen.

Matilda was as strong and resourceful as Stephen was weak and indecisive. It was she who recaptured London for him from the Empress Matilda's forces and later forced the Empress's withdrawal from the siege of Winchester, leading to Stephen's release in 1141 in exchange for Robert of Gloucester. Had she not died in 1152 the dispute over the crown might well have continued and there would have been no Treaty of Westminster. Stephen was even more of a broken reed without her and survived her by a little over two years.

THE PLANTAGENETS: THE HOUSE OF ANJOU

The male line of the Counts of Anjou is traced to Geoffrey II of Château-Landon, Count of Gatinais, who married Ermengarde, the heiress of Anjou around the first quarter of the eleventh century. There must have been a Geoffrey I before him, but he is a more than shadowy figure. Ermengarde's family had reigned in Anjou for about two hundred years and claimed descent from the fairy Mélusine.

Geoffrey and Ermengarde's grandson, Count Fulk V, resigned Anjou and Maine (the latter county acquired by his first marriage) to his eldest son Geoffrey and went off to the crusades. Here he married as his second wife Melesende, Queen of Jerusalem, an even greater heiress, becoming King in her right and dying at Acre in 1144.

Geoffrey, the son who stayed at home to rule Anjou and Maine, acquired the nickname of *Plantagenet* from the sprig of broom (*planta genista*) which he jauntily wore in his cap. It was he who married Henry I's daughter the Empress Matilda and became the ancestor of our Plantagenet kings.

| HENRY II *Curtmantle* | 1154–1189 |

Born:	Le Mans 25 March 1133	(3) Matilda: *b.* London 1156; *d.* Brunswick 28 June 1189; *m.* Minden 1 February 1168, Henry V (the Lion), Duke of Saxony and Bavaria
Acceded:	25 October 1154	
Crowned:	Westminster Abbey 19 December 1154	
Married:	Bordeaux 18 May 1152, Eleanor, Duchess of Aquitaine, formerly wife of Louis VII, King of France and elder daughter and heiress of William X, Count of Poitou, and Aënor, daughter of Aimery I, Viscount of Châtellerault	(4) Richard, later King Richard I
		(5) Geoffrey, Duke of Brittany in right of his wife: *b.* 23 September 1158; *d.* (killed in a tournament) Paris 19 August 1186; *m.* July 1181, Constance, Duchess of Brittany; one son and one daughter
Children:	(1) William: *b.* Normandy 17 August 1152; *d.* Wallingford Castle, Berkshire *ca* April 1156	(6) Eleanor: *b.* Domfront, Normandy 13 October 1162; *d.* Burgos 31 October 1214; *m.* Burgos September 1177, Alfonso VIII, King of Castile
	(2) Henry the Young King: *b.* Bermondsey 28 February 1155, crowned in his father's lifetime; *d.* Martel 11 June 1183; *m.* Neubourg, Normandy 2 November 1160, Margaret, daughter of Louis VII, King of France, and his 2nd wife Constance of Castile (she remarried with Bela III, King of Hungary)	(7) Joan: *b.* Angers October 1165; *d.* 4 September 1199; *m.* 1st, Palermo 13 February 1177, William II, King of Sicily (*d.* 18 November 1189); 2nd, Rouen October 1196, Raymond VI, Count of Toulouse
		(8) John, later King John
Died:		Chinon 6 July 1189
Buried:		Fontevraud Abbey

Henry FitzEmpress had a strong claim to the throne. His mother was the proud childless widow of the Emperor Henry V and the only surviving legitimate child of King Henry I. She had, at her father's behest, been married to Geoffrey V, Count of Anjou and Maine, with the express purpose of providing male heirs when it became obvious that no issue was likely to be forthcoming from Henry's own second marriage. Although married somewhat unwillingly to the fourteen-year-old Count, ten years her junior, she did bear him three sons, of whom Henry was the eldest.

During the civil war in England, Geoffrey Plantagenet had taken the opportunity to acquire Normandy from the preoccupied Stephen and in 1150 had invested his son Henry with the duchy. The following year, Geoffrey died and the young Duke also succeeded to the counties of Anjou and Maine. In 1152 Henry was seduced by the newly divorced Queen of France, Eleanor of Aquitaine, a woman eleven or so years his senior, and their subsequent marriage added further to his French dominions. Stephen's agreement to his claim to the English throne the next year and his accession on Stephen's death in 1154 made him the ruler of a greater empire than any of his predecessors.

The early years of the reign were spent in restoring law and order and recovering the Crown lands and prerogatives dissipated by Stephen. In this Henry was ably assisted by the Church, and a brilliant young cleric Thomas à Becket, a protégé of Archbishop Theobald of Canterbury, rose swiftly to power as the King's chief adviser. Plans to invade Ireland in 1155 fell through, but Malcolm IV, King of Scots was forced to restore the northern counties of England which had been ceded to his grandfather David I. An invasion of North Wales took place in 1157 followed in 1159 by a campaign in France to assert Queen Eleanor's claim to the county of Toulouse. This proved unsuccessful and an uneasy peace was concluded with Eleanor's former husband Louis VII, whose daughter Margaret (by his second wife) was betrothed to Henry and Eleanor's eldest surviving son.

Henry returned to England in 1163 and almost at once began a quarrel with the Church which was to occupy the next few years of his reign. Henry had raised his Chancellor Thomas à Becket to the Archbishopric of Canterbury in 1162, and in order to show that he was no mere cipher of the King, Becket set out to prove his independence. An argument developed between them over the issue of 'criminous clerks' and in 1164 Becket was forced to leave the country and Henry impounded the revenues of the archbishopric. Eventually, in spite of Henry's finesse, threat of a papal interdict forced a reconciliation and Becket returned to England in 1170. The well-known story of Henry's exasperated utterance 'will no one rid me of this turbulent priest?', leading to

Becket's murder in his own cathedral on 29 December 1170, was disastrous to Henry's cause against the Church, but he cannot be considered altogether culpable. He was stricken with remorse and his public penance at Becket's tomb, while expediently obtaining papal absolution at the price of a complete surrender over the matters in dispute, exhibited a genuine sorrow at the loss of a once dear and trusted friend.

In 1170 Henry had his eldest surviving son, a boy of fifteen also named Henry, crowned at Westminster Abbey, borrowing a custom which had grown up at the French court to ensure a peaceful succession. Louis VII took exception to the fact that his daughter Margaret, the 'Young King's' wife, had not also been crowned, and to satisfy him the ceremony was repeated at Winchester, with Margaret participating, in August 1172. At the banquet which followed the coronation King Henry II served his son himself, remarking that 'No other King in Christendom has such a butler.' 'It is only fitting', came the pert reply from his son, 'that the son of a Count

should wait on the son of a King.' Alas, young Henry did not live to become King Henry III, dying long before his father in 1183. His only child died in infancy and Margaret remarried and ended her days as Queen of Hungary.

The latter part of Henry's reign was taken up by quarrels with and between his sons, stirred into rebellion by their mother from whom he had separated. In 1189 Henry was at Tours when he received the news that his youngest and favourite son John was in league with his enemies. It broke his heart. At fifty-six he was prematurely aged, worn out by the strenuous exertion of trying to hold together his unwieldy empire. On 30 June he was struck down by fever, yet nevertheless on the 4 July set out to meet Philip of France at Colombières. While the two Kings spoke, still mounted, a sudden thunder clap caused Henry's horse to rear and throw him. He made his peace with Philip and was carried in a litter to the Castle of Chinon. His last two days were embittered by wrangling with a deputation of monks from Canterbury come to demand further concessions for their order. Nearing his end, Henry asked to be carried before the altar of the castle church where, deliriously

Henry II (left) and Richard I as depicted in a medieval manuscript in the British Library.

cursing the day he was born and calling down heaven's vengeance on his sons, he suffered a violent haemorrhage and died almost immediately. He was buried in the Abbey of Fontevraud.

Henry's effigy, though stylized, gives some impression of his appearance. Sturdily built with a large head, he was clean shaven, had grey eyes and had inherited the red hair of his Norman ancestors which he wore cut short. His nickname of 'Curtmantle' was derived from the short Continental cloak he wore, which appeared strange to English eyes. Essentially a man of action, athletic, energetic and self-disciplined, Henry stands out among his contemporaries. We are told he spoke not only Latin and French but also had a good knowledge of all languages 'from the French sea to the Jordan'. His mother, who retained a great influence on him until her death in 1167, had taken care with his education and he was well-grounded in law and history. Although a man of strong passions, hasty, and often bad-tempered, Henry's good qualities outweigh the lesser and he was undoubtedly a great king and the dominant figure of his day in western European politics.

Eleanor of Aquitaine

Born:	Bordeaux or Belin *ca* 1122
Married:	1st, Bordeaux 1137, Louis VII (le Jeune), King of France (annulled 18 March 1152); 2nd, Bordeaux 18 May 1152, Henry II, King of England
Crowned:	Westminster Abbey 19 December 1154
Died:	Fontevraud 31 March/1 April ~~1024~~ 1204
Buried:	Fontevraud Abbey

It must be admitted that Eleanor was, in her youth at any rate, a lady of easy virtue. She was the elder of two daughters of William X, Count of Poitou, and Aënor of Châtellerault. Her name is said to have been invented by adding the prefix of Ali- to that of her mother (Alienor signifying 'another Aënor'). Her parents both died when she was a child and she was brought up under the care of her grandfather, Duke William IX of Aquitaine, a renowned troubadour.

Heiress of the great house of Aquitaine, she was married first to Louis VII, King of France. She bore him two daughters, but the couple were quite incompatible. Her levity of conduct when she accompanied him to Palestine on crusade, where she is said to have had an affair with Saladin among others, led Louis on their return to seek an annulment on the grounds of their consanguinity. Consanguinity and affinity were very convenient grounds for obtaining the desired dissolution of a marriage in the Middle Ages. Such grounds could almost always be found but only needed to be invoked when things had gone wrong.

Given her freedom, Eleanor lost no time in seducing the young Duke of Normandy and Count of Anjou, who probably saw her merely as a means of adding Aquitaine to his growing dominions and annoying his enemy the King of France. When they married at Bordeaux in May 1152, Eleanor was about thirty years old and Henry just nineteen. A large family of five sons and three daughters was born over the next fifteen years. Henry's flagrant infidelities were perhaps only to be expected from the still vigorous husband of an ageing wife and Eleanor herself had never been noted for chasteness of conduct. The romantic story of Henry's love for 'The Fair Rosamund', whom he installed in a bower (the 'site' of which is still pointed out in Kent), where she was discovered by Eleanor and put to death, can safely be consigned to legend. As the children grew up the couple grew further apart and Eleanor took a delight in backing first one son and then another against his father.

After Henry's death Eleanor continued to lead a sprightly life ill-befitting her years and again visited the eastern Mediterranean when she escorted Berengaria of Navarre on part of the journey to marry her son Richard. Eleanor lived to see her favourite son John ascend the throne and when she died at Fontevraud in 1204 she was about eighty-two, an age which no other queen consort was to attain or exceed for over seven hundred years.

RICHARD I COEUR DE LION   1189–1199

Born:	Beaumont Palace, Oxford 8 September 1157
Acceded:	6 July 1189
Crowned:	Westminster Abbey 3 September 1189
Married:	Limasol, Cyprus 12 May 1191, Berengaria, daughter of Sancho VI (the Wise), King of Navarre, and Beatrice (or Sanchia), daughter of Alfonso VII, King of Castile
Died:	Châlus, Limousin 6 April 1199
Buried:	Fontevraud Abbey

It is curious that Richard Lionheart should be regarded as a national hero and have been chosen to typify English monarchy in the fine statue erected outside the Houses of Parliament, since he spent less time in and took less interest in his country than any other king before or since. As the second surviving son of Henry II, he grew up with little prospect of succeeding to the throne until the death of his elder brother Henry the 'Young King' in June 1183. Meanwhile, he had been invested as Duke of Aquitaine (his mother's inheritance) in 1172 before reaching the age of fifteen, and shown his military prowess by besieging and taking the seemingly impregnable fortress of Taillebourg in 1179.

In the autumn of 1187 news reached Europe of Saladin's crushing defeat of the Christian forces at Hattin in July, and fired with enthusiasm Richard took the Cross, vowing to devote the rest of his life to the reconquest of the Holy Land. Before leaving Europe, however, Richard had a stormy meeting with his father and King Philip of France, to whom he did homage for his French possessions much to his father's annoyance.

On Henry's death Richard set out for England, pausing at Rouen to be invested with the Duchy of Normandy and receive the fealty of his Norman barons in July. Arriving in England, he proclaimed a general amnesty and was crowned at Westminster on 3 September. A unique feature of the ceremonial, recorded by Roger of Hoveden, was that Richard himself took the crown from the altar and handed it to Archbishop Baldwin before the act of crowning. The coronation celebrations were marred, however, by a violent persecution of the London Jews, followed by similar outbreaks in Lincoln, Norwich and York. Concerned with little but raising money to pursue the Crusade, Richard paid scant heed and returned to Normandy before Christmas. At last, in July 1190 the Crusade headed by Richard and Philip of France set out and made its way across Europe. By October they had reached Messina, where further delays took place and Richard did penance for vice.

Although it has been denied by a recent biographer, it seems likely that Richard was homosexual. His marriage was probably never consummated and throughout his life preachers were to thunder at him to beware the fate of Sodom. However, he did have one well-attested illegitimate son, Philip, so there must have been some heterosexual episode in his life. Richard's mother Eleanor was probably aware of her son's weakness and hastened to join him with a young bride. Her choice fell on Berengaria of Navarre, whose own brother had probably been one of Richard's early lovers. The marriage took place in Cyprus and was followed immediately by Berengaria's coronation as Queen of England.

The Crusade proceeded but failed to recapture Jerusalem and after concluding a truce with Saladin, the Saracen leader, Richard sailed for home in October 1192. Wrecked in the Adriatic, he set out to cross Europe by land but was flung into prison for fifteen months by the Duke of Austria, whom he had rashly insulted in the Holy Land. The romantic story has often been told of how the minstrel Blondel sought out Richard's place of imprisonment by travelling throughout Austria singing one of Richard's own songs until he heard the refrain taken up from a barred window. This may be true. At any rate the ransom demand was finally met and Richard returned to London in March 1194 to find that his brother John had been depleting the

The following pictures take us from the days of William the Conqueror (the Bayeux Tapestry and Domesday Book) to eve of the Wars of the Roses. We see some fine examples of medieval craftsman in architecture, sculpture and art; and the rich, glowing colours of Richard II's portrait are reminiscent of a Greek or Russian icon.

Opposite

Above, Harold takes his solemn oath to aid William of Normandy to gain the English throne on the death of Edward the Confessor. This section of the Bayeux Tapestry gives a spirited rendering of the scene at the ducal court and manages to make Harold look none too pleased about the proceedings, while tittering Norman nobles whisper behind their hands.

Below, Domesday Book, William the Conqueror's great survey of England made in 1086.

UBI HAROLD:SACRAMENTUM:FECIT: HIC HAROLD:DV
VVILLELMO DVCI:

Dover Castle **(right)** was begun by Harold and its fortifications were improved by William the Conqueror. Stephen died in the castle in 1154 and his successor Henry II built the existing stone castle for the then enormous cost of £7000. Later Kings made further additions. Commanding the English Channel, the castle was of great strategic importance up to the Napoleonic wars when it was used to house French prisoners and extensive underground passages were constructed in the chalk cliffs on which it stands.

Below, a medieval illuminated manuscript showing the crusader King Richard I unhorsing a disgruntled Saracen.

Above, an illumination from the manuscript *De Rege Johanne* shows King John and his hounds intent on a stag hunt while the birds in the trees maintain a disdainful disapproval and the rabbits look somewhat apprehensive. Note the King's gauntlet gloves.

Right, a gold penny of Henry III. This rare coin was struck in 1257 by William the royal goldsmith and depicts the King enthroned in regal splendour with crown, orb and sceptre.

60

Left, a Victorian artist's impression of the scene at Runnymede when King John put his seal to Magna Carta. It is one of Daniel Maclise's great series of historical frescoes commissioned to decorate the walls of the Houses of Parliament when they were rebuilt after the disastrous fire of 1834.

Right, the nave of Westminster Abbey looking west. The loftiest Gothic nave in England (102 ft) is one of the glories of Henry III's rebuilding of the Abbey. The tomb of the unknown warrior of World War I can be seen in the centre surrounded by poppies. Its position, immediately inside the west door, led a wit to remark after reading the somewhat fulsome inscription: 'They buried him among the Kings – but only just!' The singularly incongruous crystal chandeliers are an infelicitous post-war addition to the Abbey furnishings.

Right, a contemporary illuminated manuscript depicting the coronation of Edward I. The crown has just been set on the King's head and he holds the sceptre with the dove while one of the attendant bishops holds aloft the ampulla of holy oil with which Edward would have been annointed at an earlier stage of the ceremony.

Below, the alabaster monumental effigy of Edward II in Gloucester Cathedral commissioned by his son Edward III. Edward's murder at Berkeley Castle led many to regard him as a martyr and his tomb became the centre of a popular cult for many years. Viewed from this side, the carved initials with which the monument has been defaced over the centuries are not visible.

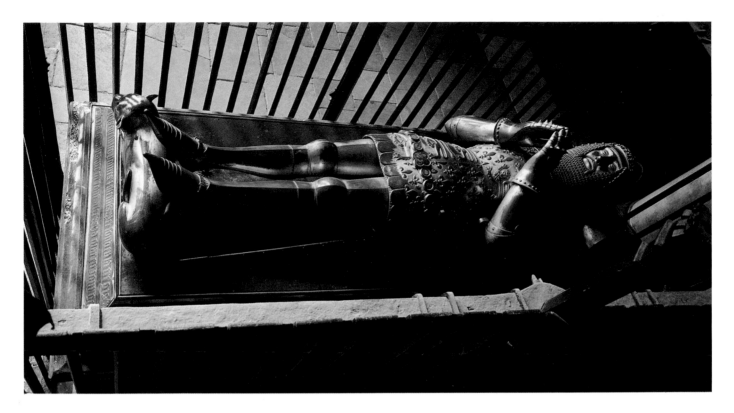

Above, the tomb of Edward the Black Prince in Canterbury Cathedral. At his own request he was buried as near as possible to Thomas à Becket's shrine, which was destroyed by Henry VIII's order in 1538.

Left, a medieval representation of the Tower of London, looking very much as it does today with Traitor's Gate easily recognisable in the foreground. In the distance is old London Bridge covered with houses, shops and a chapel.

treasury and planning to supplant him. John, like many other rogues, possessed charm and good looks and Richard readily forgave him, exclaiming, 'You are a child!'

During Richard's absence, his Continental possessions had been threatened by his enemies, including the King of France who had returned from the Crusade earlier than Richard. The years after his return from imprisonment were spent in regaining lost territory and strengthening his hold over his Continental possessions. During this period he constructed the great fortress of Château-Gaillard in Normandy and is said to have been his own architect. Its purpose was to guard the border between Normandy and France.

In March 1199 Richard was laying siege to the town of Châlus in Limousin, where he claimed possession as the ultimate suzerain, but the local landlord had refused to give it up. One morning while riding before the town walls Richard was struck on the right shoulder by an arrow loosed from the battlements by a crossbowman. He made light of the wound and continued his siege, successfully taking the town several days later. His physician Marchadeus had made a bungling job of removing the arrow and the wound turned gangrenous. The King died on 6 April, nursed at the last by his mother Queen Eleanor. Marchadeus paid for his mishandling of the case with his life a few days later. Richard was buried at Fontevraud near his father. His heart, as was then frequently the custom, was buried separately at Rouen.

Opposite

Above, King Richard II, the only contemporary painted portrait of a medieval king prior to the fifteenth century. It hangs in Westminster Abbey and may have been painted to commemorate the King's visit there on the feast of the translation of St Edward the Confessor on 13 October 1390. The portrait has been attributed to André Beau (working 1361-1400) and also to Jacquemart de Hesdin. The face accords well with descriptions of Richard and also with his monumental effigy, in which the features are older and heavier.

Below, Leeds Castle, near Maidstone, Kent, takes its name from Ledian, or Leed, a prominent Kentish magnate of the mid 9th century and the original builder. A stone castle was built by the Normans and passed into royal ownership in 1278, when it was bought by Eleanor of Castile and passed down through her to succeeding English Queens. It was the scene of a strange incident in the reign of Edward II, when his Queen Isabel of France was refused admission to the castle by Lady Badlesmere, the wife of the absent castellan. The good lady ordered her men to shoot at the royal party and a member of the Queen's entourage was actually killed by an arrow. The over zealous guardian was imprisoned in the Tower of London but eventually pardoned.

Berengaria of Navarre

Born:	Pamplona *ca* 1163
Married and Crowned:	Limasol, Cyprus 12 May 1191
Died:	L'Epau Abbey, near Le Mans after 1230
Buried:	L'Epau Abbey

Berengaria was the only English queen never to set foot in England and her name is more likely to conjure up memories of the Atlantic luxury liner which plied the seas between the two world wars than of Richard Lionheart's consort. Richard and Berengaria first met when little more than children at a tournament held at her father's court in Pamplona. Here Richard formed a strong romantic attachment (Agnes Strickland calls it 'an ardent friendship') with Berengaria's brother Sancho. Urged to marry soon after his accession by his mother and others, Richard's thoughts turned to the sister of his beloved friend, whom she may have resembled, and his mother was charged with demanding her hand on his behalf and escorting her to join him at whatever point he might have reached on the Crusade.

Queen Eleanor escorted Berengaria as far as Messina where she handed her over to her daughter, the Queen of Sicily, who accompanied her the rest of the way to Cyprus. Here they joined Richard and the marriage and coronation of Berengaria were celebrated.

Berengaria accompanied Richard throughout the Crusade and was always treated courteously by him, but it is doubtful if the marriage was ever consummated.

When Richard's party left the Holy Land to return to Europe the ladies sailed on a different ship from the King. Whereas he was shipwrecked, they landed safely at Naples and proceeded to Rome. After a year in Rome the Pope gave them a safe-conduct to travel to Marseilles. Here the widowed Queen of Sicily met Raymond de St Gilles, Count of Toulouse. They fell in love and were married shortly afterwards in Poitou.

Richard returned to his Angevin possessions in 1195 but made no attempt to rejoin his queen until exhorted to do so by a monk who railed against his irregular life. A reunion was affected and the royal couple spent the Christmas of 1196 together at Poitiers. On Richard's death Berengaria had the revenues of the tin mines in Devon and Cornwall, the county of Bigorre and the city of Le Mans settled on her as dower, and it was in Le Mans that she settled in widowhood. She founded the Abbey of L'Epau there and retired to it on its completion in 1230, dying, it is believed, soon afterwards. The abbey in which she was buried fell into ruin and in the seventeenth century Berengaria's mutilated effigy was found lying with her bones beneath a pile of wheat. It was carefully restored and provides the only known likeness of this almost unknown queen.

JOHN *Lackland*   **1199–1216**

Born:	Beaumont Palace, Oxford 24 December 1167
Acceded:	6 April 1199
Crowned:	Westminster Abbey 27 May 1199
Married:	1st, Marlebridge 29 August 1189 (annulled on the grounds of consanguinity 1200), Isabella, Countess of Gloucester (who remarried twice and *d.* November 1217) 2nd, Bordeaux 24 August 1200, Isabella, daughter of Aymer Taillefer, Count of Angoulême, and Alice de Courtenay
Children:	(1) Henry, later King Henry III
	(2) Richard, Earl of Cornwall, elected King of the Romans 1257: *b.* Winchester Castle 5 January 1209; *d.* Berkhamsted 2 April 1272; *m.* 1st, Fawley, Bucks 13 March 1231, Lady Isabella Marshal (*b.* Pembroke Castle 9 October 1200; *d.* Berkhamsted 15 January 1240); three sons and one daughter; *m.* 2nd, Westminster Abbey 23 November 1243, Sanchia of Provence, sister of Eleanor, wife of Henry III (*b.* Aix-en-Provence *ca* 1225, *d.* Berkhamsted 9 November 1261); two sons; *m.* 3rd, Kaiserslautern, Germany 16 June 1269, Beatrix of Falkenburg (*b. ca* 1253, *d.* 17 October 1277); no issue

	(3) Joan: *b.* Gloucester 22 July 1210; *d.* near London 4 March 1238; *m.* York 19 June 1221, as his 1st wife, Alexander II, King of Scots; no issue
	(4) Isabella: *b.* Gloucester 1214; *d.* Foggia 1 December 1241; *m.* Worms 20 July 1235, as his 3rd wife, Frederick II (Hohenstaufen), Holy Roman Emperor and King of Sicily; two sons and two daughters
	(5) Eleanor: *b.* Gloucester 1215; *d.* Montargis, France 13 April 1275; *m.* 1st 23 April 1224, as his 2nd wife, William Marshal, 2nd Earl of Pembroke (*d.* 24 April 1231); no issue; *m.* 2nd, Westminster 7 January 1239, Simon de Montfort, 2nd Earl of Leicester (killed at Evesham 4 August 1265); five sons and one daughter. King John also had several illegitimate children, of whom Joan *m.* 1205, Llywelyn the Great, Prince of Gwynedd, and *d.* at Aber 2 February 1237
Died:	Newark Castle 18 October 1216
Buried:	Worcester Cathedral

John has always been regarded as the archetype 'bad' king; yet he had some redeeming features and his good looks and charm induced many of those he wronged to forgive him.

The youngest child of Henry II and Eleanor of Aquitaine, John was born when his mother was well over forty and was to become and remain her favourite child. He inherited or acquired many of her characteristics. What he did not inherit or acquire was any patrimony, as did his elder brothers, and his nickname of 'Lackland' is said to have been bestowed on him by his father. John grew up a dandy, a gourmet and a womanizer, dedicated to a sybaritic existence and entirely unprincipled. His parents looked on his youthful escapades with indulgence and doubtless extricated him from many scrapes. At eighteen John was sent to Ireland to complete the conquest but was soon recalled when his ridiculing of the long beards and style of dress of the Irish princes and chieftains aggravated an already delicate situation.

Richard I seems to have had a soft spot for his young brother and on his accession conferred upon him the county of Mortain in Normandy. He also arranged a marriage with an English heiress, the granddaughter of Robert, Earl of Gloucester (Henry I's bastard), who had been such a staunch supporter of the Empress Matilda. The marriage at once encountered ecclesiastical difficulties as the couple were second cousins and the Archbishop of Canterbury declared the marriage void and placed their lands under an interdict. John at once appealed to the Pope and got the decision reversed. However, there was little or no love between the pair and they soon ceased to live together.

Though fond of John, Richard was well aware of his weaknesses and at first excluded him from any part in the government when he left for the Crusade, appointing a Norman, William de Longchamp, as Chancellor and principal regent. John lost no time in identifying himself with the people, who resented the Chancellor's arrogant French ways. With the assistance of his half-brother Geoffrey, Archbishop of York (one of Henry II's bastards), he led a force to seize London, where he promptly won over the citizens by granting them the right to elect a mayor. Longchamp fled disguised as a woman and was about to sail from Dover when the advances of an over-amorous sailor discovered him. John was so amused on hearing of this incident that he allowed him to go.

Despite John's scheming against him, Richard was ever forgiving and on his deathbed named John as heir. By the rules of primogeniture Arthur, Duke of Britanny, the posthumous son of John's elder brother Geoffrey should have succeeded, but he was only eleven years old and the succession of a child in those times was to be avoided if possible.

John was invested as Duke of Normandy at Rouen on 25 April 1199. In the course of the solemn ceremony he dropped the spear, part of the ducal insignia, and this was later to be taken as a portent of the loss of the duchy five years later. After this he set out for England and his coronation at Westminster, at which the Archbishop, Hubert Walter, delivered an oration arguing that the election of a sovereign was more important than hereditary right.

John's next step was to rid himself of his now unwanted wife, who had not been acknowledged as queen. An annulment was easily procured on the old grounds and after a whirlwind courtship John married Isabella of Angoulême, a twelve-year-old girl with whom he had become infatuated while campaigning in France. Neither was to be a model of fidelity.

The murder of his nephew and rival Arthur of Brittany at Rouen in April 1203 was carried out at John's instigation and aroused the fury of Philip Augustus of France who, as overlord of both Brittany and Normandy, declared John's duchy forfeit and began an invasion. Château-Gaillard fell in March 1204 and in June the French King entered Rouen. The once mighty Angevin empire had shrunk to a fragment.

In 1205 John began a quarrel with the Church when he refused to accept Pope Innocent III's nomination of Stephen Langton as Archbishop of Canterbury in preference to John, Bishop of Norwich, his own nominee and a personal friend. His intransigence in this matter led to a papal interdict being laid over the whole country in 1208 and his own excommunication. John was forced to submit at last and humiliatingly resign his kingdom to the Pope and receive it back again as a fief of the papacy before the interdict and excommunication were ended in May 1213.

In 1214 John conducted another campaign in France and suffered a catastrophic defeat at Bouvines. During his absence the barons banded together under the leadership of Stephen Langton to protest against the longstanding misgovernment of the realm. This culminated in the best known event of John's reign, his forced sealing of *Magna Carta* at Runnymede, near Windsor, on 15 June 1215. The charter defined the rights of the Church, the barons and the people. In essence it declared that the Church was free to choose its own bishops; that no money over and above certain regular payments was to be exacted from the King's feudal tenants without their previous consent; and that no freedom was to be punished except in accordance with the laws of the land.

John was infuriated by this forced agreement and claimed that he had acted under duress. He gained the backing of the Pope who had once excommunicated him and received his blessing to gather an army and fight the barons, who for their part called in Louis of France, the heir to the French throne. Louis landed at Sandwich and proceeded at once to London where the barons made him their leader and promised him the throne. Once again civil war was rife in the land and a year of indecisive skirmishing ensued.

Journeying through East Anglia with his band, John attempted to cross the Wash from Norfolk to Lincolnshire but misjudged the tides so that the whole of his baggage train was lost, including his crown and many valuables. The story has inspired treasure hunters ever since, but nothing was ever recovered except a small crest crown from a helmet. The loss affected John so greatly that Matthew Paris says: 'He fell into such deep despondency . . . that being seized with a sharp fever he became seriously ill. But he aggravated the discomfort of his illness by his disgusting gluttony, for that night by indulging too freely in peaches and copious draughts of new cider he greatly increased his feverishness.' Next day John was suffering from dysentery but he managed to ride as far as Sleaford, where he took to a litter and was carried to Newark Castle. Here 'in a day or two' he died on the night of 18 October 1216, aged nearly forty-nine.

John was buried in Worcester Cathedral, clad as a monk and, at his own request, as near the shrine of St Wulfstan as possible. Later his tomb was moved to the centre of the choir where his effigy may be seen today. Though not contemporary it conveys a strong impression of character.

John's personality was a complex one and latterly he has found some apologists. He was cruel and avaricious but possessed a sense of humour and could occasionally shows acts of mercy and generosity.

Isabella of Angoulême

Born:	Angoulême *ca* 1188
Married:	1st, Bordeaux 24 August 1200
Crowned:	Westminster Abbey 8 October 1200
Married:	2nd, in France before 22 May 1220, Hugh X de Lusignan, Count of La Marche, by whom she had issue
Died:	Fontevraud 31 May 1246
Buried:	Fontevraud Abbey

Isabella, the twelve-year-old heiress of the county of Angoulême, was betrothed to Hugh de Lusignan, son and heir of the Count of La Marche. She was residing at the Castle of Lusignan when John saw her, became infatuated, and carried her off 'screaming with terror' to Bordeaux. This is the romantic version of events; the reality was a little different. Dazzled by the prospect of their daughter becoming a queen, Isabella's parents connived at breaking off her betrothal to Lusignan and the compliant clergy, headed by the Archbishop of Bordeaux, declared that there was no impediment to her union with John and solemnized the marriage forthwith.

The first few years of Isabella's marriage were passed in a round of pleasure, accompanying the King on his journeys about his dominions. Her first child, the future Henry III, was not born until 1207, and the next two followed soon after. John was not a faithful husband and Isabella was, if not blatantly unfaithful herself, at least flirtatious when she fancied. John's jealousy was frequently aroused and on one occasion he is said to have hung one of his wife's supposed lovers over her bed. By 1212 John's suspicions of the Queen had become so great that he had her placed in confinement at Gloucester, but the following year a reconciliation took place after Isabella had succeeded to her father's county of Angoulême. Two more daughters were born in 1214 and 1215 respectively.

Queen Isabella was residing at Gloucester with her children when John died in 1216, and on receiving the news she at once took steps to have her elder son proclaimed king and crowned, sending Richard, the younger boy, to Ireland for safety.

In July 1217 Isabella returned to France to take up residence in her native city of Angoulême. Here she met her old fiancé Hugh de Lusignan, now Count of La Marche. He had never married, and a proposed betrothal between him and Isabella's ten-year-old daughter Joan was swiftly set aside 'because her age is so tender' and he was advised to 'take a wife from whom he might speedily hope for an heir'. Accordingly he married the mother, and Isabella became a bride again in 1220 when she was about thirty-two. The marriage took place without Henry III's consent and, although only thirteen, he found it an excuse to deprive his mother of her dower. It was a year before the breech was healed and the arrears of jointure paid.

Isabella bore a large family of five sons and at least three daughters to her second husband. Of the sons, Hugh XI succeeded his parents in La Marche and Angoulême, Guy fell at the battle of Lewes, William became Earl of Pembroke and loyally served his half-brother Henry III and nephew Edward I, and Aymer became Bishop of Winchester in 1250.

In 1242 Isabella and her husband became implicated in a plot against the life of Louis IX and were arraigned to answer before him at a court of enquiry. Isabella remained seated on her horse at the door of the court and, when she heard that matters were likely to go against her, spurred homewards in a terrible rage. When she had calmed down, after attempting to stab herself and tearing her headdress to shreds, she sought refuge in the Abbey of Fontevraud where she remained for the rest of her life. Her husband and son managed to patch up matters with Louis, while Matthew of Paris tells us that 'the Poitevins and French, considering her the origin of the disastrous war with France, called her by no other name than Jezebel, instead of . . . Isabel.'

All things considered, Isabella was a fitting mate for John. She died in May 1246 and was buried in the common graveyard of the Abbey. However, Henry III, visiting his mother's grave some years later, had her body moved into the choir of the Abbey Church and commissioned the fine effigy which is the only near contemporary likeness of her. Isabella's second husband survived until 1249, when he fell fighting in the crusades.

The head of Henry III's monumental effigy in Edward the Confessor's Chapel at Westminster Abbey. It is heavily stylized like all medieval monuments but probably has elements of a true likeness.

HENRY III		1216–1272	

Born:	Winchester Castle 1 October 1207	(4)	Edmund Crouchback, Earl of Leicester
Acceded:	19 October 1216		and Lancaster, titular King of Sicily:
Crowned:	Gloucester Cathedral 28 October 1216,		b. London 16 January 1245; d. Bayonne
	and again at Westminster Abbey 17 May		5 June 1296; m. 1st Westminster
	1220		Abbey 8 or 9 April 1269, Aveline de
Married:	Canterbury Cathedral 4 January 1236,		Forz (d. Stockwell 10 November 1274);
	Eleanor, second daughter and co-heiress of		2nd, Paris before 3 February 1276,
	Raymond Berenger V, Count of Provence,		Blanche (d. 2 May 1302), widow of
	and Beatrice of Savoy		Henry I, King of Navarre, and
Children:	(1) Edward, later King Edward I		daughter of Robert I, Count of Artois;
	(2) Margaret: b. Windsor Castle		left issue
	29 September 1240; d. Cupar Castle,	(5)	Richard: b. ca 1247; d. before 1256
	Fife 26 February 1275; m. York	(6)	John: b. ca 1250; d. before 1256
	26 December 1251, Alexander III,	(7)	Katherine: b. Westminster 25
	King of Scots		November 1253; d. Windsor Castle
	(3) Beatrice: b. Bordeaux 25 June 1242:		3 May 1257
	d. London 24 March 1275; m. St Denis	(8)	William: b. and d. ca 1256
	22 January 1260, John of Dreux, Earl	(9)	Henry: d. young
	of Richmond, later John II, Duke of	Died:	Palace of Westminster 16 November
	Brittany		1272
		Buried:	Westminster Abbey

With the accession of Henry III, the throne of England was occupied by a child for the first time since before the Conquest. Queen Isabella and her children were residing at Gloucester when John died and, since the greater part of eastern England was in the hands of Louis of France and the rebel barons, it was thought expedient to have the nine-year-old Henry crowned as soon as possible. Since the regalia was at Westminster and therefore not available, and John's personal state crown had been lost in the Wash, the young King was crowned in Gloucester Cathedral by the Bishop of Winchester with a gold torque (or bracelet, according to some accounts) belonging to his mother. The regency was exercised by William Marshal, Earl of Pembroke, until his death in 1219 and then by Hubert de Burgh. The King's person and education (his mother having retired to her native land at the first opportunity and remarried) were entrusted to Peter des Roches, Bishop of Winchester. Hubert and the Bishop were soon to become deadly rivals. The French invaders were expelled and the rebel barons brought to heel by the end of 1217 and on Whitsunday 1220 Henry was crowned for a second time in Westminster Abbey with the full ceremonial.

In order to secure the resumption of the royal castles and demesnes which had pased into private hands during the recent civil war, Henry was formally declared of age by Pope Honorius III in 1223, but his personal rule did not commence until 1227 when he was twenty. Even then, Hubert de Burgh retained a great influence until July 1232 when he was dismissed as Justiciar, accused of filling his own pockets from the royal treasury and other malpractices, and imprisoned. Although he probably was guilty of some of these charges, the King was really using him as a scapegoat for the failure of his own ineffectual expedition to France to recover some of the Continental possessions lost by John. Peter des Roches, who had prudently left the kingdom on the declaration of Henry's majority, now returned to power and appointed his fellow Poitevins to high offices, initiating the long period of bad government for which the weak-willed Henry's reign is best known.

When the barons, headed by Edmund Rich, Archbishop of Canterbury, finally demanded the expulsion of the Poitevins in 1234, Henry assumed the administration himself, filling the high offices of state with his own men. His extortionate taxation, disastrous foreign policy, and the favouritism shown to his wife's foreign relations and his own half-brothers, brought matters to a head and the lay barons of the kingdom found a leader in the person of Henry's brother-in-law Simon de Montfort, Earl of Leicester. In the ensuing civil war Henry and his son Edward were defeated and captured by de Montfort at Lewes in 1264 and the King was forced to summon a parliament and undertake to rule with the advice of a council of barons. While the King submitted, 'the Lord' Edward continued to lead the opposition and Montfort was killed at Evesham in 1265. Thereafter Edward and Henry's brother, Richard of Cornwall, concluded a peace with the remaining rebels.

For the rest of his life Henry remained but a cipher

and the forced inactivity eventually resulted in premature senility. The death of his beloved brother Richard was a mortal blow. While praying at St Edmund's shrine in Suffolk, Henry 'began to wax somewhat crasie', in the words of Holinshed. He recovered enough to call a council there, but suffered a relapse and was taken 'with all speed' to London, where he died at the Palace of Westminster. He was sixty-five, and had reigned for fifty-six years. By his own directions he was interred in the original coffin of Edward the Confessor, who had been reburied in a more magnificent one, 'having with his usual simplicity', says Agnes Strickland, 'an idea that its previous occupation by the royal saint had made it a peculiarly desirable tenement.'

If Henry was a bad king, he was not a bad man, possessing none of his father's viciousness. The troubled realm he inherited would have needed a very strong ruler indeed to restore stability. Henry was not the man for the job and it remained for his far abler son and brother to accomplish it. What Henry lacked in statesmanship was largely compensated by a cultivated mind and a patronage of literature and the arts which had been neglected by his immediate predecessors. His rebuilding of Westminster Abbey, a tribute to his profound veneration for Edward the Confessor, whose relics he personally assisted in carrying to their new shrine on 13 October 1269, was his greatest achievement and it stands today as his most eloquent memorial.

Henry was the first sovereign to use a distinguishing numeral on some of his coins, the inscription on his silver pennies reading 'Henricus Tertius'. His appearance may be deduced from his magnificent tomb effigy, which, though stylized, probably represents a genuine likeness.

Eleanor of Provence

Born:	Aix-en-Provence *ca* 1217
Married:	Canterbury Cathedral 4 January 1236
Crowned:	Westminster Abbey 20 January 1236
Died:	Amesbury, Wiltshire 24 June 1291
Buried:	Convent Church, Amesbury; heart buried in Church of Friars Minors (Minories), London

The young girl travelling from the south of France to be married to an unknown bridegroom in the rigours of an English winter must, one feels, have possessed a strength of character above the average. Eleanor, who became Henry III's queen in January 1236, was the second of four beautiful sisters, the daughters of Raymond Berenger V, Count of Provence, himself one of the last great Provençal poets, whose court was renowned for its patronage of the troubadours. All the girls made brilliant marriages: Margaret to St Louis IX, King of France; Eleanor to Henry III; Sanchia to Henry's brother, Richard of Cornwall, King of the Romans; and Beatrice to Charles of Anjou, King of Naples.

Henry III had first negotiated for the hand of Joan, Countess of Ponthieu, whose daughter Eleanor was years later to become the wife of his son Edward. However, having heard from his brother Richard of the beauty and vivacity of the Provençal ladies, he cancelled his suit and made proposals for the hand of Eleanor which were finally accepted after some haggling about her dower. This was necessarily limited because Henry's mother was still alive and in full possession of her jointure, which could only be dowered to Eleanor in reversion.

Eleanor journeyed through France, visiting the court of her sister Queen Margaret *en route*, landed at Dover, and proceeded to Canterbury where she was married to the King by Edmund Rich. Sixteen days later she was crowned at Westminster Abbey. Henry had spared no expense in having the Palace of Westminster refurbished for his young queen, installing refinements of plumbing, window-glazing and a standard of general comfort hitherto unknown in this country. Instructions remain for chambers in the Palace to 'be painted a good green colour, like a curtain.' The Queen's coronation was an occasion of great display and a large equestrian procession escorted the sovereigns from the Tower to Westminster in a splendid cavalcade.

Henry was a loving and faithful husband and the couple's married life remained a completely happy one. However, the Queen's popularity suffered when her Savoyard uncles visited England and were generously entertained, the King extracting money for that purpose from the Jews with threats of expulsion. The marriage of the Queen's sister Sanchia to the King's brother Richard was another occasion of great display, for which the Jews were again obliged to furnish funds.

On the death of Edmund Rich in 1240, Eleanor procured the Archbishopric of Canterbury for her uncle, Boniface of Savoy, writing to the Pope herself to assure the nomination.

Boniface's attempts to institute a visitation of the province of Canterbury were strongly resented, and there was an unseemly brawl when he visited St Bartholomew's Priory in the diocese of London and was told by the monks that they would only accept a visitation from their own bishop. Boniface lost his temper, personally assaulted the sub-prior, and encouraged his attendants to beat the monks savagely. The King refused to listen to the monks' complaint and the people of London chased Boniface into Lambeth Palace, where he was forced to lie low until they had calmed down.

The Queen's extravagances continued to excite the hostility of the Londoners for many years and, even after

...wer lands on the
0, she and Henry
by every possible
o France to deal
was constituted
v Richard. She
f *Aurum Reginae*
nark paid to the
old enemies the
eriffs committed to

...rickland, Eleanor 'loved power well, but pleasure better', and in 1254 she accompanied her son Edward to Spain to take part in the festivities to celebrate his marriage to the Infanta of Castile. On the way back, Henry, Eleanor and the young couple were invited to stay at the French court by Eleanor's sister and brother-in-law. After a long and pleasant sojourn the King and Queen finally returned to England in January 1255 after an absence of nearly a year.

Throughout the civil war Eleanor was active in support of her husband and son, raising money on her jewellery to aid their cause. 'This noble virago', as Matthew of Westminster termed her, was in France when the victory of Evesham was won and rejoined her husband and son as soon as a favourable wind would allow.

On Henry III's death Eleanor exercised the regency until her son Edward returned. She had the sorrow of losing her daughters, the Queen of Scots and the Duchess of Brittany, who both died in 1275. In 1280 she retired to the Benedictine convent of Amesbury, where she intended to take the veil – not, however, until the Pope had given her permission to retain her dower. This being finally granted, she was professed a nun and assumed the religious habit on 7 July 1284. Two of her granddaughters made their profession at the same time.

Eleanor continued to take an interest in the affairs of her widely dispersed family and lived on at Amesbury until 1291, dying after a short illness at the age of about sixty-seven with her son the King at her bedside. Eleanor's is not a very sympathetic character, being strong-willed, avaricious and pleasure-loving, but she was a loyal wife and mother, and her religious vocation appears to have been genuine.

Edward I presiding over the House of Lords, a drawing made in the reign of Edward IV. The King of Scots and the Prince of Wales sit in privileged positions on either side of the King and are flanked by the Archbishops of Canterbury and York; the Law Lords occupy four Woolsacks and the bishops and abbots (and possibly some abbesses) take up a lot of room. The parliamentary robes of the temporal peers are similar to those still worn today.

EDWARD I *Longshanks*   1272–1307

Born:	Palace of Westminster 17 June 1239
Acceded:	16 November 1272
Crowned:	Westminster Abbey 19 August 1274
Married:	1st, Las Huelgas October 1254, Eleanor, daughter of (St) Ferdinand III, King of Castile and Leon, and his 2nd wife Jeanne, Countess of Ponthieu
Children:	(1) Eleanor: *b.* Windsor Castle *ca* 17 June 1264; *d.* Ghent 12 October 1297; *m.* Bristol 20 September 1293, Henry III, Count of Bar
	(2) Joan: *b.* and *d.* 1265
	(3) John: *b.* Winchester or Windsor 10 June or July 1266; *d.* Westminster 1 or 3 August 1271
	(4) Henry: *b.* Windsor 13 July 1267; *d.* Merton, Surrey 14 October 1274
	(5) Julian (alias Katherine): *b.* and *d.* in the Holy Land 1271
	(6) Joan: *b.* Acre, Palestine 1272; *d.* Clare, Suffolk 23 April 1307; *m.* 1st, Westminster Abbey 30 April 1290, Gilbert de Clare, 3rd Earl of Gloucester and 7th Earl of Hertford; 2nd, January 1297, Ralph de Monthermer, 1st Baron Monthermer
	(7) Alfonso, Earl of Chester: *b.* Bordeaux 24 November 1273; *d.* Windsor Castle 19 August 1284
	(8) Margaret: *b.* Windsor Castle 11 September 1275; *d.* Brussels 1318; *m.* Westminster Abbey 8 July 1290, John II, Duke of Brabant
	(9) Berengaria: *b.* Kennington 1276; *d. ca* 1279
	(10) Mary, a nun at Amesbury: *b.* Windsor Castle 11 March 1278; *d.* Amesbury before 8 July 1332
	(11) Alice: *b.* Woodstock 12 March 1279; *d.* 1291
	(12) Elizabeth: *b.* Rhuddlan Castle August 1282; *d. ca* 5 May 1316; *m.* 1st, Ipswich 18 January 1297, John I, Count of Holland; 2nd, Westminster 14 November 1302, Humphrey de Bohun, 4th Earl of Hereford and Essex
	(13) Edward, later King Edward II
	(14) Beatrice: *b.* Aquitaine *ca* 1286; *d.* young
	(15) Blanche: *b.* and *d.* 1290
Married:	2nd, Canterbury Cathedral, 10 September 1299, Margaret, daughter of Philip III, King of France, and Marie of Brabant
Children:	(16) Thomas of Brotherton, Earl of Norfolk: *b.* Brotherton, Yorkshire 1 June 1300; *d.* August 1338; *m.* 1st, *ca* 1316, Alice Hayles (*d.* after 8 May 1326); 2nd, *ca* 1328, Mary de Ros; left issue
	(17) Edmund of Woodstock, Earl of Kent: *b.* Woodstock 5 August 1301; *d.* (beheaded) Winchester 19 March 1330; *m.* December 1325, Margaret, Baroness Wake (*d.* 29 September 1349); left issue
	(18) Eleanor: *b.* Winchester 4 May 1306; *d.* Amesbury 1311
Died:	Burgh-on-the-Sands, near Carlisle, 7 July 1307
Buried:	Westminster Abbey

Edward I is the outstanding English king of the Middle Ages. A great soldier and a wise statesman, he initiated constitutional reforms that laid the foundations of parliamentary government.

Edward, who was named after the revered Edward the Confessor, inherited none of his father's weaknesses and took far more after his very able uncle Richard of Cornwall. He also possessed his mother's strength of character without her pleasure-loving frivolity. The young 'Lord Edward', as he was known, loyally supported his father throughout the civil war and Montfort's rebellion. At the age of fifteen, Edward journeyed to Spain where he received the honour of knighthood from King Alfonso X of Castile and the hand of Alfonso's half-sister the Infanta Eleanor. She became the love of his life and, like his father before him, he was a faithful husband.

By 1270 peace had been restored to the country and Edward went off on crusades, accompanied by Eleanor. When Henry III died in November 1272, Edward was in Sicily making his slow way back. England, he felt, was safe under his mother's regency and he did not hurry, arriving in the summer of 1274. He and Eleanor were crowned together at Westminster Abbey on 19 August.

Edward's encouragement of 'parliaments', which he used to keep in touch with the problems and needs of the country, has led him to be described as the 'Father of the Mother of Parliaments'. His relentless, but unsuccessful, attempts to assert his overlordship of the Scottish kingdom have earned him the grim title of 'Hammer of the Scots', which was to be inscribed on his simple tomb in Westminster. His Welsh campaign was more successful and the country was completely subjugated in two wars, ending with the deaths of Llywellyn and David, the last two native princes. A policy of castle building ensured that Wales remained under English rule and the mighty fortresses of Rhuddlan, Conway, Denbigh, Harlech and Caernarvon still stand.

When campaigning in Scotland Edward captured and took back to England the Stone of Scone on which Scottish kings had always been crowned. This stone was said to be that on which the Patriarch Jacob had slept at Bethel when he had his vision of angels. In many adventures it travelled to Egypt, thence to Spain and to Ireland, where it was set up on the Hill of Tara and became the centre of the inauguration ceremonies of the High Kings of Ireland, being said to utter a groaning noise when the rightful monarch sat on it and to have remained silent under a usurper. Such a stone still stands at Tara, so it must have been a duplicate which, in the continuation of the legend, was taken to Scotland, built into the walls of Dunstaffnage Castle, and finally deposited at Scone by Kenneth MacAlpin in AD850. Edward dedicated the stone to Edward the Confessor, his patron saint, and commissioned Master Walter of Durham to construct a wooden chair to contain it for a fee of one hundred shillings. Since then every English sovereign has been crowned seated in the Coronation Chair, with the exception of Mary II, for whom, as joint sovereign, a duplicate chair without the stone was constructed. Both chairs are exhibited in Westminster Abbey near the Confessor's shrine and have been much defaced and vandalized by Westminster schoolboys and others who have carved their initials over the centuries.

Edward's reign was one of architectural flowering and many cathedrals and abbey churches were begun or rebuilt, including Exeter, Lichfield and York Minster, while the first scientific attempt at town planning took place at Winchelsea, which remains a delight to visitors today.

Edward's beloved Eleanor died in 1290 and nine years later, at the age of sixty, he married the twenty-year-old Margaret of France. The marriage was not unhappy, in spite of the great disparity in age, and three more children were born, making Edward the father of more legitimate children than any other English king before or since.

In June 1307 Edward was again campaigning in the north when he was struck down by dysentery. He died at Burgh-on-the-Sands, near Carlisle, on 7 July, having just completed his sixty-eighth year.

Eleanor of Castile

Born: Castile *ca* 1244
Married: Las Huelgas October 1254
Crowned: Westminster Abbey 19 August 1274
Died: Herdeby, near Grantham, Lincolnshire 24 November 1290
Buried: Westminster Abbey; heart buried in Blackfriars Church, London

Eleanor was only about ten years old when married to the fifteen-year-old Edward of Westminster at Las Huelgas in 1254. Such child marriages were commonplace in Europe in the Middle Ages and the brides were usually consigned to their husbands' families to complete their education. The marriages were not consummated until the bride reached a suitable age (usually fourteen or fifteen) and in Eleanor's case it seems to have been eighteen or nineteen, as the first of her fifteen children was born when she was twenty. Through her mother, an heiress, she brought Ponthieu and Montreuil to her husband's dominions.

Edward and Eleanor were to remain inseparable throughout their married life. In 1270 she accompanied him on a crusade, in the course of which she is said to have sucked the poison from Edward's wounded arm after an assassination attempt with a poisoned dagger. Eleanor's fifth and sixth children were born in the Holy Land, the younger being Joan of Acre (so called from her birthplace). Joan's second marriage, years later, to the squire of her first husband was to so anger her father that in a fit of rage he threw his crown on the fire and the bill for its repair ('when the King's grace was pleased to throw the coronet upon the fire') is still extant.

In 1290 news of the death of Margaret of Scotland, 'The Maid of Norway', sent Edward hastening north, leaving the Queen, who had but recently given birth to her fifteenth child (an infant which did not survive), to follow at a more leisurely pace. She had reached Lincolnshire when she fell ill with a fever and was lodged at Herdeby, near Grantham, in the house of one Master Weston. She grew worse and messengers were sent to recall the King, but before he arrived Eleanor had died. Edward's grief was expressed by the erection of Eleanor Crosses at each place where the Queen's body rested overnight on its journey to London. Thirteen of these once existed, but only those of Northampton and Waltham survive of the originals. Elsewhere replicas have been built, notably at Banbury and at Charing Cross, the last place where the cortège halted on its sad progress to Westminster. Eleanor lies at the feet of her father-in-law Henry III and her effigy manages to convey something of the serenity and beauty which so captivated a king.

It is said that to English ears Eleanor's Spanish title of Infanta of Castile sounded so strange that it became corrupted in speech to 'Elephant and Castle', giving rise to the district of south London and the many inn signs of that name.

Overleaf:
Eleanor of Castile, the beloved first wife of Edward I, from her monumental effigy in Westminster Abbey.

Margaret of France

Born: Paris (?) 1279
Married: Canterbury Cathedral 10 September 1299
Died: Marlborough Castle 14 February 1317
Buried: Grey Friars Church, London

Edward appeared to be an inconsolable widower. His second marriage, at the age of sixty to a girl forty years his junior, seems to have been at the instance of the King of France, the bride's father. Margaret's elder sister Blanche was originally intended for Edward, but Margaret was substituted for reasons that are not clear. When all was agreed she sailed for England, landing at Dover on 8 September. They were married at Canterbury two days later. In October she made her state entry into London and progressed from the Tower to Westminster accompanied by the Mayor and Aldermen and three hundred burgesses. As was customary, the conduits in Cheapside flowed with wine and rich cloths were hung from all the windows on the route. Edward never got around to arranging Margaret's

coronation and she was the first queen since the Conquest not to be consecrated and crowned.

Edward was still a handsome and vigorous man and Margaret appears to have been quite content with her elderly bridegroom. She bore him two sons, who were both to play a part in history, and a daughter (named after the lamented Eleanor), who died young. Margaret accompanied Edward on his campaigns, as Eleanor had done, and was probably with him when he died. She was on excellent terms with her stepson Edward II and travelled to Boulogne to attend his wedding to her niece in January 1308. Returning to England, she took up residence at Marlborough Castle and devoted herself to charitable works. She died there on 14 February 1317, still under forty, and was buried in the Church of the Grey Friars in London, of which she was a co-founder.

Her monument, and those of nine other members of the royal family interred there, was sold for £50 by an avaricious Lord Mayor in the reign of Queen Elizabeth I and consequently lost. Likenesses of Queen Margaret are preserved in stone carvings at Lincoln Cathedral and in Winchelsea Church and by a statuette on the tomb of John of Eltham in Westminster Abbey.

Margaret of France, the second wife of Edward I. There is a surprisingly modern air to this statue of the queen at Lincoln Cathedral.

	EDWARD II		1307–1327

Born:	Caernarvon Castle 25 April 1284	(3) Eleanor:	*b.* Woodstock 18 June 1318;
Acceded:	8 July 1307		*d.* Deventer 22 April 1355,
Crowned:	Westminster Abbey 25 February 1308		*m.* Ni jmegen May 1332, Rainald II,
Married:	Boulogne 25 January 1308, Isabella, eldest		Count (later Duke) of Gueldres
	daughter of Philip IV, King of France, and	(4) Joan:	*b.* Tower of London 5 July 1321;
	Jeanne I, Queen of Navarre		*d.* Hertford 7 September 1362;
Children:	(1) Edward, later King Edward III		*m.* Berwick-on-Tweed 17 July 1328,
	(2) John of Eltham, Earl of Cornwall:		David II, King of Scots
	b. Eltham Palace, Kent *ca* 15 August	Deposed:	20 January 1327
	1316; *d.* Perth 13 or 14 September	Died:	Berkeley Castle, Gloucestershire
	1336		September 1327
		Buried:	Gloucester Cathedral

In Edward II we can again see the phenomenon of a strong father producing a weak-willed son. In his weakness Edward resembled his grandfather Henry III, but unfortunately for him he did not possess Henry's integrity and innate goodness.

Edward of Caernarvon, as he was called from his birthplace, Edward I's mightiest Welsh stronghold, was the thirteenth child of his parents and the only son to survive infancy. The apocryphal story of his father presenting the baby on his shield to the people of Wales as a prince who could speak no word of English has often been told. In fact, Edward did not become heir apparent until he was four months old, when his elder brother Alfonso, Earl of Chester, died, and he was not created Prince of Wales and Earl of Chester until February 1301. He lost his mother at the age of six and his father did not remarry for another nine years and so Edward lacked parental guidance for most of his childhood. He was a lonely boy and his longing for companions of his own age and sex were probably engendered at this early stage of his life. His 'favourites' were badly chosen, however. The first was Piers Gaveston, a Gascon of good family, who became the Prince's inseparable companion and rendered himself odious to the court by the sarcastic and offensive nicknames he applied to its members. Indeed, things got so bad that Edward I banished him shortly before his death. Edward II recalled him immediately after his accession and bestowed the royal Earldom of Cornwall upon him.

Before his father's death Edward had been betrothed to Isabella of France and in January 1308 he sailed to Boulogne to complete the marriage, leaving Gaveston as Guardian of the Realm, or regent, in his absence. The wedding was celebrated with great splendour and the young couple returned to England early in February. Gaveston came to receive them at Dover and the slobbering display of affection with which Edward greeted him caused great dismay to the new Queen and

her two uncles who had accompanied them. Further offence was caused at the coronation on 25 February, when the high honour of carrying St Edward's Crown was assigned to Gaveston, who, it is said, in purple velvet and pearls, 'was dressed more magnificently than the sovereign himself.' The King's cousins, who had been allotted lesser honours, were so outraged that they could scarcely be prevented from coming to blows with Gaveston in the Abbey itself, and they and the rest of the nobility were further incensed when it became apparent later that Gaveston had bungled the arrangements for the coronation banquet, which was badly cooked and not served till after dark.

The feeling against the favourite was such that Edward, who had recently married him off to his niece Margaret (the daughter of Joan of Acre), found it politic to send him to Ireland. He soon found he could not live without him, however, and recalled him the following year. Gaveston regained his old ascendancy over Edward and continued his offensive ways for the next three years until Guy, Earl of Warwick, whom he had nicknamed 'The Black Dog of Arden', kidnapped and murdered him on Blacklow Hill in June 1312. Edward hid his feelings by the seemingly callous comment: 'By God, what a fool he was! I could have told him never to get into Warwick's hands.'

In 1314 Edward took up arms in an attempt to complete his father's Scottish campaign and suffered a complete and ignominious defeat at Bannockburn at the hands of Robert the Bruce, who thus finally secured Scottish independence.

A new favourite now arose in the person of Hugh le Despenser, who was appointed the King's Chamberlain in 1313. He and his father, Hugh 'the elder', Earl of Winchester, had both been supporters of Gaveston and gained the royal favour thereby. They now supported the King against the coalition of nobles, the 'Lords Ordainers', which had been constituted in 1310. They

also intrigued against the Queen and induced Edward to deprive her of her estates in 1324. For her, it was the last straw. She left for France in 1325 and with Roger Mortimer, who became her lover, raised an army in Germany and the Low Countries and returned in 1326. She swept all before her, the Despensers were captured and executed, and the wretched Edward, deposed in favour of his son, was confined in Berkeley Castle.

Edward's end at the hands of his gaolers was horrific. Holinshed describes it thus:

> With heavy feather beds or a table (as some write) being cast upon him they kept him down ... put into his fundament an horn and through the same they thrust up into his body an hot spit or (as others have) through the pipe of a trumpet, a plumber's instrument of iron made very hot, the which passing up into his entrailes and being rolled to and fro burnt the same, but so as no appearance of any wound or hurt outwardlie might be perceived.

The ghostly screams of the dying King were long reputed to be heard ringing through Berkeley Castle.

It is related that Edward once dined with the Abbot of Gloucester, who possessed a collection of royal portraits, and asked him if he proposed to add one of himself. The Abbot courteously replied that the King's likeness would appear in a more distinguished position than those of his predecessors. His utterance was prophetic, for Edward's body was brought to Gloucester Cathedral for burial and a fine alabaster effigy was raised over his tomb by Edward III. Popular disgust at the manner of Edward's death caused his tomb to become the centre of a popular cult and the offerings of the pilgrims were

A 17th century painting of Berkeley Castle, Gloucestershire, where Edward II was so cruelly murdered in 1327.

sufficient to enable the rebuilding of the choir of the Cathedral in Perpendicular style.

Isabella of France

Born: Paris (?) 1295
Married: Boulogne 25 January 1308
Crowned: Westminster Abbey 25 February 1308
Died: Castle Rising, Norfolk 22 August 1358
Buried: Grey Friars Church, London

Isabella, the 'she-wolf of France', is remembered as the wicked Queen of English history. The daughter of two sovereigns and the sister of three kings, she was affianced to the future Edward II at the age of four. Papal dispensation for the marriage was obtained in 1303 and it was solemnized at Boulogne in January 1308. The bride's portion from her father was £18,000 (a vast amount in those days), and she was to have the reversion of the dower settled on her aunt Queen Margaret by Edward I. The bride's trousseau was magnificent and contained two gold crowns set with jewels, gold and silver cups, gold spoons, fifty silver porringers, and twelve large and twelve small silver dishes, as well as dozens of dresses of cloth of gold, cloth of silver, velvet, taffetta, and other materials, furs, household linen, and much more. The presents which her father bestowed on Edward were promptly passed to Gaveston, 'whose passion for finery was insatiable', and the King's marked

Isabella of France, from a roof boss in Bristol Cathedral. This likeness of Edward II's queen conveys something of the sensuality and ruthlessness which earned her the sobriquet of 'the she-wolf of France.'

partiality for his favourite started the rift which was to exist throughout the marriage.

Isabella gave birth to her first child, the future Edward III, in 1312. Three more children followed at well-spaced intervals, a sign that relations between husband and wife were not all they should be, in an age when annual pregnancy was the norm.

The Tower of London was a royal palace as well as a prison at this period and it was there that Isabella first saw and fell in love with a state prisoner, Roger Mortimer. He was under sentence of death but the Queen used her influence to have this sentence commuted to life imprisonment and in August 1323 she connived at his escape from the Tower and flight to France. The following year things came to a head between the Queen and the Despensers and she left the King, who nevertheless foolishly despatched her and their son Edward on a mission to France in September 1325. She at once joined her lover Mortimer in Paris and commenced the long and sordid process which was

to end in Edward II's deposition and murder. Her duplicity and mendacity were such that when her brother the King of France finally had her conduct brought to his notice, he at once ordered her to quit the country and she was compelled to go to Hainault, where the Count and Countess gave her a good reception.

When Isabella had gathered an army she set sail for England, landing at Harwich on 25 September 1326. She was joined by Henry of Lancaster and many barons and knights and was, of course, accompanied by Mortimer, whom she placed in command of her forces. Events moved swiftly and the King's deposition was accomplished by January 1327.

Isabella shed hypocritical tears for her husband at the coronation of her son Edward III, but the murder of Edward II later in the year brought about a reaction of public feeling against her. She was by now living openly with Mortimer. Eventually Edward III was forced to take action and, in spite of his mother's cry, 'Fair son, have mercy on the gentle Mortimer!', as he was literally snatched from her arms at Nottingham Castle, Mortimer was taken and paid for his crimes at Tyburn, having the distinction of being the first person to be executed there. Edward spared his mother a public disgrace but she was obliged to take up residence at Castle Rising in Norfolk and live there quietly, occasionally visited by the King, until her death in August 1358.

Her body was taken to London and buried in Grey Friars Church, where Mortimer's body had been consigned many years previously. 'Carrying her characteristic hypocrisy even to the grave,' says Agnes Strickland, 'she was buried with the heart of her murdered husband on her breast.' Isabella's statuette forms one of the 'weepers' on the tomb of her son John of Eltham and her head also appears as a carving in Winchelsea Church.

EDWARD III   1327–1377

Born: Windsor Castle 13 November 1312
Keeper of
the Realm: 26 October 1326
Proclaimed
King: 25 January 1327
Crowned: Westminster Abbey 2 February 1327
Married: York Minster 24 January 1328, Philippa, third daughter of William III, Count of Holland and Hainault, and Jeanne of Valois

Children:
(1) Edward Prince of Wales (The Black Prince): b. Woodstock 15 June 1330; d. Palace of Westminster 8 June 1376; m. Windsor 10 October 1361, Joan, Countess of Kent (b. 29 September 1328; d. Wallingford Castle, Berkshire 8 August 1385), widow of Thomas de Holand, and only daughter of Edmund of Woodstock, Earl of Kent, son of King Edward I
Children: (a) Edward: b. Angoulême 27 January 1365; d. Bordeaux 1372
(b) Richard, later King Richard II

(2) Isabella: b. Woodstock 16 June 1332; d. London before 7 October 1382; m. Windsor 27 July 1365, Enguerrand VII, Sire de Coucy, created Earl of Bedford

(3) Joan: b. Woodstock ca February 1335; d. Bayonne 2 September 1348

(4) William of Hatfield: b. Hatfield, Herts before 16 February 1337; d. before 8 July 1337

(5) Lionel of Antwerp, Duke of Clarence: b. Antwerp 29 November 1338; d. Alba, Piedmont 17 October 1368; m. 1st, Tower of London 9 September 1342, Lady Elizabeth de Burgh (d. Dublin, 10 December 1363); left issue; 2nd, Milan 28 May 1368, Violante Visconti

(6) John of Gaunt, Duke of Lancaster, titular King of Castile and Leon: b. Abbey of St Bavon, Ghent, March 1340; d. Leicester Castle 3 February 1399; m. 1st, Reading 13 May 1359, Blanche of Lancaster (d. Bolingbroke Castle 12 September 1369), great-great granddaughter of Henry III; 2nd, Roquefort September 1371, Constance, titular Queen of Castile and Leon (d. Leicester 24 March 1394); 3rd, Lincoln 13 January 1396, Catherine (d. Lincoln 10 May 1403), widow of Sir Hugh Swynford, and daughter of Sir Payn Roet; left issue by all three marriages
His eldest surviving son by his first marriage later became King Henry IV. From the legitimated issue of the third marriage descend the Tudors and later sovereigns (see Appendix)

(7) Edmund of Langley, Duke of York: b. King's Langley, Herts 5 June 1341; d. there 1 August 1402; m. 1st, Hertford ca 1 March 1372, Isabel of Castile (d. 23 November 1393), sister of his brother John's 2nd wife (see above), left issue from whom the Yorkist Kings, Edward IV, Edward V and Richard III descend (see tables in Appendix); 2nd, before 4 November 1393, Joan de Holand

(8) Blanche: b. and d. Tower of London March 1342

(9) Mary: b. Waltham, near Winchester, 9 or 10 October 1344; d. 1361 or 1362; m. Woodstock summer 1361, as his 1st wife, John V, Duke of Brittany

(10) Margaret: b. Windsor Castle 20 July 1346; d. after 1 October 1361; m. Reading 19 May 1359, as his 1st wife, John Hastings, 2nd Earl of Pembroke

(11) William of Windsor: b. Windsor Castle before 24 June 1348; d. September 1348

(12) Thomas of Woodstock, Duke of Gloucester: b. Woodstock 7 January 1355; d. Calais 8 or 15 September 1397; m. 1374, Lady Eleanor de Bohun (d. Barking Abbey, Essex 3 October 1399); left issue

Died: Sheen Palace 21 June 1377
Buried: Westminster Abbey

An impression of the great seal of King Edward III.

Edward of Windsor, the eldest child of Edward II and Isabella of France, was the first English king to have the time of his birth noted exactly. He was born at 5.40 am on Monday 13 November 1312 and baptized four days later in the old chapel of St Edward in Windsor Castle. The names of seven godfathers are recorded, but no godmother. A few days later his father created him Earl of Chester, but not, for some reason, Prince of Wales.

The events leading to Edward's proclamation as Keeper of the Realm and then as king have already been described. The principal preoccupation during his long reign of fifty years was to be his claim to the throne of France, which began the Hundred Years' War. Edward assumed the title of King of France in 1340, claiming the crown through his mother, as heir of her brother Charles IV, who had died in 1328. The French barons, however, did not recognize the principle of inheritance through the female line and Charles had been succeeded by his cousin Philip VI, the nearest male heir. Edward did homage to him for his French fiefs in 1329 and 1331. Some years later, English commercial interests connected with the wool trade in Flanders precipitated a commercial crisis. Flanders had passed under French administration in 1328 and it was the powerful Flemish weavers who persuaded Edward to advance his claim to France after concluding a commercial treaty with him in 1338.

Philip's answer to Edward's pretensions was to declare his French fiefs forfeited and invade Guienne. Edward, no less a warrior than his grandfather Edward I, took up arms to defend his title by sea and land. The great naval battle of Sluys in 1340 gave England control of the Channel and this was followed by the land victories of Crécy (1346) and Poitiers (1356), in which the superiority of the English longbowmen over the heavily armoured French cavalry won the day. Calais was taken after a long siege in 1347, thus giving the English an important economic and military base.

The hero of the wars was Edward's eldest son, Edward, Prince of Wales, later known as 'The Black Prince', who came to be regarded as the 'model of chivalry', but who was in reality bad-tempered, foul-mouthed and cruel. It was perhaps a mercy that he died a year before his father and never lived to become king.

In the years 1348–50 northern Europe was ravaged by the Black Death, an outbreak of bubonic plague, which is said to have halved the population of England and served greatly to undermine her military strength.

The Treaty of Brétigny in 1360 ended the wars for a time and Edward renounced his claim to the French crown. King John of France, the son and successor of Philip, was released from prison in England, where he had been held since his capture at Poitiers, and allowed to return home.

In 1369 Edward renewed his claim and resumed the title of King of France after the Black Prince had refused to appear at the court of Charles V (John's successor) to answer complaints brought against him by the Count of Armagnac. Poitou was reconquered but the French regained control of the Channel, with Castilian aid, at the battle of La Rochelle (1372) and successfully blocked English transport. When the Black Prince died of dysentery in 1376, English fortunes were at their lowest ebb and all that remained were the five fortified towns of Bordeaux, Bayonne, Brest, Calais, Cherbourg and their coastal lands. France, however, was in a ruinous state.

At home, Edward III's reign saw many changes. English replaced French as the official language of the law courts (and Chaucer commenced writing his *Canterbury Tales* in English), the office of Justice of the Peace was created, and Parliament divided into two houses.

In 1348 Edward founded the Order of the Garter which was to become (and still remains) one of the leading orders of chivalry in Europe.

Edward was a tall, dignified man of regal bearing. Though sometimes given to violent outbursts of temper, a Plantagenet characteristic, his charm, generosity, and affinity with the baronial classes helped him to retain his popularity for most of his reign. He was happily married to the plump and somewhat stolid Philippa for over forty years.

After her death in 1369, he acquired a rapacious mistress, Alice Perrers – 'that wanton baggage' as a contemporary account describes her – who rendered the declining years of the senile though lecherous King a thorough misery. She and her daughter Isabella were in the habit of sleeping with the King together and it seems highly probable that one or the other of them infected the old man with gonorrhoea. Edward was taken ill in September 1376 and only partially recovered in the following spring when an abscess (the locality of which is not specified) burst and gave him some relief. He was able to attend Parliament, but towards the end of May suffered a stroke and died at Sheen Palace in June. His body was left unattended for several hours and Alice Perrers is said to have robbed it of its rings and personal jewellery. She lived comfortably on her ill-gotten gains until her death in 1400.

Edward was buried in Westminster Abbey beside Philippa. The wooden head of the effigy carried on the coffin at his funeral in accordance with custom is preserved in the Abbey museum and appears to have been modelled from a death mask as the mouth shows signs of the characteristic distortion suffered by some stroke victims. The impressive effigy on his tomb was probably derived from the same source although it is more stylized.

Philippa of Hainault

Born: Valenciennes 24 June 1311
Married: York Minster 24 January 1328
Crowned: Westminster Abbey March 1330
Died: Windsor Castle 14 August 1369
Buried: Westminster Abbey

Philippa of Hainault was first considered as a possible bride for the future Edward III when she was only eight. Bishop Stapeldon of Exeter was sent to inspect her on behalf of Edward's parents and reported back in minute detail:

The lady ... has not uncomely hair, betwixt blue-black and brown. Her head is clean-shaped; her forehead high and broad, and standing somewhat forward. Her face narrows between the eyes, and the lower part of her face is still more narrow and slender than the forehead. Her eyes are blackish-brown and deep. Her nose is fairly smooth and even, save that it is somewhat broad at the tip and flattened, yet it is no snub-nose. Her nostrils are also broad, her mouth fairly wide. Her lips somewhat full, and especially the lower lip. Her teeth which have fallen and grown again are white enough, but the rest are not so white. The lower teeth project a little beyond the upper; yet this is but little seen. Her ears and chin are comely enough. Her neck, shoulders, and all her body and lower limbs are reasonably well shapen; all her limbs are well set and unmaimed; and nought is amiss so far as a man may see. Moreover, she is of brown skin all over, and much like her father; and in all things she is pleasant enough, as it seems to us.

The Bishop goes on to add that she was 'neither too tall nor too short' for her age, and that she was 'of fair carriage, and well taught in all that becometh her rank.'

Edward was able to check the truth of this report for himself when he and his mother were guests at the Court of Hainault in 1326. Philippa was then fifteen and Edward fourteen. Evidently he liked what he found and after a papal dispensation for the marriage (the couple being second cousins) had been sought and obtained from Avignon in September 1327, Philippa set out for England arriving in London two days before Christmas. Edward was in the north with his army and Philippa, with a large suite in attendance, rode to meet him. The marriage took place in York Minster on 24 January 1328. They dallied in York until after Easter, then moved south to the royal manor of Woodstock, which was to become Philippa's favourite residence and the birthplace of four of her twelve children. The Queen's coronation at Westminster was delayed until March 1330, only three months before Philippa gave birth to her first child, the Black Prince. She chose to feed the baby herself going against the current fashion for wet-nurses.

Like other medieval queens, Philippa accompanied her husband on his campaigns and the birthplaces of her children testify that she was not to be deterred by pregnancy. She had a kindly nature and was able to restrain her husband and eldest son on many occasions when their tempers got the better of them. She interceded for the lives of the carpenters whose stand collapsed at the great tournament in Cheapside held to celebrate the birth of the Black Prince and later, in an episode celebrated as a subject for pictures and statues, pleaded successfully for the lives of the six burghers of Calais who came to surrender the town to Edward III.

The Queen's great amiability gained her a popularity not enjoyed by any of her predecessors. Her homely features and comfortable motherly figure are well apparent in Master Hennequin of Liège's fine alabaster effigy on her tomb in Westminster Abbey. A lively carving of the younger Philippa, wearing an elaborate crown, is to be seen on one of the misericordes in the Chapel of the Royal Foundation of St Katherine in east London.

Philippa died in her late fifties of 'a dropsical malady' which had afflicted her for about two years. Froissart describes her deathbed, with her hand in that of the King, and her youngest son Thomas, a boy of fourteen, standing by her bed.

Queen's College, Oxford was founded in Philippa's honour by her chaplain Robert d'Eglesfield and established by Royal Charter in 1341.

Agnes Strickland, ever one to point a moral, ends her life of Philippa with this paragraph:

> The close observer of history will not fail to notice that with the life of Queen Philippa the happiness, the good fortune, and even the respectability of Edward III and his family departed; and scenes of strife, sorrow and folly distracted the court where she had once promoted virtue, and presided with well-regulated magnificence.

The alabaster effigy of Philippa of Hainault on her tomb in Westminster Abbey, is the work of Master Hennequin of Liège and although damaged gives a vivid impression of the motherly and kind-hearted queen.

RICHARD II — 1377–1399

Born:	Bordeaux 6 January 1367
Acceded:	21 June 1377
Crowned:	Westminster Abbey 16 July 1377
Married:	1st, St Stephen's Chapel, Palace of Westminster 14 or 20 January 1382, Anne, daughter of Charles IV, Holy Roman Emperor and King of Bohemia, and his fourth wife Elizabeth of Pomerania; 2nd, Calais 1 November 1396, Isabella, second daughter of Charles VI, King of France, and Isabelle of Bavaria
Deposed:	29 September 1399
Died:	Pontefract Castle 6 January 1400
Buried:	Westminster Abbey

On Edward III's death the crown passed to a child of ten. Richard of Bordeaux was the only surviving son of the Black Prince and the Fair Maid of Kent. His father entrusted his education to an old soldier, Sir Simon Burley, who instilled in him a love of literature and music, as well as a sense of the importance of his royal office. Richard could have had no memories of his grandmother Queen Philippa, who died when he was only two years old, and whatever impressions he had of family would have been derived from memories of his stern father, who died when he was nine, his lecherous old grandfather King Edward, his flighty but loving mother, and his assortment of uncles and half-siblings.

After his father's death Richard was created Prince of Wales, but only held the dignity for a few months before succeeding his grandfather. The dignitaries of the day saw nothing incongruous in submitting a boy of ten to the long ceremonial of anointing and coronation preceded by fasting, and the little King was so exhausted that he had to be carried from the Abbey to Westminster Hall on the shoulders of his attendants.

In 1381 the Peasants' Revolt led by Wat Tyler against the imposition of a tax of a shilling a head on all persons over fifteen, was the occasion of a remarkable act of bravery from Richard, who rode out to meet them at Smithfield and was personally able to pacify them.

The minority ended in 1382 and the King was married to Anne of Bohemia, with whom he fell deeply and passionately in love. Unfortunately the marriage was to remain childless and the Queen's death, probably from plague, in 1394 drove Richard so wild with grief that he had Sheen Palace, where she died, razed to the ground.

Richard's reign was a troubled one throughout, his uncles of Lancaster, York and Gloucester continually vying for power with an eye on the eventual succession. While Richard remained childless the heir to the throne was Roger Mortimer, Earl of March, the grandson of his uncle Lionel, Duke of Clarence, but his claim, although officially recognized by Richard in 1387, was hardly likely to remain uncontested.

In 1396 Richard married again, but his bride was a child and not likely to produce an heir for several years. Richard became fond of her, but she filled the position of a sister more than a wife. Undoubtedly what Richard needed emotionally was a father-figure, and this was supplied, after Sir Simon Burley had been impeached and beheaded by the King's opponents in 1388, by Robert de Vere, 9th Earl of Oxford, successively created Marquess of Dublin and Duke of Ireland. The King worshipped this dashing figure who was only five years older than himself. Their association was probably quite innocent but it aroused intense jealousy and hostility from the royal uncles and others who had Robert charged with treason. He managed to escape to the Continent where he was killed in a boar hunt in 1392. The sorrowing Richard had his body brought back to England and buried with great solemnity.

In 1396 Richard concluded peace with France but his attempt to do away with parliamentary government and establish a royal autocracy proved his final undoing and he was deposed by his cousin Henry Bolingbroke and imprisoned in Pontefract Castle. Here he completely lost the will to live and, refusing to eat, starved himself to death. Inevitably false rumours that he had been murdered were circulated and to refute them his body was brought to London and paraded through the streets on an open bier. He was buried beside his beloved Queen Anne in the tomb he had carefully ordered for them both in Westminster Abbey.

Richard is perhaps the most tragic of all our kings. His reign began with great promise but after he attained his majority it proceeded from failure to failure, not always of his making. He is a sad, lonely figure and his portrait in Westminster Abbey and tomb effigy both have an air of melancholy. He was only thirty-three when he died.

A cast of the monumental effigy of Anne of Bohemia made for the National Portrait Gallery from her tomb in Westminster Abbey.

Anne of Bohemia

Born: Prague 11 May 1366
Married: St Stephen's Chapel, Palace of
            Westminster 14 or 20 January 1382
Crowned: Westminster Abbey 22 January 1382
Died: Sheen Palace before 3 June 1394
Buried: Westminster Abbey

Richard's first queen was a brilliant match, even though she brought no dowry, for she was the daughter of the Emperor Charles IV. Richard's tutor Sir Simon Burley was sent to negotiate the marriage and escort the bride to England. She duly landed at Dover in December 1381, was met at Canterbury by the King's uncle Thomas and at Blackheath by the Mayor and citizens of London. The marriage was solemnized in the new Chapel of St Stephen at Westminster and the Queen's coronation followed a few days later.

Contemporary chroniclers speak of Anne's beauty, but her only known likeness, her tomb effigy at Westminster, gives the impression of a plump, expressionless young woman. She brought a large retinue with her to England and the expenses of her household aggravated the struggle between Richard and Parliament. She pleaded unsuccessfully for the life of Sir Simon Burley and after his execution retired with the King to Bristol for a time. In 1392 the Queen acted as a successful mediator between Richard and the citizens of

An 18th century print of Pontefract Castle. It was here that Richard II met his untimely and mysterious end.

London and staged a spectacular royal progress through the city with him, mounted and wearing their crowns. Anne is credited with having introduced the side-saddle into England.

At Whitsuntide 1394 Anne was struck down by plague and died, after an illness of a few hours only, in the presence of her inconsolable husband. The funeral procession wound its way from Sheen to Westminster lit by flambeaux and torches made from wax imported from Flanders which provided, so Froissart tells us, an 'illumination so great that nothing was seen like it before'.

Isabella of France

Born: Hôtel du Louvre, Paris 9 November 1387
Married: 1st, Calais 1 November 1396
Crowned: Westminster Abbey 8 January 1397
Married: 2nd, Compiègne 29 June 1406, Charles, Duke of Orleans
Died: Blois 13 September 1409
Buried: Abbey of St Saumer, Blois; transferred to the Celestines, Paris ca 1624

Richard's second queen was twenty years his junior and the marriage was arranged to cement the peace with France in 1396. The twenty-nine-year-old King and the nine-year-old Queen were married in the Church of St Nicholas at Calais on All Saints' Day and embarked for England a few days later. Isabella made her state entry into London on 13 November and the crowd which collected to see her was so great that nine people were crushed to death on London Bridge. One might have thought that Richard, mindful of the ordeal of his own coronation, would have spared his child-bride from undergoing the same, but strangely he did not and she was duly crowned on 8 January 1397, although no details of the ceremony have been preserved.

Isabella's chief residence in England was at Windsor Castle, where one of the King's de Coucy cousins was her chief companion and preceptress. Richard visited her frequently and a strong affection and companionship grew up between the disparate couple of this unconsummated marriage.

On Richard's deposition Isabella was confined at Sonning by Henry IV and to her great distress kept in ignorance of her husband's fate. Henry seized her jewels and divided them among his own children and induced the Council to declare that she had no right to any dower as Queen Dowager. Her return to France was eventually arranged and she sailed from Dover on 1 July 1401. In the succeeding years Henry IV made several attempts to procure her in marriage for the future Henry V, but the French royal family declined and in 1406 Isabella was betrothed to her cousin Charles of Angoulême, son of Louis, Duke of Orleans, amid 'banquets', dancing, jousts, and other jollities'. In 1407 she became Duchess of Orleans when her father-in-law was murdered in the streets of Paris by the Duke of Burgundy.

Isabella enjoyed a short but happy married life with her second husband, dying at Blois within a few hours of the birth of her first child, a little girl who later became Duchess of Alençon. Her husband survived her by many years, twenty-three of them spent as a prisoner in the Tower of London following his capture after the Battle of Agincourt. He was a poet of some merit and composed several verses in Isabella's memory.

The Plantagenets: The House of Lancaster

The murder of Edward II and the deposition and premature death of Richard II weakened the developing principle of primogeniture in the royal succession and initiated a period of violence and a struggle for supremacy between the Houses of Lancaster and York.

Henry Bolingbroke's claim to the throne was through his father John of Gaunt, the fourth son of Edward III. If succession through the female line was accepted in England, as Edward III claimed in his attempts to wrest the French crown from Philip IV, then the descendants of Lionel, Duke of Clarence, Edward's third son, had a stronger claim than Henry Bolingbroke, and this was the basis of the struggle fought out in the Wars of the Roses.

The royal House of Lancaster is so-called because in 1359 John of Gaunt married Blanche, heiress of the great Lancastrian inheritance, and in 1362 was created Duke of Lancaster. His eldest son Henry succeeded to the dukedom on his father's death in early 1399.

HENRY IV   1399–1413

Born:	Bolingbroke Castle 4 April 1366
Acceded:	29 September 1399
Crowned:	Westminster Abbey 13 October 1399
Married:	1st, Arundel Castle 1380 or 1381, Lady Mary de Bohun (d. Peterborough Castle 4 July 1394); 2nd, by proxy Eltham Palace 3 April 1402, in person, Winchester Cathedral 7 February 1403, Joan, widow of John V, Duke of Brittany, and second daughter of Charles II, King of Navarre, and Joan of France
Children:	(1) A son: b. April 1382; d. in infancy
	(2) Henry, later King Henry V
	(3) Thomas, Duke of Clarence: b. Kenilworth 1388; d. (killed in battle) Beaugé 22 March 1421; m. 1412, Margaret (d. 31 December 1439), widow of his father's half-brother John Beaufort, Earl of Somerset, and daughter of Thomas de Holand, Earl of Kent (half-brother of King Richard II); no issue
	(4) John, Duke of Bedford, Regent of France and Protector of England 1422–35: b. 20 June 1389; d. Rouen 15 September 1435; m. 1st, Troyes 17 April 1423, Anne of Burgundy (d. Paris 14 November 1432); 2nd, Thérouenne 22 April 1433, Jacquette of Luxembourg (who m. 2nd, Richard Woodville, 1st Earl Rivers, and became the mother, among others, of Queen Elizabeth Woodville, wife of King Edward IV); no surviving issue
	(5) Humphrey, Duke of Gloucester, Regent of England, 1420–21, Protector 1422 and 1427–29, Lieutenant of the Kingdom 1430–32: b. August/September 1390; d. Bury St Edmunds 23 February 1447; m. 1st, 1422 (m. annulled 1428), Jacqueline, Countess of Holland; 2nd, before 1431 (divorced 1441), Eleanor de Cobham (d. Beaumaris Castle 7 July 1452); no legitimate issue
	(6) Blanche: b. Peterborough Castle, spring 1392; d. Germany 21 May 1409; m. Cologne 6 July 1402, Ludwig III, Elector Palatine of the Rhine
	(7) Philippa: b. Peterborough Castle 4 July 1394; d. Convent of Vadstena 5 January 1430; m. Lund 26 October 1406, Eric of Pomerania, King of Denmark, Sweden and Norway
Died:	Jerusalem Chamber, Westminster Abbey 20 March 1413
Buried:	Canterbury Cathedral

Henry of Bolingbroke was as unprepossessing in person as his predecessor had been attractive. Short, stout, red-haired and bearded, he was altogether lacking in kingly grace and dignity and entirely uninspiring. He was styled Earl of Derby and created a Knight of the Garter in 1377 and was married at the age of fourteen to a ten-year-old heiress Mary de Bohun, whose father Humphrey was 7th Earl of Hereford, 6th Earl of Essex and 2nd Earl of Northampton. She bore seven children in quick succession and died at the birth of the last.

Mary's elder sister had married Henry's uncle, Thomas of Woodstock, Duke of Gloucester, and Henry supported his uncle and brother-in-law in his armed revolt against Richard II in 1387, but was later induced by his father to change sides. The spirit of adventure sent him to serve with the Teutonic Knights in Lithuania for a while and to visit Venice, Cyprus and Jerusalem. On his return to England he joined his father and the King against Gloucester and as a reward was created Duke of Hereford. Early in 1398, however, he quarrelled with the Duke of Norfolk, who accused him of treason, and challenged him to settle the matter by combat at

Coventry. As the fight was about to start the King intervened and banished both contestants from the kingdom. Henry went to Paris and bided his time. On his father's death in February 1399 he found the excuse to return secretly to recover his estates, which the Crown had confiscated in spite of promises to the contrary from Richard. While the King was in Ireland, Henry landed in Yorkshire and was joined by the Percys. Richard was abandoned by his followers, surrendered at Flint in August, and forced to resign the crown to Henry by Parliament on 29 September 1399.

The crown gained by usurpation was indeed an uneasy one, as Shakespeare was to point out. The thirteen years of Henry's reign were occupied by warfare of one sort or another. Owen Glendower's spirited bid for Welsh independence made in 1400 took ten years to put down. The French plundered the south coast and the Scots made incursions in the north. The Percys and the Mortimers organized two rebellions and Archbishop Scrope of York, who gave them support, was among those executed for treason, an act for which Henry was regarded as an impious monster. To add to Henry's troubles, Henry's second wife, Joan of Navarre, was suspected of witchcraft, and he himself was afflicted with a disfiguring skin disease, probably a form of eczema but called 'leprosy' by his contemporaries.

It had been prophesied that Henry would die in Jerusalem and he comforted himself with the knowledge that his death would thus be deferred until he went on his long-projected crusade to the Holy Land. In March 1413 he was praying at the Confessor's shrine in Westminster Abbey when he had a seizure and was carried unconscious to the Jerusalem Chamber near the west door. Here he recovered consciousness and asked in what room he was. On being told its name, Holinshed tells us, he said: 'Lauds be given to the Father of Heaven, for now I know that I shall die here in this chamber; according to the prophecy of me declared, that I should depart this life in Jerusalem.'

Although Henry died in Westminster Abbey, where so many of his ancestors lay, his body was, at his own request, taken to Canterbury for burial. It was taken as far as Faversham by water and Clement of Maidstone relates that a fierce storm sprang up during the journey and caused the superstitious crew to throw the King's body overboard and later substitute another. The King's tomb was opened in 1832 and the account given in *Archaeologia* states that the outer coffin was of entirely different shape from that of the inner and that the space between them was filled with straw. No regalia was found with the body and on the inner coffin lay a cross fashioned from twigs bound together.

Henry's portraits are of one type only and probably based on a contemporary original. The effigy on his tomb at Canterbury accords well with the descriptions of him.

Joan of Navarre

Born:	Pamplona *ca* 1370
Married:	1st, Saillé, near Guerrand 11 September 1386, John V, Duke of Brittany (*d.* 1 November 1399), and had issue; 2nd, by proxy Eltham Palace 3 April 1402, in person Winchester Cathedral 7 February 1403, King Henry IV
Crowned:	Westminster Abbey 26 February 1403
Died:	Havering atte Bower, Essex 9 July 1437
Buried:	Canterbury Cathedral

An electrotype cast of the alabaster effigy of Joan of Navarre from her tomb at Canterbury Cathedral. She wears a crown almost identical in form with that of her husband Henry IV, who lies at her side.

Henry's first wife died before he became king and it was during his exile in France in 1399 that he first met the Duchess of Brittany who was to become his second wife nearly four years later. Joan was the daughter of Charles the Bad, King of Navarre, and her mother was a daughter of King John of France who had lived so long as a prisoner in England. In 1386 she was married to John the Valiant, Duke of Brittany, by whom she had nine children.

On the death of the Duke of Brittany in November 1399, Joan became regent of the duchy for her eldest son until he came of age (at twelve) and was invested at Rennes on 22 March 1401. Evidently Henry's visit to the Breton court in 1399 had made a great impression on the Duchess, in spite of his rather unattractive appearance, and she determined to marry him should the opportunity ever arise. Now freed of her responsibilities she applied to the Pope at Avignon for a dispensation to marry anyone she pleased within the fourth degree of consanguinity and it was granted on 20 March 1402. She then sent an emissary to England to conclude matters with Henry, who appears to have been quite compliant, and the proxy marriage (with her male emissary standing in for the bride) took place at Eltham Palace on 3 April. Matters were now complicated by the fact that whereas Joan supported and had obtained her dispensation from Pope Benedict XIII at Avignon, Henry supported the rival Pope Boniface IX at Rome. Eventually things were settled to the satisfaction of all parties. Joan assumed the title of Queen and set out for England, accompanied by her two youngest daughters and a large Breton and Navarrese suite. The crossing, in January 1403, was a rough one taking five days and the party was forced to land at Falmouth rather than at Southampton as had been intended. They then went on to Winchester where Henry met them and the marriage took place. A feature of the elaborate wedding-breakfast was a pair of crowned panthers and a pair of crowned swans formed out of sweetmeats. Such things were known as 'subtleties' and were produced in between courses in much the same way as a sorbet might be today. Joan's entry into London and her coronation were celebrated with all the customary ceremonies.

Although Joan was no more than thirty-five at the time of her marriage and Henry about thirty-seven, she bore no more children and one cannot help wondering if some early form of birth control was used, since both had had large families by their previous partners. The seemingly unnatural lack of progeny may well have contributed to the suspicion of witchcraft which the people entertained against the Queen. In this connection it must be remembered that Joan had been Duchess of Brittany, where many curious old superstitions and ceremonies are held and observed to this day.

Joan maintained an excellent relationship with her stepchildren and was frequently visited by her own children. She obviously held her first husband in high regard as in 1408 an alabaster monument was made for him at her behest and shipped to Brittany to be erected over his tomb at Nantes. Agnes Strickland states that Joan's 'besetting sin' was avarice and she certainly amassed a large fortune, being liberally dowered both in Brittany and in England.

The high esteem in which Joan was held by her stepson Henry V is evidenced by the fact that he appointed her, whom he termed 'his dearest mother', to act as regent when he departed to continue the war in France in 1415. When the news of the victory of Agincourt was received in London, Joan, with the Mayor and Aldermen and a large retinue, walked in solemn procession from St Paul's to Westminster to make a thanksgiving offering at St Edward's shrine. Her feelings must have been very mixed as her brother the King of Navarre and one of her sons-in-law (the Duke of Alençon) both fell fighting on the French side, while her son Arthur, Duke of Brittany had been taken prisoner, and was to be brought back to England to languish many years in the Tower and later at Fotheringay.

In 1417 Henry was still referring to Joan as 'that excellent and most dear lady, the Queen our mother', but in the following year, when Henry was again absent in France and his brother John, Duke of Bedford was acting as regent, she was suddenly arrested at Havering atte Bower in Essex and taken to Pevensey Castle, 'being accused by certain persons of an act of witchcraft, which would have tended the King harm.' Joan's accuser was her own confessor, John Randolf, whose motivation is not clear. The Queen was deprived of all her property and dower and kept in close confinement without trial until July 1422 when she was released and her dower was restored.

The rest of Joan's life was lived out quietly and she died at her favourite residence Havering atte Bower on 9 July 1437, aged about sixty-seven. 'Also the same year', adds the Chronicle of London, 'died all the lions in the Tower, the which was nought seen in no man's time before out of mind.' The implication is that the Witch-queen's familiars did not survive her!

Joan was buried with Henry IV at Canterbury. Her alabaster effigy depicts a small, well-made woman with a trim figure and a long slender neck.

HENRY V   1413–1422

Born:	Monmouth 9 August 1387
Acceded:	20 March 1413
Crowned:	Westminster Abbey 9 April 1413
Married:	Troyes 2 June 1420, Catherine, youngest daughter of Charles VI, King of France, and Isabelle of Bavaria
Child:	Henry, later King Henry VI
Died:	Bois de Vincennes 31 August 1422
Buried:	Westminster Abbey

Henry V was the last great warrior king of the Middle Ages. His personality is not attractive and he appears stern and humourless. His portrait shows a lean, ascetic face with an over-large nose beneath a monkish haircut. There is an air of fanaticism about him and one is not

Henry V, a portrait by an unknown artist in the National Portrait Gallery. It is one of a set of Kings and Queens made in Tudor times but probably derives from a contemporary likeness.

surprised at the singleness of purpose with which he pursued the continuation of the French war.

The story of Henry's riotous youth is mostly an invention of Shakespeare and is not substantiated by any contemporary record. His profession of arms started early when he took part in the suppression of Owen Glendower's rebellion. His father's increasing ill-health obliged him to take a share in the government with his half-uncles Henry and Thomas Beaufort, but his policies differed from those of the King, who dismissed him from the Council in 1411. There was, however, no personal quarrel between father and son.

On his accession in 1413, Henry set about restoring and maintaining order at home by cleverly diverting the interest of the great nobles to a renewal of the French war begun by Edward III. His expedition was crowned with success and the great victory of Agincourt on 25 October 1415 was followed by two years of careful preparation for further activity. Normandy was conquered and by August 1419 the English forces had reached the walls of Paris. Negotiations for peace led to the Treaty of Troyes, whereby Henry was recognized as heir and Regent of France, to the exclusion of the Dauphin, and received in marriage the mad King Charles VI's daughter Catherine.

Henry was now at the height of his power and a force to be reckoned with throughout western Europe. His influence, combined with that of the Emperor Sigismund, brought about the end of the Great Schism with the election of Pope Martin V, and Henry's next ambition was to launch a new crusade to the Holy Land.

Death overtook him before this could be accomplished. He had long been prone to suffer attacks of dysentery, an almost unavoidable accompaniment to life on campaign in those insanitary days, and a particularly virulent attack struck him down at Bois de Vincennes on 31 August 1422. 'Death overcame the King when he was speaking to his nobles', says the author of the *Memorials of Henry V*. His last words are said to have been to express the wish that he might live to rebuild the walls of Jerusalem. He was just thirty-five years old.

Henry's body was brought back to England for burial in Westminster Abbey. His chantry chapel lies immediately east of the Confessor's shrine. The tomb was despoiled at the Reformation and at some stage the head of the effigy disappeared. It has recently been carefully restored.

Catherine of France

Born: Hôtel de St Pol, Paris 27 October 1401
Married: 1st, Troyes 2 June 1420
Crowned: Westminster Abbey 24 February 1421
Married: 2nd, *ca* 1428, Owen Tudor (d. [beheaded] Hereford 2 February 1461); had issue, including Edmund Tudor, Earl of Richmond, father of King Henry VII
Died: Bermondsey Abbey 3 January 1437
Buried: Westminster Abbey

Catherine of France, or Catherine of Valois as she is more often called, was the youngest child of the mad King Charles VI of France and his rapacious, nymphomaniac queen, Isabelle of Bavaria. An elder daughter of this couple was Isabella, who had already been Queen of England as the young wife of Richard II.

Catherine's childhood was passed at her birthplace, the Hôtel de St Pol, where she and her sister Michelle lived in a deplorable condition of squalor, dirty and half-starved, while their mother disported herself with her paramour and brother-in-law the Duke of Orleans. Charles VI's madness is now believed to have been occasioned by porphyria, 'the royal malady', which also afflicted George III. In a period of lucidity he became aware of the state of his unfortunate children and, having no other resources, gave their governess a gold cup to sell to provide for their necessitities. The King's temporary recovery lasted several years, during which the Duke of Orleans was assassinated by the Duke of Burgundy, Queen Isabelle was imprisoned at Tours, and Catherine was educated in the convent of Poissy, where her sister Marie was a nun.

The first demand for Catherine's hand in marriage was made by Henry V soon after his succession in 1413, but it was not until after the Treaty of Troyes had been signed that the couple were married in St Peter's Church in that town. The betrothal ring which Henry gave to his bride was to be used as the coronation ring of succeeding queen consorts, and was presumably broken up with the rest of the old regalia under the Commonwealth rule in the seventeenth century. The couple did not return to England for Catherine's coronation until the following February. There is the usual detailed description of the coronation banquet, which included 'dead eels stewed', jelly coloured with columbine flowers, and the usual 'subtleties', this time a figure of St Catherine, and a tiger looking in a mirror. At the banquet the new Queen interceded for the release of the King of Scots, James I, who had been imprisoned in the Tower and elsewhere since 1406, although he had accompanied Henry to France in 1420.

Towards the end of 1421 Catherine gave birth to her first child, the future Henry VI, at Windsor, and the following May crossed to France to join her husband and effect a reunion with her parents (now reconciled) at Paris. Catherine and her mother were both present at Henry V's deathbed and after only eighteen months of marriage she found herself a widow at the age of twenty.

Catherine accompanied Henry's body back to England

and busied herself with the upbringing of the infant Henry VI. Baynard's Castle on the Surrey side of the Thames was assigned to her as a residence in 1424. She had barely settled in when rumours were heard of her intrigue with Owen Tudor, a handsome young Welsh squire of good family but little fortune. A secret marriage was alleged, although no proof has ever been forthcoming. There were, however, three sons, Edmund, Jasper and Owen, and we shall hear more of the first two later.

Catherine accompanied Henry VI to Paris for his French coronation and again visited her mother, now, to quote Agnes Strickland, 'full of years, and it must be added, of dishonours'. The old Queen died in 1436 and Catherine only survived her mother a year. In the summer of 1436 she gave birth to a daughter, Margaret, who survived only a few days. This event appears to have alerted the King's guardians to his mother's ménage and she was forced to withdraw to Bermondsey Abbey, her three young sons being taken from her. Although only thirty-five, the Queen's spirit broke, she fell into some sort of decline, made her will, and died in the Abbey on 3 January 1437.

Catherine's body was buried in the old Lady Chapel of Westminster Abbey and a tomb was erected by Henry VI. The Latin inscription referred to her only as the widow of Henry V, but when her grandson Henry Tudor had become King Henry VII, he had it replaced by another acknowledging her Tudor marriage. Catherine's mummified body was disinterred when Henry VII was buried and remained above ground in a chest near Henry V's tomb for the best part of three centuries. Here it was shown to the curious for a few pence, and Samuel Pepys recorded in his Diary on 23 February 1669, when he visited the Abbey with his wife and a party of friends: 'I had the upper part of her body in my hands, and I did kiss her mouth, reflecting upon it that I did kiss a Queen, and that this was my birthday, thirty-six years old, that I did first kiss a Queen.'

HENRY VI	1422–1461 AND 1470–1471

Born:	Windsor Castle 6 December 1421	Child:	Edward, Prince of Wales: *b.* Palace of
Acceded:	31 August 1422		Westminster 13 October 1453; *d.* (killed)
Crowned:	Westminster Abbey 6 November 1429		Tewkesbury 4 May 1471; *m.* Amboise
	(and as King of France at Nôtre Dame,		August 1470, Lady Anne Nevill (who
	Paris 16 December 1431)		*m.* 2nd, Richard, Duke of Gloucester, later
Married:	by proxy at Nancy March 1445, in person		King Richard III)
	at Titchfield Abbey, Hants 22 April 1445,	Deposed:	4 March 1461
	Margaret, daughter of René, Duke of	Restored:	3 October 1470
	Anjou, titular King of Naples and Sicily,	Deposed:	11 April 1472
	and his 1st wife Isabelle, Duchess of	Died:	Tower of London 21 May 1471
	Lorraine	Buried:	Chertsey Abbey, later transferred to St
			George's Chapel, Windsor

Henry VI succeeded to the throne at the age of eight months and was thus younger than any other English sovereign. His reign was one long tragedy and he himself a pathetic figure afflicted in the same way as his maternal grandfather Charles VI of France, though not perhaps to such a great degree.

The baby King presided over Parliament seated in his mother's lap, but he was not always well behaved and threw a great tantrum in November 1423 when he was being brought from Windsor and lodged overnight at Staines. In the morning he was being carried to his mother's litter when 'he skreeked, he cried, he sprang, and would be carried no further; wherefore they again bore him to the inn, and there he abode ... all day.' The next day he was 'glad and merry of cheer' and the journey continued by extraordinarily slow stages with further overnight stops at Kingston and at Kennington.

Henry was crowned at Westminster Abbey exactly one month before his eighth birthday and two years later was crowned as King of France at Paris. He had the dubious distinction of being the only English claimant to the French throne to become *de facto* sovereign.

Before Henry was of age on 12 November 1437, English rule in France had begun a steady decline with Joan of Arc's campaign and the death of the regent Duke of Bedford. By 1453 only Calais remained of Henry V's conquests.

At home Henry concerned himself with his two great scholastic foundations, Eton College and King's College, Cambridge, laying the foundation stones of both buildings. This 'good and gentle creature' was better fitted for a life of piety and learning than that of a monarch. At the age of twenty-three he was married to Margaret of Anjou, who was to prove as strong as he was

Henry VI, another portrait painted in Tudor times but probably based on a lost original. The costume dates it to about 1450 and the King is wearing a collar of SS, a Lancastrian symbol of unknown origin.

The English coronation of Henry VI from the Rous Roll in the British Library. Note the peers' coronets, which bear very little resemblance to those of today.

weak, being cast in the mould of Eleanor of Provence and Isabella of France, though without their worse features. After eight years of marriage a son was born, the birth following almost immediately Henry's first attack of insanity. It lasted for over a year, during which time Richard, Duke of York, the next in line after Henry's son, reigned as Protector.

On Henry's recovery in 1455, the Queen and Edmund Beaufort, Duke of Somerset, became all-powerful. Things came to a head between the rival Lancastrians and Yorkists and open warfare broke out, Somerset being killed at the first battle of St Albans on 22 May 1455. A peace of sorts was patched up, but four years later hostilities recommenced and on 10 July 1460 Henry was captured at Northampton and forced to recognize the Duke of York as his heir to the exclusion of his own son. The Queen rallied the Lancastrian forces and won a victory at Wakefield in which Richard of York was slain (29 December 1460). The second battle of St Albans (17 February 1461) secured Henry's freedom, but the Lancastrian triumph was short-lived. On 29 March 1461 the new Duke of York, Edward, defeated the King's forces in a snowstorm at Towton and Henry fled to take refuge in Scotland. The Duke of York had already been

proclaimed King Edward IV on 4 March, when Henry was formally deposed.

Henry returned from Scotland to take part in an abortive rising in 1464. A year later he was captured and brought as a prisoner to the Tower of London, where he lived until a brief restoration engineered by Warwick 'the King-maker', and known as the 're-adeption', brought him back as puppet sovereign in October 1470. Edward, who had fled to Burgundy, returned early in 1471 and in two battles regained the throne. His final victory at Tewkesbury was followed by the murder of Henry's son Edward on 4 May 1471.

The hapless Henry was returned to the Tower from whence his own death was announced on 21 May 1471. He was, it appears, stabbed to death and the perpetrator of the crime was popularly believed to have been Edward's brother, Richard, Duke of Gloucester, later King Richard III.

Henry was first buried at Chertsey Abbey, his corpse being conveyed up the Thames by night, but it was later removed to St George's Chapel, Windsor, where he lies near his rival Edward, his tomb consisting of a plain black marble tablet bearing his name and the date in brass lettering.

Henry remains one of the saddest figures in English history. He was well-meaning, courteous and honest and could have made a good king in different times had he not been cursed with a recurring inherited mental affliction.

Margaret of Anjou

Born:	Pont-à-Mousson, Lorraine 23 March 1429
Married:	by proxy Nancy March 1445, in person Titchfield Abbey, Hants 22 April 1445
Crowned:	Westminster Abbey 30 May 1445
Died:	Château de Dampière, near Saumur 25 August 1482
Buried:	Angers Cathedral

Henry VI's strong-minded queen was the second daughter and fifth child of 'le bon roi René', Count of Anjou and titular King of Naples and Sicily, by his first wife Isabelle, in her own right Duchess of Lorraine. Her childhood must have been unsettled as her parents went through many vicissitudes as sovereigns without a throne. Her education was partly entrusted to her paternal grandmother Yolande of Aragon. Her marriage to Henry VI was negotiated by Beaufort and after the proxy marriage at Nancy the sixteen-year-old bride set out for England. The Channel crossing was a rough one and Margaret was violently sea-sick, being carried ashore at Porchester in the middle of a thunderstorm on 8 April 1445. She rested for a few days at Portsmouth and then went to Southampton where she fell ill with what appears to have been chickenpox. Recovered from this, she joined Henry and the marriage was solemnized at Titchfield Abbey.

Margaret was generally acknowledged to be a beauty, but Henry does not appear to have been a very demanding husband. Probably he was not highly sexed and it was eight years before the first and only child of the marriage appeared. As an intelligent and energetic woman, Margaret soon realized that she would have to take on most of the sovereign's duties, and she allied herself to the Beaufort-Suffolk faction. She also shared Henry's scholastic interests to some extent and in 1448 founded Queen's College, Cambridge.

The birth of Margaret's son Edward in 1453 followed closely on Henry's mental aberration. Richard, Duke of York, superseded in the succession by the Queen's child, lost no time in spreading rumours to the effect that the boy was either the result of an intrigue between Margaret and Somerset, or an entirely supposititious child of low birth. These she angrily refuted. The King's condition appeared so hopeless that Richard of York was constituted Protector by Parliament on 27 March 1454. By November Henry's condition began to improve and by Christmas he was almost entirely recovered and saw his infant son with joy for the first time.

The Queen now took over the management of affairs, caused the King to dissolve Parliament, and mustered an army to attempt to crush the Yorkists. Her efforts on behalf of her husband and son were indefatigable, but doomed to failure. She must often have felt exasperated and frustrated by her husband's inertia.

The defeat at Towton sent Margaret into exile in Scotland with Henry and the young Edward, but her restless, questing spirit soon sent her to France to appeal for aid to Louis XI, who was her first cousin as well as being first cousin to Henry VI. She returned after five months with Pierre Brezé, the Seneschal of Normandy, and a company of French, and attempted to invade Northumberland but was beaten at Hexham. After being befriended and protected by a robber, she made good her escape to France, accompanied by her son. They possessed only the clothes they stood up in and were practically destitute.

The exiled Queen did not give up hope. After living

Henry VI and Margaret of Anjou being presented with a book, from a 15th century manuscript. Note the head-dresses of the Queen's ladies, reminiscent of the Duchess in 'Alice in Wonderland', the garter-studded gown of the donor, and the frisky little dog determined to get into the picture.

for nearly seven years in reduced circumstances near Verdun, her father and other members of her family finally arranged a meeting with Louis XI at Tours. On his persuasion she was reconciled with the Earl of Warwick and their alliance was cemented by the marriage of the Prince of Wales to Warwick's daughter Anne. Warwick and his force landed at Dartmouth. Edward IV, unable to oppose them, fled to Holland, and Henry VI's brief restoration ensued.

The final defeat of the Lancastrians at Tewkesbury followed by the murder of the Prince of Wales ended all Margaret's hopes. She was brought before Edward IV at Coventry and despatched to London forthwith. Henry VI's murder took place on the very night his wife entered the Tower as a prisoner, and she is said to have seen his body carried past her window.

Margaret was removed from the Tower to Windsor and thence to Wallingford Castle, where the sum of five marks weekly was allotted for her maintenance. Her father King René worked tirelessly to procure her release and finally by surrendering some of his Provençal possessions to Louis XI was able to raise the ransom of 50,000 crowns demanded by Edward IV. The tragic Queen was released in November 1475 and escorted by slow stages to Sandwich, where she embarked for France and landed at Dieppe early in January 1476. She went to Rouen and there signed a renunciation of her dower. Only then was she allowed to join her devoted father at his country retreat, La Maison de Reculée, near Angers. Her tribulations had left their mark and the Queen's once lovely face was disfigured by a scaly eczema.

In 1480 Margaret's father died and she went to live with an old family retainer, François de la Vignolles, at his Château de Dampière, near Saumur, and there, after a residence of less than two years, she died on 25 August 1482. She was only fifty-three but had the appearance of a worn-out old woman. The saddest of England's queens was buried with her parents in Angers Cathedral. She has no memorial.

The Plantagenets: The House of York

The Yorkist claim to the throne was not through direct descent from Edward III's son, Edmund of Langley, Duke of York, for he was born after John of Gaunt, from whom Henry VI derived his Lancastrian claim. In order to assert precedence over the House of Lancaster the claim had to derive from John of Gaunt's elder brother Lionel of Antwerp, Duke of Clarence, through the female line. Lionel's only child Philippa had married Edmund Mortimer, Earl of March, the great-grandson of Queen Isabella's lover. Their son had fathered Edmund Mortimer (*d.* 1425) and Anne, who married Richard, Earl of Cambridge, the second son of Edmund of Langley. Edward IV, the first Yorkist king, was the grandson of Richard and Anne.

Edward IV   1461–1470 and 1471–1483

Born:	Rouen 28 April 1442
Acceded:	4 March 1461
Crowned:	Westminster Abbey 28 June 1461
Deposed:	3 October 1470
Restored:	11 April 1471
Married:	Grafton Regis, Northants 1 May 1464, Elizabeth, widow of Sir John Grey, and eldest daughter of Richard Woodville, 1st Earl Rivers, and Jacquette of Luxembourg (widow of John, Duke of Bedford, 4th son of King Henry IV)
Children:	(1) Elizabeth, later wife of King Henry VII
	(2) Mary: b. Windsor Castle August 1466; d. Greenwich 23 May 1482
	(3) Cicely: b. 20 March 1469; d. Quarr Abbey, Isle of Wight 24 August 1507; m. 1st, before December 1487, John Welles, 1st Viscount Welles (d. London 9 February 1499); 2nd, before January 1504, Thomas Kyme
	(4) Edward, later King Edward V
	(5) Margaret: b. 10 April 1472; d. 11 December 1472
	(6) Richard, Duke of York: b. Shrewsbury 17 August 1473; d. in or after 1483; m. St Stephen's Chapel, Westminster 15 January 1478, Lady Anne Mowbray (d. Greenwich 19 November 1481)
	(7) Anne: b. Palace of Westminster 2 November 1475; d. 23 November 1511; m. 4 February 1495, Thomas Howard, 3rd Duke of Norfolk
	(8) George, Duke of Bedford: b. Windsor Castle March 1477; d. Windsor Castle March 1479
	(9) Catherine: b. Eltham Palace ca 14 August 1479; d. Tiverton 15 November 1527; m. before October 1495, William Courtenay, Earl of Devon
	(10) Bridget, a nun at Dartford: b. Eltham Palace 10 November 1480; d. Dartford 1517
Died:	Palace of Westminster 9 April 1483
Buried:	St George's Chapel, Windsor

Edward was the second son of Richard, Duke of York, and Cicely Nevill, an elder brother Henry having died in infancy. He was born at Rouen when his father was acting as Lieutenant and Captain-General of the Duchy of Aquitaine and Chief Commissary, Ambassador and Deputy to treat with France, a sonorous array of titles. Edward and his brother Edmund, his junior by one year, were installed at Ludlow Castle, whence they wrote letters to their campaigning father, thanking him for such things as 'our green gowns now late sent unto us to our great comfort', and requesting him to send 'some fine bonnets ... by the next sure messenger, for necessity so requireth.' They also complained bitterly about their tutor Richard Crofte. Edward grew up a burly, blond giant, over six feet tall, skilled in military arts and with an eye for the ladies, who found him an amusing companion and accomplished dancing partner. In courtly pursuits he was trained by his mother 'The Rose of Raby', also known as 'proud Cis', who through her mother, Joan Beaufort, was a granddaughter of John of Gaunt, bringing to her children yet another line of descent from Edward III.

As soon as they were old enough, Edward and Edmund took up arms in their family cause. Edmund perished with his father at Wakefield in December 1460, but Edward lived to triumph over his enemies and was finally declared king in Parliament on 4 March 1461, and crowned at Westminster Abbey on the St Peter's Day following.

Three years later the King married in a somewhat furtive manner. While hunting on May Day 1464, he slipped away to Grafton Regis and was married in the parish church to the widowed Lady Grey, five years his senior. Her maiden name was Elizabeth Woodville and she had been a maid of honour to Margaret of Anjou. On her father's side she belonged to an obscure enough family, but her mother was Jacquette of Luxembourg, Duchess of Bedford, the widow of Henry IV's doughty son. Nevertheless, Elizabeth was hardly a suitable match for the King, who did not make his marriage public until the autumn, when he was pressed to seek the hand of a foreign princess. The newly acknowledged Queen was brought to London and the ceremonies of her state entry and crowning were observed with more than usual magnificence. In spite of his marriage and the large family Elizabeth bore him, Edward remained a philanderer and was wont to boast of his three concubines, 'one the merriest, the other the wiliest, the third the holiest harlot in the realm.' He had, however, only two proven bastards, one being Arthur Plantagenet, Viscount Lisle, who was to serve his half-nephew Henry VIII as Deputy of Calais.

Edward's marriage alienated many of his supporters, including Warwick 'the King-maker', who joined the

Edward IV, a portrait by an unknown artist in the National Portrait Gallery. It is easy to trace the King's features recurring in those of his grandson Henry VIII.

Lancastrians and reopened the civil war, defeating the King near Banbury in 1469. He then went to France to raise more troops and returned to effect the brief 're-adeption' of Henry VI. Edward was forced to fly to France and his wife and family to take refuge in Sanctuary at Westminster. He returned and regained the throne in April 1471. Warwick was defeated and killed at Barnet soon after, while the battle of Tewkesbury and the deaths of Henry VI and his son ended all Lancastrian hopes for the foreseeable future. Edward's brother George, Duke of Clarence, had sided with his father-in-law Warwick and was declared a traitor and imprisoned in the Tower. There he is alleged to have been drowned in a butt of malmsey wine on 18 February 1478. How far Edward and his youngest brother, Richard, Duke of Gloucester, were implicated in his death is not known.

Although apparently a popular and pleasure-loving king, Edward possessed all the ruthlessness and strong will of a Renaissance despot. Had he lived longer he might well have become one of the most powerful of English kings. He died a few weeks before his forty-first birthday, probably of pneumonia, although very few details of his last illness have been recorded. He was buried in St George's Chapel, Windsor, where his tomb is marked by a simple monument of black marble.

Elizabeth Woodville

Born: Grafton Regis, Northants ca 1437
Married: 1st, Sir John Grey (d. killed at the second
            battle of St Albans 17 February 1461), and
            had issue two sons
            2nd, Grafton Regis 1 May 1464, King
            Edward IV
Crowned: Westminster Abbey 26 May 1465
Died: Bermondsey Abbey 8 June 1492
Buried: St George's Chapel, Windsor

Elizabeth Woodville, whose story almost rivals that of Cinderella, was of comparatively humble origin. She was born on her father's estate at Grafton Regis, Northamptonshire in about 1437 and as a young girl became, probably through her mother's grand court connections, a maid of honour to Margaret of Anjou, who appears to have held her in some affection. A marriage was arranged for her with Sir John Grey, sometimes styled 2nd Baron Grey of Groby. Two sons were born before Grey died in the second battle of St Albans in February 1461. Edward IV is said to have fallen in love with Lady Grey's cool, blonde beauty when she presented a petition for the restoration of her husband's forfeited lands. He paid ardent suit to her, but she steadfastly refused to become his mistress, saying 'that she did account herself too base to be his wife, so she did think herself too good to be his harlot.' The King's passion was so great that he married her secretly and declared her to be his queen some months later.

The sudden arrival of this stately, cool and aloof unknown put many noses out of joint at court, including that of the King's brother Richard of Gloucester, who heartily disliked his new sister-in-law and showed it at every opportunity. The advancement of the Woodville family also caused grave offence. They had, of course, been Lancastrians and Elizabeth's father had been created Baron Rivers and a Knight of the Garter by Henry VI in 1448. He was now advanced to an Earldom by his new son-in-law and also made Lord High Constable of England. Brilliant marriages were arranged for Elizabeth's sisters, Margaret becoming Countess of Arundel, Anne becoming Countess of Kent, Jacquetta becoming Lady Strange of Knokyn, Mary becoming Countess of Huntingdon, and Catherine becoming Duchess of Buckingham, while Elizabeth's elder son, Thomas Grey, was created Marquess of Dorset.

Elizabeth bore Edward a large family of three sons and seven daughters. During Edward IV's flight and the 're-adeption' of Henry VI she took refuge in Sanctuary at

Westminster with her mother and children and it was there that she gave birth to Edward, Prince of Wales.

The death of Edward IV in April 1483 forced his queen to again seek refuge in Sanctuary with her younger children, fearing the enmity of her brother-in-law Richard of Gloucester and Buckingham. After Edward V had been lodged in the Tower of London, Elizabeth was persuaded by Cardinal Bourchier to allow her son Richard, Duke of York, to leave Sanctuary to join his brother, who was lonely without a companion. She did so reluctantly and was never to see him again.

In 1484 Parliament declared Elizabeth's marriage to Edward IV to have been invalid on the grounds of his having been previously contracted to marry Lady Eleanor Butler, who was still living when he married Lady Grey. This, of course, automatically bastardized all Elizabeth's children by Edward IV and upheld Richard III's title to the throne. Richard III eventually persuaded his sister-in-law to leave Sanctuary with her daughters on a promise of providing for them, which, to his credit, he did; Elizabeth and her daughters are even reputed to have graced his court with their presence, the girls joining in the dancing.

After Henry VII's accession and marriage to her eldest daughter, Elizabeth was reinstated as Queen Dowager in 1486, but in the following year her lands were forfeited for her alleged perfidy in attending Richard's court in 1484 and she was obliged to retire in reduced circumstances to Bermondsey Abbey, where she died in June 1492, aged about fifty-five. She was buried with Edward in St George's Chapel Windsor.

Elizabeth's character is a difficult one to assess. Edward was infatuated with her, yet she appears strangely cold and aloof. Her daughters were not fond of her and cared little that she spent the greater part of her widowhood within the grim walls of Bermondsey Abbey. Although assiduous in her advancement of her brothers and sisters and her sons from her first marriage, her royal children seemed to mean less to her and she was unconcerned about the fate of Edward V and his brother to an extent which inclines one to judge her one of the most enigmatic of queens.

EDWARD V   APRIL–JUNE 1483

Born:	in Sanctuary at Westminster 4 November 1470
Acceded:	9 April 1483
Deposed:	25 June 1483
Died:	place and date uncertain

Edward V, the 'Boy King' who was never crowned, is a figure who never really comes to life. To most people his name will conjure up a sentimental vision of two pale fair-haired little boys in black velvet, looking wistful and pensive in the grim surrounding of a room in the Tower.

Edward was born in Sanctuary at Westminster at a moment when his parents' fortunes seemed at their lowest ebb, but in a few months all had changed. Edward IV was back in power and able to create his first-born son Prince of Wales and Earl of Chester, Duke of Cornwall, a Knight of the Garter, Earl of March and Earl of Pembroke successively. The young Prince was placed in the charge of his paternal uncles, the Dukes of Clarence and Gloucester, and his maternal uncle, Earl Rivers.

When Edward IV died in April 1483, Edward was at Ludlow and on receipt of the news that he was now King set out for London, being met on the way at Stony Stratford by his uncle Richard of Gloucester who was coming from York. Richard conducted him to London with every sign of loyalty and they were met outside the city by the Lord Mayor and leading citizens, who escorted them to the Tower, which it is alleged the young Edward V never left again.

Some weeks later Robert Stillington, Bishop of Bath and Wells, who had been Chancellor from 1467 to 1475 and was openly hostile to the Woodvilles, dropped his bombshell regarding the validity of Edward IV's marriage. The fact that Edward had been pre-contracted was good enough reason in Canon Law to invalidate any subsequent marriage contracted by him during the lifetime of Lady Eleanor Butler. The Bishop's allegation may have had some justification, or may have been a complete fabrication, but it served to induce Parliament to declare Elizabeth Woodville's marriage to Edward invalid and their children bastards. It therefore followed that Edward V was no longer king and he was declared deposed on 25 June 1483, after a reign of only two months. Richard of Gloucester was proclaimed king in his place the following day.

There now ensues one of the greatest historical mysteries of all time: 'what became of the Princes in the Tower?' Tudor propaganda, engineered by Henry VII, would have us believe that Edward and his brother Richard were smothered in their sleep by Sir James Tyrrell (note the similarity of the surname to that of the alleged slayer of William Rufus), who was later induced by torture to confess the deed and was beheaded in 1502. It seems strange that no search for the Princes' bodies was made at that time and it was not until the reign of Charles II that the bones of two children were found beneath a staircase in the Tower and solemnly deposited in an urn in Westminster Abbey. These pathetic remains were medically examined in 1933 by Professor William Wright. He concluded that they came from the skeletons of two boys aged approximately 12 and 9 or 10, their heights being 4 feet 9½ inches and 4 feet 6½ inches respectively. Were they the Princes? Who can say? If so, who was responsible for their murder? Richard III or Henry VII? As long as they lived they provided rivals to both. There are many who believe that Richard had them moved to Middleham Castle in Yorkshire and that they were still alive there at the time of Bosworth. If that is true, the implications are obvious.

RICHARD III   1483–1485

Born:	Fotheringay Castle 2 October 1452
Lord High Protector:	9 April 1483
Proclaimed King:	26 June 1483
Crowned:	Westminster Abbey 6 July 1483
Married:	Westminster 12 July 1472, Anne, widow of Edward, Prince of Wales (only son of King Henry VI), and younger daughter of Richard Nevill, 1st Earl of Warwick, and Lady Anne Beauchamp
Child:	Edward, Prince of Wales: *b.* Middleham Castle, Yorkshire *ca* December 1473; *d.* Middleham Castle 9 April 1484
Died:	Bosworth 22 August 1485
Buried:	Grey Friars Abbey, Leicester; later disinterred and bones thrown in River Soar

Richard was the eleventh child and eighth and youngest son of Richard Plantagenet, 3rd Duke of York, and the redoubtable Lady Cicely Nevill. He was born at Fotheringay Castle on 2 October 1452. All that remains of Fotheringay today is a single lump of masonry in the middle of a field. Attached to it are two plaques commemorating the two most notable events to take place within its walls, the birth of Richard and the beheading of Mary, Queen of Scots.

Richard was only eight years old when his brother Edward IV was proclaimed king in March 1461, and he was created Duke of Gloucester on the eve of Edward's coronation. He proved himself a loyal and loving brother and fought bravely in the later stages of the civil war culminating in the battle of Tewkesbury. The deaths of Edward, Prince of Wales, and Henry VI have both been laid at his door, but the evidence is circumstantial and like everything else to Richard's discredit highly coloured by the Tudor propagandists, Polydore Vergil and Sir Thomas More.

In 1472 Richard married the widow of Edward, Prince of Wales, Anne Nevill, the younger daughter of Warwick 'the King-maker'. Her elder sister, Isabel, had married Richard's brother George, Duke of Clarence,

three years earlier. These marriages caused a rift between the brothers as George was desirous of retaining all the Warwick estates for himself. Richard was suspected of being implicated in Clarence's death in the Tower in 1478, but the charge remains unproven.

Edward IV's death made Richard Lord High Protector of the Realm for his nephew Edward V, and he set out from York to meet Edward, who was coming from Ludlow, and proceeded to London. Edward was conducted by his maternal uncle Earl Rivers and his half-brother Lord Richard Grey. When the parties met up at Stony Stratford, these two were seized by Richard,

A processional cross found on Bosworth Field. It was probably carried into battle and abandoned when its bearer was slain.

who had long chafed under the ascendancy of the Woodville faction, and he took charge of the young King. On entering London, Richard presented Edward to the Lord Mayor and citizens as their King, himself evincing complete loyalty.

The Woodville party was completely overthrown and Lord Hastings, who had previously supported Richard, grew apprehensive as he gained power and sought, with some members of the Council, to wrest Edward from Richard's control. The result was dramatic. Apprised of their intentions, Richard had Hastings and his fellow plotters arrested at a sitting of the Council and summarily beheaded on 13 June 1483. Their executions were followed twelve days later by those of Rivers and Grey, also without trial.

On 22 June 1483 Dr Shaw preached a sermon at St Paul's Cross, London, declaring Edward IV's marriage invalid and his children bastards, based on the information revealed by Bishop Stillington of Bath and Wells. As a result, Richard was offered the crown by Parliament and proclaimed king on 26 June. Ten days later Richard and Anne were crowned in Westminster Abbey by Cardinal Bourchier.

A great sorrow was the death of Richard's only legitimate son, another Edward, Prince of Wales, whose shadowy, sickly life of ten years ended at Middleham Castle in Yorkshire on 9 April 1484, and was followed a year later by that of Queen Anne. Richard then designated his nephew, John de la Pole, Earl of Lincoln, as heir-presumptive. He was the eldest son of Richard's second sister, Elizabeth, Duchess of Suffolk. The possibility of a female succeeding to the throne in her own right was still considered unfeasible.

Meanwhile, the Lancastrians were being rallied under the leadership of Henry Tudor, who landed at Milford Haven on 7 August 1485 and travelled through Wales gathering support. Richard was in the north and proceeded to Leicester with his army. On 21 August he rode out to meet Henry, who was encamped near Market Bosworth. Battle was joined on the morning of 22 August. The King's army was twice the size of Henry's, but the turning point of the battle came when Lord Stanley and his 7000 men deserted Richard and went over to Henry. Richard fought bravely to the last. He could have escaped, but proudly declared: 'I will not budge a foot; I will die King of England.' And so he did. The crest crown from his helmet fell or was hacked off and rolled away under a hawthorn bush, where Stanley picked it up and placed it on the head of the victorious Henry. The battle had only lasted two hours.

Richard's body, stripped of its armour, was laid across the back of a pack-horse and a sad little procession wended its way back to Leicester, arriving at nightfall. He was buried in Grey Friars Abbey in Leicester, but it proved a temporary resting place for at the Reformation Richard's bones were dug up and thrown into the River Soar. In recent years the Richard III Society has placed a memorial to the King in Leicester Cathedral and there is also an inscription adjacent to the bridge over the River Soar.

Richard was a small, slightly built man, a complete contrast to his brother Edward. He had one shoulder slightly higher than the other, a malformation which has been magnified into the hump and crooked back so maliciously described by his detractors. His portraits reveal a not unpleasant face with a rather worried expression. It is hard to believe that he was only thirty-two when he died.

That Richard III has gone down in history as the archetype 'wicked uncle' and an evil monster is due almost entirely to the effective hatchet job carried out by Tudor propagandists in the reigns of Henry VII and Henry VIII and perfected by Shakespeare in the reign of Elizabeth I. He had to wait nearly 300 years for his first apologist and found a doughty champion in the person of Horace Walpole, who in 1768 published his *Historic Doubts on Richard III*, in which he questioned Richard's guilt. Thereafter the move towards his rehabilitation has grown steadily and in the present century Josephine Tey's ingenious novel *The Daughter of Time*, in which a detective whiles away a forced sojourn in hospital by studying Richard's story and finding him innocent of all charges brought against him, has done more to win over people to Richard's cause than anything else. A flourishing Richard III Society, appropriately under the patronage of another Richard, Duke of Gloucester, holds regular meetings and lectures to promote the cause and enthusiastically visits Ricardian sites.

Anne Nevill

Born:	Warwick Castle 11 June 1456
Married:	1st, Amboise August 1470, Edward, Prince of Wales, only son of King Henry VI; 2nd, Westminster 12 July 1472, Richard, Duke of Gloucester, later King Richard III
Crowned:	Westminster Abbey 6 July 1483
Died:	Palace of Westminster 16 March 1485
Buried:	Westminster Abbey

Richard III's queen has been depicted as yet another victim of the 'monster'. In fact her marriage to him appears to have been a happy one and his love and regard for her quite genuine.

The younger daughter and co-heiress of the great 'King-maker' was born at Warwick Castle on 11 June 1456. Her marriage at Amboise in August 1470 to Henry VI's son, Edward, Prince of Wales, was made in anticipation of the success of her father's expedition to restore Henry, and she was with Queen Margaret at

Tewkesbury when her father and young husband were both slain. The consummation of the marriage was not to have taken place until the restoration had been fully effected, so Anne remained a virgin bride.

Anne's elder sister Isabel had married Edward IV's brother George, Duke of Clarence, in 1469, and Anne's hand was now sought by Edward's youngest brother, Richard, Duke of Gloucester. The marriage took place at Westminster on 12 July 1472, and at the end of the following year Anne's only child, Edward, was born at Middleham Castle, one of Richard's northern possessions. The marriage led, as we have seen, to a dissention between the brothers over the Warwick inheritance.

Richard and Anne were crowned together and the Rous Roll has an engaging full-length picture of them both, robed and crowned. Anne has long, flowing fair hair and a serene and happy expression which belies the stories of Richard's ill-treatment and neglect. He did have some bastards, it must be admitted, but they were almost certainly born before his marriage.

Anne's health was never good (she may have been consumptive) and that of her son was even worse. He spent much of his life in the north and died at his birthplace on 9 April 1484. His beautiful little tomb with his effigy, though badly damaged, may still be seen in Sheriff Hutton Church. The Queen survived her child by less than a year, dying in the Palace of Westminster on 16 March 1485. She was buried in Westminster Abbey, where she had no monument until a few years ago when the Richard III Society commissioned a handsome wall plaque with her arms enamelled in colour to be affixed near her burial site.

Anne remains a shadowy figure and it seems fairly obvious that she was a negative personality, placid and uncomplaining while great events passed by leaving little mark on her life.

THE HOUSE OF TUDOR

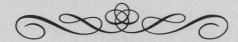

The male line of the House of Tudor, which
ascended the throne in the person of Henry VII in
1485, is traced back, probably fairly reliably,
through many generations to none other than 'Old
King Cole', the Romano-British chief Coel Hen
Godebog or Caelius Votepacus, who held sway in
Colchester in the fourth century AD. Henry VII's
great-grandfather Maredudd ap Tudur was a first
cousin of the great Welsh hero Owen Glendower,
who made the last bid for Welsh independence in
1400, and Henry was the representative of several
lines of Welsh kings and princes as can be seen from
the genealogical table in Appendix B.

Henry VII's grandfather Owen Tudor either
married, or formed an alliance with, Catherine of
Valois, widow of Henry V, and their eldest son
Edmund was therefore a half-brother of Henry VI.
Edmund Tudor, Earl of Richmond, married
Margaret Beaufort, the only child of John Beaufort,
Duke of Somerset and Henry was their only son.
Henry's slender claim to the English throne was
through his mother, the genealogical representative
of John of Gaunt, Duke of Lancaster (the fourth son
of Edward III) and his third wife Katherine
Swynford. Their children had all been born before
their marriage, but were legitimated by Richard II
and this was confirmed by Henry IV, but with the
addition of a new clause *excepta dignitate regale*,
which excluded them from any right of succession
to the throne.

HENRY VII	1485–1509

Born: Pembroke Castle 28 January 1457
Acceded: 22 August 1485
Crowned: Westminster Abbey 30 October 1485
Married: Westminster 18 January 1486, Elizabeth (of York), eldest daughter of King Edward IV
Children:
(1) Arthur, Prince of Wales: *b.* St Swithin's Priory, Winchester 20 September 1486; *d.* Ludlow Castle 2 April 1502; *m.* St Paul's Cathedral, London 14 November 1501, Catherine of Aragon (who remarried with his brother Henry)
(2) Margaret: *b.* Westminster Palace 28 November 1489; *d.* Methven Castle 18 October 1541; *m.* 1st, Holyrood Abbey 8 August 1503, James IV, King of Scots; 2nd, Kinnoull 4 August 1514 (*m.* dissolved 1527), Archibald Douglas, 6th Earl of Angus; 3rd, March 1528, Henry Stewart, 1st Lord Methven

(3) Henry, later King Henry VIII
(4) Elizabeth: *b.* 2 July 1492; *d.* Eltham Palace 14 September 1495
(5) Mary: *b.* Richmond Palace 18 March 1496; *d.* Westhorpe, Suffolk 25 June 1533; *m.* 1st, Abbeville 9 October 1514, Louis XII, King of France; 2nd, Paris 3 March (secretly) and Greenwich 13 May 1515, Charles Brandon, 1st Duke of Suffolk, KG
(6) Edmund: *b.* Greenwich Palace 21/22 February 1499; *d.* Bishop's Hatfield, Herts 19 June 1500
(7) Katherine: *b.* Tower of London 2 February 1503; *d.* later the same year

Died: Richmond Palace 21 April 1509
Buried: Henry VII's Chapel, Westminster Abbey

Henry VII was born three months after the death of his father Edmund Tudor, who was probably killed fighting for the Lancastrian cause at Carmarthen Castle on 3 November 1456. His pregnant widow, the thirteen-year-old, orphaned heiress Lady Margaret Beaufort, sought the protection of her brother-in-law Jasper Tudor, who held Pembroke Castle as Constable for the Lancastrians and it was there that her son Henry was born and spent his early years.

The Castle was captured for the Yorkists by Lord Herbert on 30 September 1461 and Henry's custody and marriage were sold to Herbert for £1000 early the following year. His life appears to have continued much as before and he resided either at Pembroke or at the Herberts' castle at Raglan for the next few years. His mother had left to remarry (first to Henry Stafford, who died in 1471, then to Thomas, Lord Stanley), and Lord and Lady Herbert proved kind foster parents, bringing Henry up in their household as the intended husband of their daughter Maud and providing him with a good education.

The 're-adeption' of Henry VI in October 1470 brought Jasper Tudor back to Pembroke to bring his nephew to London to meet the King and there is a tradition that Henry pursued his studies at his royal half-uncle's foundation at Eton. If so, it must have been for a very short time, for early in 1471 he returned to Wales with Jasper, who had received a commission to array Welsh forces. The battles of Barnet (14 April) and

Lady Margaret Beaufort, mother of Henry VII, a portrait by an unknown artist in the National Portrait Gallery. A very learned lady, she was the founder of Lady Margaret Hall at Oxford.

Tewkesbury (4 May) proved fatal to the Lancastrian cause and Jasper and Henry, who had been unable to join forces with Queen Margaret and her other supporters, headed back for Pembroke, where they were besieged in the Castle. They were allowed to escape through the good offices of a friend and make their way to Tenby where they took a ship with the intention of going to France. Stormy weather conditions drove them to land in Brittany, where they were accorded the protection of Duke Francis II. The next thirteen years of Henry's life were passed in Brittany and little is known of this period during which he grew to manhood. Edward IV made several attempts to extradite the exiles, being particularly anxious to get 'the only imp now left of Henry's brood' into his clutches, but Jasper and Henry succeeded in evading all such efforts.

The details of the rising against Richard III, culminating in the Battle of Bosworth in August 1485, have already been told. The victor of Bosworth lost no time in consolidating his position. No one questioned his claim to be considered the heir of the House of Lancaster, though his mother had a prior one. He at once ordered the arrest and imprisonment in the Tower of his chief rival, Edward, Earl of Warwick, the son of the ill-fated Duke of Clarence, and then made his way to London where he was received by the Mayor and Aldermen and escorted by them to St Paul's Cathedral. There he deposited his standards on the high altar and a solemn *Te Deum* was sung. At the end of October Henry's coronation took place at Westminster Abbey. He was crowned by the octogenarian Cardinal Bourchier, Archbishop of Canterbury, who had officiated at the coronations of both Edward IV and Richard III. The new king did not neglect to reward his supporters, among them his uncle Jasper, who became Duke of Bedford and was married to a sister of the Queen Dowager (Elizabeth Woodville), and his stepfather Lord Stanley, who became Earl of Derby.

Henry's first Parliament had been called for November and one of its first acts was to pass a bill confirming Henry's right to the throne and settling it on 'the heirs of his body lawfully comen'. The session ended in December with a petition from the Lords and Commons begging the King to marry Elizabeth, the eldest daughter of King Edward IV, to which he was graciously pleased to accede. Henry had, in fact, already pledged himself to this marriage at Rennes in 1483. Now it remained to remove the stigma of bastardy from the intended bride and to obtain a papal dispensation for the marriage of persons related 'in the fourth degree of kinship and perhaps in the fourth degree of affinity'. Both these formalities being complied with, the marriage took place at Westminster on 18 January 1486.

Henry, apart from seeing himself as the lawful heir of the House of Lancaster and the husband of the lawful

Henry VII's portrait by Michiel Sittow in the National Portrait Gallery gives a strong impression of his shrewdness of character.

heiress of the House of York, also laid claim to a much older tradition. Through his Welsh grandfather he traced descent from ancient British kings and saw himself as the lawful successor of the semi-mythical Arthur. It was almost a restoration! He adopted the red dragon of Wales as one of the supporters of the royal coat of arms and named his eldest son and heir 'Arthur' to boost the tradition. Although Henry was only one-quarter Welsh by blood, it must be remembered that he was born and spent his earliest years in Wales and then in Brittany, where the same traditions prevailed and the same language was spoken. In many ways he was a typical Celt, both in appearance and temperament.

During his reign Henry had to deal with two pretenders to the throne. The first was Lambert Simnel who personated Edward, Earl of Warwick, the son of Edward IV's brother George, Duke of Clarence. Simnel gained the support of his putative aunt Margaret, Duchess of Burgundy, and repairing to Ireland was actually crowned in Dublin as Edward VI in 1487. On invading England in the same year, however, he was defeated and captured by Henry at Stoke-on-Trent. Henry showed great magnanimity in pardoning him and putting him to work as a turnspit in the royal kitchens. He was still living in 1525. The second pretender was Perkin Warbeck, a native of Tournai, who pretended to be Richard, Duke of York, the younger son of Edward IV. He gained support in Europe, and Margaret of Burgundy, the Emperor Maximilian and James IV, King of Scots, all recognized him as Richard IV of England. At the Scottish court he received the hand of Lady Catherine Gordon in marriage. After rallying support in Ireland, he landed in Cornwall and advanced as far as Exeter before he was captured in September 1497. He confessed his imposture, was imprisoned in the Tower of London, and was eventually hanged after an attempted escape in 1499. The real Earl of Warwick, who made a bid for freedom at the same time, perished with him, but on the block as befitted his royal birth.

Henry's health, never very robust, began to fail in 1507, when he became subject to recurrent attacks of gout and asthma. His condition worsened steadily and he died at his new palace at Richmond, a place not ideally situated for a sufferer from respiratory troubles, on 21 April 1509, aged fifty-two. His tough old mother survived him until the June following, when she died at

A 17th century drawing of Richmond Palace, where Henry VII and his granddaughter Elizabeth I both died. According to legend it was from the window over the gate that the waiting Sir Robert Carey received the news that Queen Elizabeth I had died and set out on his journey to Scotland to inform the new king of his accession. The gatehouse and the window are still much the same today, but there is little left of the rest of the palace.

the age of sixty-six, which was considered quite a venerable one in those days.

Although the Venetian Ambassador was to sum up Henry after his death as 'a very great miser but a man of vast ability', it was a facile judgement. Henry, although parsimonious by nature, maintained a splendid court and spent lavishly on the building of Richmond Palace (the old palace of Sheen having been destroyed by fire in 1497), and the rebuilding of Baynard's Castle and Greenwich Palace. He also founded several religious houses and actively supported his mother's religious and educational foundations; but his greatest achievement and everlasting memorial is the exquisite chapel known by his name which he added to Westminster Abbey, and in which he and his queen lie entombed beneath Torrigiano's magnificent bronze monument.

Henry VII is the first English monarch whose portrait reveals something of his character. From the surviving contemporary portrait by Michael Sittow in the National Portrait Gallery, painted in 1504 or 1505, his lean Welsh face peers out at us through shrewd blue-grey eyes and the thin-lipped mouth speaks of his parsimony. It is the face of a lonely man, wise, but neither loved nor loving. An impression of majesty, not apparent in the painted portrait, is present in the magnificent poly-chrome bust by Torrigiano and the tomb effigy, wherein he is the personification of the Renaissance prince. Henry's death mask also survives at Westminster Abbey, but the nose has been restored, not very successfully, leaving the impression of a flawed likeness. Henry's coins were the first to carry a portrait of the monarch which is more than a stylized representation of a king.

Elizabeth of York

Born: Westminster Palace 11 February 1466
Married: Westminster 18 January 1486
Crowned: Westminster Abbey 25 November 1487
Died: Tower of London 11 February 1503
Buried: Henry VII's Chapel, Westminster Abbey

Elizabeth of York was one of history's pawns from the day of her birth. This event took place when the 'sun of York' was very much in the ascendant; her father Edward IV had secured the throne and her mother Elizabeth Woodville had been crowned queen. Her governess at this time was her future mother-in-law Margaret Beaufort, Countess of Richmond. At five years of age she accompanied her mother and sister into Sanctuary at Westminster during the short-lived restoration of Henry VI.

By the time of her father's death in 1483 she had already been promised in marriage three times, first to Henry, Earl of Richmond (her eventual bridegroom), then to the son of Henry VI, and lastly to the Dauphin Charles, son of Louis XI. The negotiations for the last

Elizabeth of York, a late 16th century version of the only known portrait type of the queen.

match were abruptly broken off on Edward's death. Thereafter, Elizabeth's mother and the Countess of Richmond came to a private agreement that she should be betrothed to her first suitor, Henry Tudor, then still exiled in Brittany.

Henry's victory at Bosworth paved the way for the conclusion of the secret agreement made between the Queen Dowager Elizabeth Woodville and the Countess of Richmond, and Elizabeth's marriage to Henry took place at the Palace of Westminster in January 1486. As she became pregnant almost immediately, her coronation was deferred until November 1487.

If Henry was not a particularly good husband, he was at least a faithful one, a rare thing in those times. Cold and unloving by nature, only one illegitimate child has been attributed to him, falsely as it has now been proved. Elizabeth bore him seven children, it is true, but their begetting would almost certainly be considered a matter of duty on the part of both parents. There is, however, one rather touching account of the King and Queen comforting each other after they received the news of the death of their eldest son Prince Arthur, which shows them in a more human light. Altogether, Elizabeth does not emerge as a personality. She appears to have taken every change of fortune placidly, never demurring for an instant when first one marriage then another was proposed for her by her father. In her final acceptance of Henry VII she again acquiesced willingly, probably for the sake of her mother and sisters, who were well nigh destitute. As Queen she led a dull existence, albeit a comfortable and often splendid one.

No contemporary portraits of Elizabeth have survived. Her tomb effigy depicts a figure of serenely calm majesty, but the carved wooden funeral effigy (partially restored) and the portrait in the National Portrait Gallery (probably a late sixteenth century copy of a contemporary original) both give the impression of a stolid plump-cheeked, pouting woman, listless and cow-eyed. Her whole life was in fact dominated by women of stronger character: her mother, of whom in later life she does not seem to have been particularly fond; her formidable grandmother 'proud Cis', the old Duchess of York, and her mother's sworn enemy; and most of all her mother-in-law, the energetic, forthright, bluestocking Countess of Richmond and Derby, with whom she got on remarkably well.

Elizabeth's health was tolerably good for the period. She bore seven children, three of whom died in childhood, and died nine days after the birth of the last, probably of puerperal fever. If Henry had not been a demonstratively loving husband, he mourned her sincerely and only contemplated remarriage as a political expedient some years after her death. His own breakdown in health was to prevent these plans from ever coming to fruition.

HENRY VIII   1509–1547

Born:	Greenwich Palace 28 June 1491		Marchioness of Pembroke, daughter of
Acceded:	21 April 1509		Thomas Boleyn, 1st Earl of Wiltshire and
Crowned:	Westminster Abbey 24 June 1509		Ormonde, and Lady Elizabeth Howard
Married:	1st, Grey Friars Church, Greenwich	Children:	(7) Elizabeth, later Queen Elizabeth I
	11 June 1509 (m. declared null and void		(8) A stillborn son at Greenwich
	23 May 1533 and 'utterly dissolved' by Act		29 January 1536
	of Parliament March 1534), Catherine	Married:	3rd, York Place 30 May 1536, Jane,
	widow of his brother Arthur, Prince of		daughter of Sir John Seymour and Margery
	Wales, and youngest daughter of		Wentworth
	Ferdinand II, King of Aragon, and	Children:	(9) Edward, later King Edward VI
	Isabella, Queen of Castile	Married:	4th, Greenwich, 6 January 1540
Children:	(1) A stillborn daughter: 31 January 1510		(m. annulled 9 July 1540), Anne, 2nd
	(2) Henry, Duke of Cornwall:		daughter of John III, Duke of Cleves, and
	b. Richmond Palace 1 January; d. there		Marie of Jülich
	22 February 1511	Married:	5th, Hampton Court Palace 28 July 1540,
	(3) Henry (?), Duke of Cornwall: b. and		Catherine, daughter of Lord Edmund
	d. Richmond Palace, November 1513		Howard and Joyce Culpeper
	(4) A stillborn son: December 1514	Married:	6th, Hampton Court Palace 12 July 1543,
	(5) Mary, later Queen Mary I		Catherine, widow of John Nevill, 3rd
	(6) A stillborn daughter: 10 November		Baron Latimer, previously of Sir Edward
	1518		Borough, and daughter of Sir Thomas Parr
Married:	2nd, Whitehall or Westminster 25 January		and Maud Green
	1533 (m. declared valid 28 May 1533 and	Died:	Whitehall 28 January 1547
	invalid 17 May 1536), Anne Boleyn,	Buried:	St George's Chapel, Windsor

Henry VIII is the one king whose likeness is instantly recognizable in his portraits, almost all of which evolve from the type made so familiar by the genius of Holbein. The large square face, the little pig eyes staring out morosely beneath the feathered hat, the red-gold beard, the slashed and bejewelled attire, the bulging codpiece, and the stance with hands on hips and legs well splayed are familiar to all. The second Tudor monarch is undoubtedly the best known English king; the story of his six wives has fired the popular imagination for four centuries and will continue to do so for centuries to come.

The third child and second son of Henry VII and Elizabeth of York, Henry was born at Greenwich Palace on 28 June 1491. Before he was five years old he had a goodly string of honours heaped upon him: Constable of Dover Castle and Lord Warden of the Cinque Ports, Lieutenant of Ireland, Knight of the Bath, Duke of York, Warden of the Scottish Marches, Knight of the Garter and Earl Marshal of England. At the age of ten he played a prominent part in the marriage ceremonies of his brother Arthur, Prince of Wales to Catherine of Aragon. It is said to have been his father's intention that he should enter the Church and eventually become Archbishop of Canterbury, but the death of Arthur less than five months after his marriage changed all this. Henry became heir apparent and automatically Duke of

Henry VIII, painted by an unknown artist about 1520.

Henry VIII processing to Parliament in 1512. The Cap of Maintenance and the Sword of State are borne before him, but although robed and carrying the orb and the sceptre with the dove, the King is wearing an ordinary hat instead of a crown.

Cornwall. On 18 February 1503 his patent as Duke of York was cancelled and he was created Prince of Wales and Earl of Chester.

Henry was well educated in the classics, his tutors being John Skelton, the Poet Laureate, and William Hone. He was also a good linguist and musician, playing several instruments and composing both religious music and secular songs. The well-known air 'Greensleeves' is attributed to him. When he succeeded his father in April 1509, Henry was regarded as the most accomplished prince of the age. Handsome and athletic, he bore a strong resemblance to his maternal grandfather Edward IV and there was none of his father's lean asceticism about him.

One of Henry's first acts was to marry his widowed sister-in-law, Catherine of Aragon, the necessary papal dispensation being first obtained. The new King and Queen then proceeded from Greenwich to the Tower and thence to Westminster for their crowning with all the usual ceremonies. Days were passed in jousting and making royal progresses and the reign of 'Bluff King Hal', the first English king to be styled 'Majesty', had begun.

Three years after his accession Henry reopened the Hundred Years War, invading France and winning the Battle of the Spurs with the aid of Austrian mercenaries. At home, the Scots invaded England but were soundly beaten at Flodden Field, where Henry's brother-in-law James IV (the husband of his sister, Margaret) and the 'flower of the Scots nobility' were slain on 9 September 1513.

These years saw the rise of Thomas Wolsey, the son of an Ipswich butcher, who, through the patronage of Sir Richard Nanfan, Deputy of Calais, had been brought to the notice of Henry VII, who gave him several ecclesiastical preferments. He was appointed Almoner to Henry VIII in 1509 and Canon of Windsor and Registrar of the Order of the Garter and a Privy Councillor in 1511. Other appointments followed and in 1513 he accompanied Henry to Calais and became his chief adviser. In 1514 he became Archbishop of York and in 1515 received the Cardinal's hat from Pope Leo X. He became all powerful and the King relied on him in all things.

Henry thought of himself as no mean theologian and in 1520 published a book *The Defence of the Seven Sacraments (Assertio Septem Sacramentorum)* to refute the heresies of Martin Luther, which were beginning to gain ground on the Continent. The book was presented to Pope Leo X who rewarded its author with the new title of Defender of the Faith (*Fidei Defensor*) conferred by Papal Bull on 11 October 1521. It has been proudly borne by all Henry's successors to the present day regardless of all the religious changes which have taken place.

It was also in 1520 that Henry held his famous meeting with Francis I of France at the Field of the Cloth of Gold at Ardres, where in a stage-managed setting of unparalleled magnificence the two sovereigns took part in a solemn act of reconciliation and concluded an uneasy and short-lived peace.

Henry's marriage to Catherine of Aragon was initially a happy one, but out of six children born to them only one sickly girl survived. By the mid 1520s it became obvious that Catherine, who was five and a half years older than Henry, was now unlikely at the age of forty to bear any more. Henry was desperate for a male heir. He toyed with the idea of making his illegitimate son Henry FitzRoy, Duke of Richmond, his heir but then thought better of it and decided that the only way was to divorce the Queen and marry again. But on what grounds? Henry was soon able to delude himself that his lack of a son was a sign of divine retribution for marrying his brother's widow, albeit the necessary dispensation had been obtained, and instructed Wolsey to open negotiations with the Holy See to have the marriage annulled. Catherine fought the petition tooth and nail and was supported by her nephew the Emperor Charles V. Wolsey's failure to procure the divorce from Rome after several years of protracted negotiations earned him the animosity of the King's paramour, Anne Boleyn, who was eager to become queen, and brought about his dismissal as Chancellor. A more far-reaching consequence of the whole business was the exasperated Henry's break with Rome which was to lead to the establishment of the Reformation in England.

In 1533 Henry nominated Thomas Cranmer to the primatial see of Canterbury and the appointment was confirmed by Rome. Cranmer begged the King to be allowed to decide Henry's 'great matter', as the divorce suit had come to be called, and in May he took it upon himself to declare the marriage to Catherine null and void. Henry, however, had already jumped the gun for Anne had become pregnant by him in December 1532 and on 25 January 1533 he had gone through a secret marriage ceremony with her, which Cranmer's pronouncement validated retrospectively. The new Queen's coronation was rushed through on 1 June and on 7 September she gave birth to a daughter, much to Henry's disappointment.

Henry's Reformation Parliament confirmed his title as 'of the Church of England on Earth Supreme Head' and copies of the new English translation of the Bible were ordered to be placed in every church. In all other respects, however, there was little alteration in the old order of worship, the Latin mass and all other ceremonies being retained.

The year 1536 saw the death of Catherine of Aragon, which her cruelly insensitive ex-husband celebrated by dressing in bright yellow and ordering a thanksgiving mass followed by feasting, dancing and jousting. It also saw the execution of Anne Boleyn, who had been superseded in the King's affections by one of her own maids of honour, the sly Jane Seymour. The delivery of a stillborn son had sealed Anne's fate, and she had been accused of adultery and incest.

The same year saw the commencement of the Dissolution of the Monasteries, which had become immensely rich and powerful. Henry desperately needed money, as always, and aided by his new Chancellor, Thomas Cromwell, saw the spoliation of the monasteries as an easy means of obtaining it. There was the added factor, too, that the religious foundations were likely to be hotbeds of pro-Roman intrigue.

Henry married Jane Seymour as his third wife and in due course she produced the longed for male heir, unfortunately dying twelve days later. Because she was the mother of his son, Henry was to regard her more highly than any of his other wives, but he was not inconsolable and ambassadors abroad were instructed to make inquiries at the courts to which they were accredited for a possible fourth bride. Henry's choice at first alighted upon the sixteen-year-old widowed Duchess of Milan, Christina of Denmark, whose splendid portrait which Holbein was commissioned to paint for the King now hangs in the National Gallery. Christina was a great-niece of Catherine of Aragon. She was a spirited girl and is said to have refused Henry's suit

Henry VIII's meeting with Francis I of France at the Field of the Cloth of Gold in 1520. This picture was severely damaged in the fire at Hampton Court Palace in March 1986.

by remarking that if she had two heads the King of England might be welcome to one of them, but, alas, she had only one.

Henry was to remain a widower for over two years and his fourth marriage was to prove the shortest of the six. He married Anne of Cleves in January 1540, found her not to his liking, and had the marriage annulled in the July. The event coincided with the fall of Thomas Cromwell, who was arrested, charged with treason and heresy, and executed on 28 July. This was also the day on which Henry married his fifth wife, Catherine Howard, a cousin of Anne Boleyn.

Catherine was nearly thirty years the King's junior and the once-handsome and much-admired King was now an obese monster, prematurely senile and stinking from an ulcerated left leg, the result of syphilis, which he had acquired early in life. Syphilis had first appeared in Spain in 1493, when Columbus returned from America with several members of his crew infected and it soon spread throughout Europe. The hypothesis has been put forward that Arthur, Prince of Wales, was infected and passed the disease on to Catherine of Aragon (in spite of the marriage never being properly consummated), who in turn infected Henry. Catherine's maternity record and the fact that her only surviving child Mary was an obvious congenital syphilitic tend to bear this out, while Henry's physical and moral degeneration throughout his reign leave little doubt as to the cause. As one writer has put it, he changed 'from a young man of great promise into a violent, brutal and ill-balanced tyrant'. Henry's fifth marriage was to founder in less than two years and Catherine, convicted of adultery, was to find her way to the block on Tower Green.

Henry now required a nurse rather than a wife and hearing good reports of the twice-widowed Catherine, Lady Latimer, who had devotedly cared for her second husband and his family, made her his sixth and last wife in July 1543. It is an indication of the extent to which the blood of our medieval kings had become diffused that all Henry's six wives descended (as did he, of course) from King Edward I, and also, perhaps, noteworthy that his four English wives are all (with a varying number of 'greats') aunts of HRH The Princess of Wales. Catherine Parr proved the good nurse Henry had hoped for and a kind stepmother to her three oddly assorted stepchildren. Nevertheless, her downfall was plotted and almost accomplished by opponents of her enthusiasm for the Protestant faith.

Henry's health was not helped by his excessive gluttony and in his fifty-sixth year he was to succumb at last to his many ailments. In January 1547 he was dying and was able to ponder aloud on his misdoings. After some urging, he agreed that Cranmer should be sent for, but when the Archbishop arrived at Whitehall he found the King beyond speech and only able to press his hand when asked to give a sign that he trusted in God. He died soon afterwards early in the morning of 28 January 1547. The news of his death was withheld for three days, while the Council debated the fate of the Duke of Norfolk, under sentence of death in the Tower, and finally decided to spare him.

Henry's embalmed body in its massive coffin was conveyed to Windsor and buried beside that of Jane Seymour. He had made plans for a magnificent tomb to be erected for them both, but they were never carried out. There is an unsubstantiated story that Mary I had her father's body disinterred and burnt.

Henry was the founder of Trinity College, Cambridge and endowed five regius professorships at the University, redistributing some of the monastic revenues gained through the Dissolution. He was also a builder and embellisher of palaces, Bridewell, Whitehall, St James's, Hampton Court (acquired from Cardinal Wolsey) and Nonsuch all being built or enlarged at his behest.

Henry VII, Elizabeth of York, Henry VIII and Jane Seymour, a picture in the Royal Collection which was commissioned by Charles II from Remigius van Leemput in 1667. It is a copy of an original wall-painting executed by Holbein for Henry VIII at Whitehall Palace and destroyed by fire in 1698. Van Leemput received £150 for his work.

Catherine of Aragon, Henry VIII's first Queen, by an unknown artist.

Catherine of Aragon

Born:	Alcalá de Henares, near Madrid 15 December 1485
Married:	1st, St Paul's Cathedral, London 14 November 1501, Arthur, Prince of Wales (d. 2 April 1502) 2nd, Grey Friars Church, Greenwich 11 June 1509, King Henry VIII
Crowned:	Westminster Abbey 24 June 1509
Divorced:	Marriage declared null and void 23 May 1533 and 'utterly dissolved' by Act of Parliament March 1534
Died:	Kimbolton Castle, Hunts 7 January 1536
Buried:	Peterborough Cathedral

Like Isabella of France, Catherine of Aragon was the offspring of two sovereigns, Ferdinand II, King of Aragon and Isabella, Queen of Castile, whose marriage had effectively united Spain into one kingdom. She was the fourth and youngest of their daughters and was born at Alcalá de Henares in December 1485. She was only two years old when Henry VII made overtures to her parents for her hand on behalf of his son Arthur, her junior by nine months, and the marriage treaty was concluded in 1500.

On her wedding day, 14 November 1501, Catherine was escorted to St Paul's by the ten-year-old Duke of York, her future brother-in-law and eventual husband. Immediately after the marriage the young couple took up residence in Ludlow Castle, where Arthur presided over the council of the Marches of Wales. He was an immature fifteen and apart from being racked with consumption was very probably infected by syphilis as the result of some youthful escapades. The marriage was almost certainly never consummated in the fullest sense, a matter which was to be of the utmost importance in the future, but Arthur's coarse braggings ('last night I was in Spain') indicate that some attempt at intercourse was probably made, enough at any rate to infect Catherine with syphilis if we accept that hypothesis. Catherine steadfastly maintained that she was still a virgin when she married Henry and as her integrity is beyond question, we must accept that she was, or believed that she was.

The damp atmosphere of Ludlow Castle swiftly proved fatal to Arthur and he died there on 2 April 1502 nearly five months after his marriage. The young widow, now known as the Dowager Princess of Wales, was almost at once proposed as a bride for Prince Henry and at the beginning of the following year, Henry VII having become a widower, there was even some talk of her marrying her father-in-law. However, the treaty of her marriage to the younger Henry was concluded on 23 June 1503 and papal dispensation for the marriage between sister-in-law and brother-in-law was obtained from Pope Julius II in 1504. Once this had been done, however, Henry VII was in no hurry to complete the marriage and, characteristically, kept Catherine so short of money and the common necessities of life, that she was obliged to apply to her father for the wherewithal to pay the members of her household. Henry VII's motivation in delaying matters was the hope that a better match might turn up for his son, in which case Catherine could quietly be discarded altogether.

Once Henry VII was dead, matters moved swiftly. Henry VIII was ardently in love with his betrothed, a tall blonde girl who matched him well for grace and looks, and the marriage took place at Greenwich on 11 June 1509, being followed two weeks later by the coronation of the young King and Queen at Westminster Abbey.

Catherine's first child, a daughter, was prematurely stillborn at the end of January 1510, but the following 1 January she gave birth to a living son, Henry. The birth was celebrated with jousts and tournaments, but sadly the baby survived barely two months. A second boy was born in November 1513 and died at once, and a third was stillborn in December 1514. In February 1516,

The following colour section takes us from the Wars of the Roses to "Good King Charles's Golden Days". It includes some architectural glories and works of high renaissance art in several media; and the austere portrait of the thrice widowed Mary, Queen of Scots contrasts strikingly with that of her great-grandson, the restored Charles II in the full panoply of royalty.

Above, an illuminated initial depicting the presentation of a book to Henry VI. Note the lack of concern exhibited by the forerunner of the royal corgis in the foreground.

Right, Henry IV's monumental effigy in Canterbury Cathedral. His tomb is on the north side of the site of Becket's shrine, opposite that of his uncle the Black Prince.

Below, the west front of King's College Chapel, Cambridge, one of Henry VI's great scholastic foundations and perhaps the finest example of perpendicular style in England.

Right, the presentation of a book to Edward IV from an illuminated manuscript.

Below, King Richard III, the standard portrait type from which all existing portraits of him are derived. Though careworn and looking far older than his thirty-two years, he does not appear the deformed monster of popular legend.

Opposite
Above, the east end of Tewkesbury Abbey. The name of Tewkesbury is derived from that of Theoc, a missionary monk who built the first church there in the 7th century. The Abbey was founded in the 12th century, but the monastic buildings were destroyed after the Dissolution of the Monasteries and today only the church remains. It is the burial place of the unfortunate George, Duke of Clarence (*d.* 1477) and his wife Isabel Nevill, and also reputedly of Edward, Prince of Wales, the son of Henry VI, who was murdered after the Battle of Tewkesbury in 1471, but no trace of his burial was found when the church was restored in the 19th century.

Below, the choir of St George's Chapel, Windsor showing the banners of the Knights of the Garter hanging over their stalls. The slab in the centre of the pavement covers the vault containing the remains of King Henry VIII, Jane Seymour and King Charles I. The wooden structure which can be seen projecting to the left of the altar is the Royal Closet from which the widowed Queen Victoria watched the wedding of her son Bertie to Alexandra of Denmark in 1863.

116

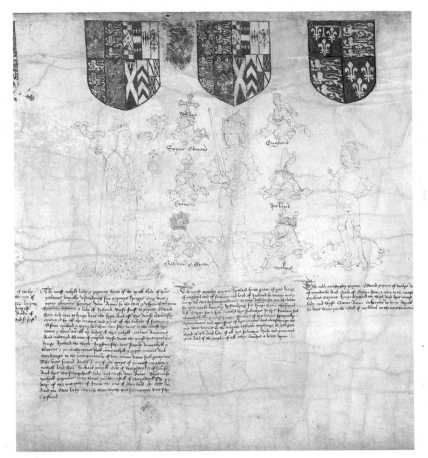

Above, Fotheringay Church, Northants, originally a collegiate church founded by Edward, 2nd Duke of York, who was killed at Agincourt in 1415. It contains monuments to the founder and to Richard, 3rd Duke of York and his wife Cicely, the parents of Edward IV and Richard III. Richard III was born in Fotheringay Castle nearby and may have been baptized in the church.

Left, a page from the Rous Roll showing Richard III with his Queen Anne Nevill and their son Edward, Prince of Wales. The King and his son are both depicted in armour, the Queen in royal robes. Note the white boars, an allusion to Richard's heraldic badge.

Above, Hever Castle, Kent, possibly the birthplace and certainly the childhood home of Anne Boleyn. Henry VIII is said to have courted her in the grounds of this fine moated manor house.

Left, Henry VIII masquerading as the psalmist David, but fooling nobody, including his jester Will Somers, who looks uneasy in the role of Saul. Note that the King is wearing the Garter on his right leg instead of the left. Could it be that his ulcers were troublesome?

Mary, Queen of Scots, a posthumous portrait full of allegories and
allusions, including a representation of her execution at Fotheringay.

The Armada Jewel, an exquisitely wrought piece of jewellery made to commemorate the defeat of the Spanish Armada in 1588.

Top, a seventeenth century view of the old royal palace of Placentia at Greenwich.

Above, the children of King Charles I by Van Dyck. The future Charles II is in the centre, James and Mary to his left, Elizabeth and the baby Henry to his right.

Right, King Charles II in the full majesty of his parliamentary robes by Michael Wright. The King is adorned with the new regalia made for his coronation to replace that melted down and sold under the Commonwealth. The orb remains almost exactly the same today, but St Edward's crown and the sceptre have both undergone considerable remodelling.

Opposite
The royal arms of Scotland, a painting dating from the time of King James IV and his wife Margaret Tudor.

Hampton Court Palace. The building of Hampton Court was begun by Cardinal Wolsey, who found it expedient to present it as a gift to Henry VIII when he began to feel the mark of royal displeasure. The pleasant riverside palace became a favourite residence of William and Mary and was added to by Sir Christopher Wren, whose splendid baroque additions blend well with the original Tudor red brick. William III intended it to rival Versailles, but on a much smaller scale. The palace remained a favourite royal residence until the reign of George II, but fell into disfavour with George III and Queen Charlotte, who preferred the more homely Kew. The state apartments were first opened to the public in the reign of Queen Victoria, and the palace houses an important part of the royal art collection permanently on show there. It also contains a number of 'grace and favour' apartments and it was a fire started in one of these in March 1986 which caused severe damage to one wing of Wren's building.

Right, one of the painted ceilings in the state apartments depicting the apotheosis of William and Mary.

Below, the river frontage of the palace showing Wren's style.

Catherine again become a mother and this time the baby, a girl named Mary, though sickly, survived. Two miscarriages followed in 1517 and Catherine's last pregnancy in 1518 ended in the birth of a stillborn daughter.

When Henry left on his French campaign in 1513, Catherine was constituted Governor of the Realm and Captain-General of the Forces and left in charge during his absence. Following the defeat of the Scots at Flodden, Catherine sent James IV's blood-stained coat to Henry in Flanders, a grim souvenir of the victory achieved under her regency. In 1520 the Queen accompanied Henry to France and was present at the Field of the Cloth of Gold.

By 1525 Catherine was forty and the likelihood of further issue seemed remote. Furthermore, her looks had faded and the King, a vigorous thirty-four, had become infatuated with Anne Boleyn. Husband and wife ceased to cohabit in 1526 and in the following year the long divorce process began. Henry's suit was for nullity on the grounds of the affinity existing between him and Catherine as the widow of his brother. Catherine had powerful support on the Continent from her nephew the Emperor, who was influential at Rome, and the Pope refused to concede that the dispensation granted by his predecessor could have been invalid. This stalemate resulted in Henry's breach with Rome and the declaration of a compliant Cranmer and Parliament that his marriage to Catherine was null and 'utterly dissolved'. Henry's sickening hypocrisy in referring to her as 'so good a lady and loving companion' and expressing regret that he must 'put her away' after living in sin with her for nearly twenty years makes sorry reading.

Catherine had her daughter taken from her in 1531 and was removed to Moor Park, Hertfordshire and thence to Bishop's Hatfield. Following the annulment, she was deprived of the title of queen and again styled Princess Dowager of Wales. She enjoyed great personal popularity and was constantly moved about for fear of an uprising in her favour. She had the hollow satisfaction of knowing that the Pope had pronounced her marriage to be valid on 23 March 1534 and resolutely refused to accept the Act of Succession which bastardized Mary and placed Anne Boleyn's daughter Elizabeth first in line to the throne.

Catherine's spirit remained unbroken to the last. She died at Kimbolton Castle, where she was confined, after an illness of about a month's duration in January 1536. Poison was rumoured, but the embalmer's account makes it clear that she died of cancer, her heart being described as 'quite black and hideous to look at' with a 'black round body stuck to the outside', an indication of a secondary melanotic sarcoma. The other organs were described as being 'as healthy and normal as possible', so the embalmer evidently did not recognize the primary

growth which must have existed. Catherine had just completed her fiftieth year. She was buried in Peterborough Cathedral, where, in Victorian times, the subscriptions of 'English ladies bearing the name of Catherine' paid for a handsome black marble slab to mark her grave opposite that in which Mary, Queen of Scots, lay before her removal to Westminster.

Anne Boleyn

Born:	Blickling Hall, Norfolk, or Hever Castle, Kent *ca* 1501/2
Married:	Whitehall or Westminster 25 January 1533 (*m.* declared valid 28 May 1533)
Crowned:	Westminster Abbey 1 June 1533
Divorced:	17 May 1536
Died:	Beheaded on Tower Green 19 May 1536
Buried:	Chapel Royal of St Peter – ad – Vincula, Tower of London

Anne Boleyn was probably born in 1501 or 1502, not, as usually stated, in 1507. Her parents were Sir Thomas Boleyn, later created Earl of Wiltshire and Earl of

Anne Boleyn, by an unknown artist. This is the standard portrait type of Henry VIII's second Queen.

Ormonde, and Lady Elizabeth Howard, daughter of Thomas Howard, 2nd Duke of Norfolk. Anne's father was appointed Ambassador to France in 1519 and Anne accompanied him there and entered the household of Queen Claude, the wife of Francis I. She remained there, acquiring the polished manners of the French court, until her father was recalled on the outbreak of hostilities in 1522.

Anne's portraits confirm contemporary descriptions of her. She had a rather pointed face with fine eyes and a long, slender neck, and possessed an abundance of long dark hair. She was marred, however, by a blemish on one hand resembling a rudimentary sixth finger and her enemies were later to point to this as a sign of her being a witch.

Returned to the English court, Anne's vivacity and acquired French *chic* soon brought her an admiring circle of young men, including the poet, Sir Thomas Wyatt, who was her cousin. The King, too, began to pay her attention, transferring his affections from her elder sister Mary, who had been his mistress both before and after her marriage to William Carey. Anne kept Henry at bay for several years, flirting coquettishly and entering into an amorous correspondence with him. It does not appear that she became his mistress until 1527 or later. In September 1532 she was created Marchioness of Pembroke and it was when she became pregnant in December 1532 that the matter of the divorce from Catherine had to be precipitated.

In her own and Henry's eyes, Anne became queen from the moment of their secret marriage in January 1533, but she was not openly acknowledged as such until 28 May. She was crowned on Whit Sunday 1 June. Her progress through the City, although staged with all the customary magnificence, met with a sullen silence from many of the crowd. Anne was the last queen consort to be accorded a separate coronation. She was six months pregnant and the coronation banquet proved something of an ordeal, two of her ladies having to sit under the table at her feet with a suitable receptacle in order that she might relieve herself frequently as she felt the need.

On 7 September Anne's child was born at Greenwich Palace. To Henry's chagrin it was a girl. He was so disappointed that he could not bring himself to attend the christening. The letters which had been prepared to announce the birth to foreign courts had not left enough room for the word 'Princess' to be written in full, so certain had Henry been of a male heir. Henry's passion for Anne began to wane from the moment of Elizabeth's birth. She was to find herself supplanted by another even as she had supplanted Catherine. Among her ladies-in-waiting was the scheming Jane Seymour who went out of her way to attract the King's attention from 1534 onwards.

Anne was pregnant again when the King had a bad fall from his horse in January 1536 and lay unconscious for two hours. The shock brought on a premature labour and she miscarried a male child. The loss of this possible heir sealed Anne's fate. Henry determined to rid himself of her and set up a commission to enquire into her conduct and find some fault in her. Anne had undoubtedly indulged in light-hearted flirtations both before and after her marriage, but there is no real evidence that she was guilty of the charges brought against her of adultery with Henry Norris and an incestuous relationship with her own brother Viscount Rochford.

On 1 May 1536 Anne presided over the jousts at Greenwich; the next day she was arrested and taken to the Tower. She and Rochford were tried on 15 May and inevitably found guilty and condemned to death. Two days later, as if this was not enough, an ecclesiastical court, convened at Lambeth under Cranmer, declared Anne's marriage to the King to have been null and void *ab initio* on account of the affinity created between them by his former relationship with her sister Mary.

Anne faced death bravely, even finding the courage to say of Henry that 'a gentler nor a more merciful prince was there never; and to me he was ever a good, a gentle and sovereign Lord.' She was beheaded on Tower Green by a headsman brought from Calais who used a sword rather than an axe. Her body was unceremoniously bundled into an oak chest and buried in the Chapel of St Peter-ad-Vincula in the Tower, where it still remains.

Jane Seymour

Born:	Wolf Hall, Savernake, Wilts *ca* 1505
Married:	York Place 30 May 1536
Died:	Hampton Court Palace 24 October 1537
Buried:	St George's Chapel, Windsor

Jane Seymour was of comparatively humble birth, being the daughter of a simple knight, Sir John Seymour and his wife Margery Wentworth, whose family came from Nettlestead in Suffolk. There were, however, court connections on both sides and Jane served as a maid of honour to both Catherine of Aragon and Anne Boleyn. In her portraits she does not appear attractive, with her large nose and runaway chin, but she set out to ensnare Henry and seduce him from Anne Boleyn in a manner which does her no credit. She evidently knew how to appeal to the King in a way he found irresistible by striking a simple little-girl pose.

During Anne's trial and execution, Jane discreetly withdrew from court to her father's house, Wolf Hall, near Savernake, in Wiltshire. Henry set out for there the moment he heard the guns at the Tower announcing Anne's death and they were formally betrothed on the

Jane Seymour, Henry VIII's third Queen, a version of the portrait by Hans Holbein.

Anne of Cleves

Born:	Düsseldorf 22 September 1515
Married:	Greenwich 6 January 1540
Marriage annulled:	9 July 1540
Died:	Chelsea 17 July 1557
Buried:	Westminster Abbey

The quest for a fourth bride for Henry began within a week of Queen Jane's death. Cromwell pressed for an alliance with a foreign royal house and English ambassadors on the Continent were instructed to look for likely candidates. It was in 1538 that the suggestion was first made that Henry should marry a sister of the Duke of Cleves, who had become one of the most ardent and powerful supporters of the Protestant Reformation. Henry sent for portaits of the ladies, Anne and Amelia, and when they were not forthcoming despatched Hans Holbein to paint them. He had been assured that Anne surpassed the Duchess of Milan in looks 'as the golden sun excelleth the silver moon', and he found her portrait (a version of which is now in the Louvre in Paris) pleasing in spite of the 'monstrous habit and apparel', which his ambassadors complained had prevented them from seeing the sisters properly.

Duke William of Cleves sent an emissary to England to negotiate the marriage treaty and it was concluded on

Henry VIII's fourth Queen, Anne of Cleves, an 18th century engraving by J. Houbraken based on the portrait by Holbein painted in 1539.

following day. Ten days later, on 30 May 1536, the marriage took place quietly in the Queen's Closet at York Place. Henry's plans for the coronation of his new queen had to be postponed because of an outbreak of plague in London and were later deferred on account of her pregnancy, so in the event she was never crowned. Jane's one memorable act in the seventeen months she was queen was to effect a reconciliation between Henry and his daughter Mary, whom she had known in her days as maid of honour to Catherine of Aragon.

Early in 1537 Jane became pregnant and on 12 October, to Henry's unspeakable joy, she gave birth to a much longed for son and heir at Hampton Court. Henry at once ordered celebrations on a massive scale and the infant Prince's christening was attended by both his half-sisters Mary and Elizabeth and by his mother, who was carried on a litter with her long train looped over the back. The excitement was too much for her, she became feverish and died twelve days after her son's birth. She was buried in St George's Chapel, Windsor on 12 November 1537. In less than ten years and three wives later, Henry was to be laid at her side.

6 October 1539. Anne set out for England and landed at Deal on 27 December, proceeding to Rochester on 1 January 1540. The eager bridegroom rushed to Rochester to take a look at her unbeknown. What he saw did not please him. He found her 'nothing so well as she had spoken of' and referred to her as 'the Flanders mare'. Had he been able to back out of the marriage at this stage he would have done so, but there was nothing for it but to go through with it. The marriage was solemnized on 6 January.

Although Henry slept at Anne's side, the marriage was never consummated and the couple are said to have spent the night hours playing cards together. It took Henry but a short while to think of grounds for an annulment: his own lack of consent, witnessed by his failure to consummate the marriage, and Anne's pre-contract to the son of the Duke of Lorraine. On these grounds Convocation pronounced the marriage null and void on 9 July 1540. It was to be the shortest of Henry's six marriages, having lasted just six months.

Anne, who had been sent to Richmond Palace for 'her health, open air and pleasure', raised no objection to the divorce proceedings. She elected to stay in England and one can well imagine that to return to her brother's court, as he wished her to do, would have been an insufferable humiliation. Henry showed his appreciation of her ready compliance by giving her two houses, a household in keeping with her rank, and an annual income of £500 (the equivalent of about £50,000 today).

It is difficult, when looking at Anne's portait, to see why Henry took such great exception to her as her face is distinctly pleasant. One can only conclude that she was a dull, unaccomplished young woman without conversation or wit and the very opposite of what Henry sought and found most attractive in women.

Once divorced, Henry remained on good terms with Anne and they became what can only be described as good friends. He referred to her as his 'beloved sister', visited her frequently and exchanged presents with her at the New Year. After Catherine Howard's execution there were even rumours that Henry and Anne were about to remarry. She also proved a good friend to her stepchildren, Mary, Elizabeth and Edward, and was to share a litter with Elizabeth in Mary's coronation procession.

Anne died at the house Henry had given her in Chelsea on 17 July 1557. She was buried on the north side of the sacrarium in Westminster Abbey, where the top of her plain but handsome table tomb has come to provide a convenient surface for the tastelessly vulgar display of the Abbey plate, which successive Deans and Chapters see fit to put out on the occasions of coronations and royal weddings.

Catherine Howard

Born:	Lambeth (?) ca 1520
Married:	Hampton Court Palace 28 July 1540
Died:	Beheaded on Tower Green 13 February 1542
Buried:	Chapel Royal of St Peter-ad-Vincula, Tower of London

Henry's fifth wife was a first cousin of his second and resembled her in her sensuality and high spirits. Catherine Howard was the daughter of Lord Edmund Howard, a younger son of the 2nd Duke of Norfolk. Her mother died when she was still a child and she was brought up at Horsham, Norfolk, and later at Lambeth, by her grandmother the Dowager Duchess of Norfolk. She was a highly sexed girl and indulged in torrid affairs with Henry Manox, her music teacher, with Francis Dereham, one of her grandmother's retainers, and with her cousin Thomas Culpeper. Henry met her at the London house of Stephen Gardiner, Bishop of Winchester, and was immediately so smitten that he arranged for her to be appointed a maid of honour to Anne of Cleves.

Catherine, well aware of the King's interest, set out to captivate him and was, of course, aided by his distaste for Anne. Her relations encouraged her scheming and the King's intentions were made plain by the favours showered on Catherine. On the day after the annulment of Henry's marriage to Anne, the Council, headed by Gardiner and Catherine's uncle Norfolk, implored the King to marry again 'to the comfort of his realm', and following their advice Henry and Catherine were married in a quiet ceremony at Hampton Court on 28 July 1540.

For a while Henry seemed to regain the vigour of his youth. He rose early, hunted, made royal progresses about the country and lavished lands and jewellery on his bewitching young bride. She, for her part, could have found little joy in a husband who was by now gross and repugnant, and unwisely turned again to her old lovers Dereham and Culpeper. She was aided and abetted by Viscountess Rochford, one of her ladies-in-waiting and the widow of Anne Boleyn's brother, who had suffered death for his supposed incest with her. Lady Rochford smuggled Culpeper into the Queen's apartments at every opportunity during the course of a progress to the north which she made with Henry in August and September 1541. An informer told the Council and Cranmer was delegated to tell the King of his wife's infidelities. Henry at first refused to believed any of the accusations against Catherine, but, finally convinced, indulged in an orgy of self-pity and took himself off on a long hunting expedition.

Catherine was placed under guard at Syon House after she had been removed from Hampton Court, where a distressing episode had taken place when she ran through the palace, shrieking her denials, to throw herself at Henry's feet as he heard mass in the Chapel Royal. The gallery through which she passed is known as the Haunted Gallery and her ghost is reputed to re-enact the scene.

The wretched Queen's lovers were brought to trial with several members of the Howard clan, and Dereham and Culpeper were executed. A bill of attainder against Catherine was introduced into Parliament and received the royal assent (through a commission appointed to spare Henry's feelings) on 11 February 1542. Two days later Catherine and her accomplice Lady Rochford were beheaded on Tower Green. The Queen was buried near her cousin Anne Boleyn in the Chapel of St Peter-ad-Vincula.

The sordid affair had made Henry an old man. His disillusionment in Catherine almost broke him, but his usual resilience saved him once again and within a week of her death he was feasting to celebrate the pre-Lenten carnival.

Catherine Parr

Born: Kendal Castle *ca* 1512
Married: 1st, *ca* 1529, Sir Edward Borough (*d.* before April 1533)
2nd, 1533, as his 3rd wife, John Nevill, 3rd Baron Latimer (*d.* London 2 March 1543)
3rd, Hampton Court Palace 12 July 1543, King Henry VIII
4th, April/May 1547, Thomas Seymour, 1st Baron Seymour of Sudeley, Lord High Admiral, brother of Queen Jane Seymour
Died: Sudeley Castle, Gloucestershire 5 September 1548
Buried: Chapel of Sudeley Castle

A contemporary described Catherine Parr as being plainer than Anne of Cleves and by the time he married her Henry, wracked by syphilis and prematurely aged, sought only a nurse and a kindly stepmother for his children, all hopes of a young wife to bring him further heirs having perished on the scaffold with Catherine Howard. Catherine, Lady Latimer, recently widowed of her second husband at the age of thirty-one, had proved herself as the third wife of a husband nearly twenty years her senior and was loved and esteemed by her stepchildren.

Catherine was the daughter of Sir Thomas Parr, of Kendal, and his wife Maud Green. She was born at Kendal Castle in about 1512 and when she was about seventeen she married Sir Edward Borough (or Burgh), the eldest son of Thomas, 3rd Lord Borough of Gainsborough. There were no children of the marriage and Edward died sometime before April 1533. In the same year his widow became the third wife of John Nevill, 3rd Lord Latimer, a man of forty. The marriage was childless but happy, and Catherine was a good nurse to her ailing husband and an understanding friend to the children of his first marriage, some of whom were little younger than she was.

Lord Latimer died in March 1543, leaving Catherine a widow for the second time at the age of thirty-one. Now, it would seem, she fell in love for the first time in her life with the dashing Thomas Seymour, a brother of the late Queen Jane and therefore Henry VIII's brother-in-law, and it was anticipated that they would marry, when the King intervened and carried off the widow for himself. The marriage, at which Stephen Gardiner officiated, took place quietly at Hampton Court on 12 July 1543.

Catherine may be considered the first Protestant Queen of England. She cultivated the friendship of the reformers Coverdale and Latimer and entered into long theological discussions with the King, who still retained his old interest in such matters.

Catherine Parr, Henry VIII's sixth and last Queen. This portrait in the National Portrait Gallery is attributed to William Scrots and was painted about 1545. It is the only authentic likeness of the Queen.

The Christmas of 1543 saw a reunion of the royal family brought about by Catherine's influence. Her three ill-assorted stepchildren, Mary, Elizabeth and Edward, came together for the first time and soon developed a genuine affection for their father's kind wife. She was assiduous in her efforts to provide for their education and further their intellectual pursuits and personally chose the tutors for Prince Edward.

In 1544 the war with France was again renewed and Henry departed for Calais, leaving Catherine as Governor of the Realm and Protector during his absence of two months, a duty which she discharged with her customary diligence.

Catherine's religious leanings incited a pro-Roman faction, led by Gardiner and Wriothesley, to bring a charge of heresy against her in 1546, going so far as to draw up a bill against her and persuading the near senile King to sign it. A copy of the bill came into Catherine's hands by accident and in a state of great trepidation she went to throw herself upon Henry's mercy. She pleaded cleverly and eloquently that she had talked theology with the King, to whom she was ever obedient in all matters concerning religion, to ease his infirmity, and elicited the reply: 'And is it even so, sweetheart, and tended your argument to no worse end? Then perfect friends we are now again as ever at any time heretofore.' The next day Henry and Catherine were walking in the gardens of Whitehall when a party arrived to arrest the Queen and take her to the Tower. Henry sent them packing forthwith, calling Wriothesley 'Knave, arrant knave, beast and fool!'

Henry's death in January 1547 left Catherine free to renew her friendship with Thomas Seymour, and she married for the fourth and last time in May the same year. As an uncle of the new King Edward VI, Seymour had been created Baron Seymour of Sudeley very soon after his nephew's succession. He was now aged about thirty-nine and had the reputation of being a rogue and a womanizer. Catherine, whose first three marriages had remained childless, found herself pregnant for the first time at the age of thirty-six in 1548. On 29 August 1548 Catherine was safely delivered of a daughter, but puerperal fever ensued and she died on 5 September. She was buried in the chapel of Sudeley Castle but the coffin was reburied in the Chandos vault in 1817.

EDWARD VI   1547–1553

Born:	Hampton Court Palace 12 October 1537
Acceded:	28 January 1547
Crowned:	Westminster Abbey 20 February 1547
Died:	Greenwich Palace 6 July 1553
Buried:	Westminster Abbey

It would be easy to dismiss Edward VI as a precocious, Protestant prig. He was, undoubtedly, all three but, had he lived and lost some of the priggishness of youth, he might well have approached the same heights of greatness as his half-sister Elizabeth.

The birth of a seemingly healthy son to his third wife Jane Seymour brought Henry VIII to a state of felicity only slightly clouded by the death of the mother two weeks later. The motherless child was confided to the care of nurses and as he grew older was tutored by four of the greatest scholars of the kingdom, carefully chosen by his stepmother Catherine Parr. These were Sir John Cheke, Professor of Greek at Cambridge; Richard Cox, Head Master of Eton; Sir Anthony Cooke, a politician; and Roger Ascham, another Cambridge classical scholar and educationist. These men imparted not only a sound knowledge of Greek, Latin and French, but also the tenets of the Protestant Reformation which had swept Germany and the Netherlands. For relaxation Edward played the lute and studied the stars. It is astounding that a young boy could have assimilated so much knowledge and Edward must have been something of a prodigy. Deprived of the company of children of his own age, he was surrounded by scholarly men and took on the character of a scholarly, rather humourless, man in a child's body.

Edward could have known no family life until Catherine Parr gathered the King's children together for the first time at Christmas 1543, when he was six years old. His half-sisters Mary and Elizabeth became genuinely fond of him and Elizabeth, who was only four years older, shared his tutors. Henry must have been sadly disappointed to see his son growing up a sickly, pale boy, so different from what he himself had been.

On the ten-year-old Edward's succession to the throne in January 1547 his maternal uncle Lord Hertford became Protector of the Realm and was created Duke of Somerset. Edward had imbibed the Protestant leanings of his stepmother, and John Knox, Ridley, Latimer and Hooper, all zealous reformers, were appointed as court chaplains, while Archbishop Cranmer was authorized to compile the first English Prayer Book, which appeared in 1548.

Edward was forced to agree to the execution of his uncle Thomas Seymour (who had married the Queen Dowager Catherine Parr) for alleged high treason early

Edward VI, by an unknown artist. The boy King is trying to emulate his father's stance.

in 1549. The attractive, swashbuckling Thomas was his favourite uncle and the incident may well have embittered him towards his other uncle, the Protector, as he was to view the latter's fall and subsequent execution with a show of indifference. Somerset was replaced as Protector by John Dudley, Earl of Warwick, who was at once created Duke of Northumberland.

Edward's love of learning induced him to found numerous grammar-schools which bore his name. He also gave the old palace of Bridewell to the corporation of London to provide a workhouse, and converted the Grey Friars' monastery into Christ's Hospital. He received instructions in political matters from his Clerk of the Council, Wiliam Thomas, who drew up a series of discourses for his use.

So much learning forced into a delicate boy was bound to have an adverse effect. In 1552 Edward supposedly suffered from measles and then from smallpox, both doubtful diagnoses. Early in the following year it became apparent that he was suffering from pulmonary tuberculosis. In addition to the normal symptoms of that

disease, 'eruptions came out over his skin, his hair fell off, and then his nails, and afterwards the joints of his toes and fingers'. All this indicates that his condition was complicated by congenital syphilis, Henry's legacy to his children. The boy King, still only fifteen, died at Greenwich Palace after great suffering on 6 July 1553. He was buried near the tomb of his grandfather Henry VII in Westminster Abbey, but has no memorial.

JANE   10–19 July 1553

Born:	Bradgate, Leicestershire October 1537
Proclaimed Queen:	10 July 1553
Dethroned:	19 July 1553
Married:	Durham House, London 21 May 1553, Lord Guildford Dudley, 6th son of John Dudley, 1st Duke of Northumberland
Died:	Beheaded on Tower Green 12 February 1554
Buried:	Chapel Royal of St Peter-ad-Vincula, Tower of London

When Edward VI lay dying, the Protector Northumberland, well knowing and fearing the Catholic reaction which would come about under the Princess Mary, induced the King to nominate Lady Jane Grey, the granddaughter of Henry VIII's sister Mary, as heiress-presumptive on 21 June 1553. This nomination excluded not only the King's half-sisters Mary and Elizabeth and the descendants of his aunt Margaret, Queen of Scots, but also Lady Jane's own mother, Frances, Duchess of Suffolk. Just one month before the nomination, the wily Northumberland had arranged Lady Jane's marriage to his own son, Lord Guildford Dudley, a callow youth of sixteen or seventeen.

Lady Jane was born in the same month as the King she was now to succeed and for whom she had at one time been suggested as a possible bride. She was something of a bluestocking, learned in Greek, Hebrew and Latin, and, of course, a staunch adherent of the Protestant Reformation. Roger Ascham, visiting her parents' house at Bradgate in Leicestershire, reported how he found her reading Plato's *Phaedo* in Greek, while the rest of her family were disporting themselves in the park.

Jane was reluctant to accept the crown forced upon her by her ambitious father-in-law, but was publicly proclaimed queen with much pomp after Edward VI's death had been made public on 10 July 1553. At her state entry into the Tower of London her train was carried by her mother, and the diminutive Jane wore specially raised shoes to give her height. Jane showed some spirit in adamantly refusing the suggestion that her

Lady Jane Grey, the 'nine days queen', a painting attributed to Master John. She looks conscious of her superior learning.

husband, for whom she apparently had little affection, should be proclaimed king with her. Whether or not she would have remained unyielding on this point is academic, for her reign only lasted nine days. The nobility were incensed by Northumberland's presumption and the people on the whole wanted Mary, not Jane, as their queen.

Northumberland's army was dispersed without bloodshed and he was beheaded. Jane and Guildford were arraigned, convicted of high treason, and confined in the Tower. They were innocent victims of the overwhelming ambition of their parents and it was only

with reluctance and after much heart-searching that Mary agreed to their execution. The young couple had been drawn closer together in their adversity and as Lord Guildford walked to his death on Tower Hill on the morning of 12 February 1554, Jane bade him farewell from her window. She was accorded the privilege of a more private execution on Tower Green later the same day and met her end with calm fortitude. The luckless pair were buried in the Chapel of St Peter-ad-Vincula.

MARY I   1553–1558

Born:	Greenwich Palace 18 February 1516
Acceded:	6 July 1553
Crowned:	Westminster Abbey 1 October 1553
Married:	Winchester Cathedral 25 July 1554, as his 2nd wife, Philip II, King of Spain
Died:	St James's Palace 17 November 1558
Buried:	Westminster Abbey

Mary Tudor, whose whole life was an unmitigated tragedy, has gone down in history as 'Bloody Mary', an unjust epithet, for she was not by nature a cruel or vindictive woman, albeit a bigoted one determined to bring England back into the papal obedience.

The only child of Henry VIII and Catherine of Aragon to survive infancy, Mary was born at Greenwich Palace on 18 February 1516. Her father's initial disappointment at her being a girl was tempered by his hope of further issue to come, but Catherine's later pregnancies all ended in miscarriages or stillbirths. Mary was given her own court at Ludlow Castle with many of the prerogatives usually given to a Prince of Wales. She was placed in the charge of the Countess of Salisbury, a Plantagenet cousin and the mother of Cardinal Pole, who was to play such a leading part in Mary's later life. She studied Greek, Latin, French, Italian, science and music. There were some tentative marriage plans to Francis I of France and to her cousin the Emperor Charles V (whose son she was eventually to marry), but they came to nought.

Mary was a sickly child and suffered from severe headaches and defective eyesight, being almost certainly a congenital syphilitic. All her portraits confirm this and Dr Maclaurin wrote in his book *Mere Mortals*: 'Any doctor looking at the portrait of her wizened, lined, and prematurely aged face would probably say "That woman must have been a hereditary syphilitic".' Mary's childhood and young womanhood were made wretched not only by her ill-health but by the protracted divorce proceedings of her parents and the subsequent

Queen Mary I with her husband Philip of Spain and two pet dogs. This picture in the National Maritime Museum is after Hans Eworth.

humiliations to which she and her mother were subjected. She was devoted to her mother but was not allowed to be with her at her death.

In 1533 Mary was declared illegitimate and sent to Hatfield to live with her baby half-sister Elizabeth under the care of Anne Boleyn's aunt Lady Shelton. She seems to have borne no grudge against the baby and even to have had some genuine sisterly feeling for her, which speaks well for her character. After the execution of Anne Boleyn, Mary was reconciled to her father and induced to acknowledge that her mother's marriage to him had been unlawful and she herself, therefore, illegitimate. She also outwardly acknowledged the King as head of the Church and on these terms was received back at court. In 1537 she stood as godmother to her half-brother, the future Edward VI, and acted as chief mourner at the funeral of her stepmother, Queen Jane Seymour.

Catherine Parr's influence drew the royal family closer together in 1544 and Mary was reinstated in the line of succession to the throne. It was with Catherine's encouragement, too, that she translated Erasmus's Latin paraphrase of St John at this time. After Henry VIII's

death his three children remained on friendly terms with each other in spite of their great differences in age and religious belief. When the Act of Uniformity in 1549 made use of the new Prayer Book compulsory, Mary refused to comply and continued to have the Latin mass celebrated in her household. The attempt to divert the succession to Lady Jane Grey on Edward VI's death was a direct result of this intransigence.

When Edward VI died in June 1553, Mary was at Framlingham Castle, Suffolk, and on hearing that the country was in her favour, set out for London, where she made a triumphant entry accompanied by her half-sister Elizabeth. All support for Jane melted away and Mary's succession was unchallenged. She at once ordered the release of the Duke of Norfolk and Stephen Gardiner from the Tower, restoring the latter to the see of Winchester and making him Chancellor. It was Gardiner, too, who officiated at her coronation on 1 October.

Throughout her reign Mary devoted herself single-mindedly to the restoration of the old order, the Latin mass and papal supremacy. Her first Parliament abolished Edward VI's religious laws and firmly re-asserted her own legitimacy.

It was essential that the new Queen, already thirty-seven, should marry as soon as possible to provide an heir to the throne other than her half-sister Elizabeth, whose religious leanings were doubtful. The Earl of Devon was suggested as a possible bridegroom, but Mary had set her heart on marrying the heir to the Spanish throne, Philip, son of her one-time suitor Charles V, who was a widower, eleven years her junior. The Commons, backed by Gardiner, begged her to reconsider, fearing the threat to English independence which might be caused by such a match. Mary was adamant and her persistence led to a rebellion headed by Sir Thomas Wyatt, who marched on London, but was promptly defeated and executed. The marriage plans went through and Mary and Philip were married in Winchester Cathedral on 25 July 1554. At Mary's instance Philip received the title of king and all official documents and Acts of Parliament were to be dated in their joint names. His head also appeared on the coinage, face to face with hers. Jointly the King and Queen had the longest style of any British sovereign:

> Philip and Mary, by the Grace of God, King and Queen of England and France, Naples, Jerusalem and Ireland, Defenders of the Faith, Princes of Spain and Sicily, Archdukes of Austria, Dukes of Milan, Burgundy and Brabant, Count and Countess of Flanders, Habsburg and Tyrol.

The marriage was not a success, for although Mary fell deeply in love with Philip, he found her repellent and complained of the disgusting odour emanating from her nose. This was another indication of her congenital syphilis resulting from syphilitic rhinitis attended by bone ulceration and the forming of malodorous crusts. After fourteen months Philip returned to Spain in August 1555 leaving a disconsolate Mary deluding herself with a false pregnancy.

Mary's rigorous attempts to eradicate Protestantism resulted in the so-called 'Marian Persecutions', in the course of which some 300 Protestants including Cranmer, Ridley, Latimer and Hooper suffered death for their faith. Bishop Bonner of London was particularly active in the persecutions. He was later to be deprived of his bishopric under Elizabeth and to die in prison. It must be stated, however, that the number of Protestants who suffered death or persecution under Mary was more than balanced by the number of Catholics who were to suffer under Elizabeth.

In 1557 Philip returned to England and was joyfully received by Mary at Greenwich. She at once agreed to join with Spain in war against France and as a result lost Calais, England's last remaining Continental possession. Philip left again in July 1557 and was never to return.

Mary had come to rely heavily on her kinsman Cardinal Pole, who became Archbishop of Canterbury in 1556 in succession to Cranmer and had acted as the Pope's Legate in reconciling the Church of England to Rome. In November 1558, both Queen and Cardinal fell ill with influenza. In the Queen's case her condition was aggravated by her grief over Philip's absence and the loss of Calais. 'When I am dead,' she said, 'you will find the words "Philip" and "Calais" engraved upon my heart.' She died at St James's Palace on 17 November 1558 and Cardinal Pole died at Lambeth the following day.

Mary's character has been so obscured by the reports of her ferocious persecutions in pursuit of her fanatical mission to restore Catholicism, that the pathetic, frustrated, chronically sick, unloved woman has been overlooked. She had some of her father's fire and greatness and blessed with health might have achieved her design.

Philip of Spain

Born: Valladolid 21 April 1527
Married: 1st, 13 November, 1543, Maria of Portugal
           (d. 16 July 1543); had issue
           2nd, 25 July 1554, Queen Mary I of
           England (d. 17 November 1558)
           3rd, 27 June 1559, Elizabeth of France (d.
           3 October 1568)
           4th, 12 November 1570, Anna Maria of
           Austria (d. 26 October 1580)
Died: El Escorial 13 September 1598
Buried: El Escorial

Philip of Spain occupies a unique position in English history, as the only King Consort. Mary chose to follow the Spanish custom by which the husbands of titled ladies took on their spouse's rank (a custom which still obtains in Spain) and in her eyes at least he was co-regent with her.

To us Philip's portraits do not show him as very prepossessing and contemporary accounts of his character only serve to confirm this; yet he captivated Mary, who after the years of frustration fell in love with all the ardour of a young girl. His callous and cruel treatment was to break her heart. Not least of his misdemeanours was his outrageous flirting with Elizabeth. Once having got a foothold in England, Philip was determined to keep it and thought it expedient to pave the way for a possible future matrimonial alliance with his sickly wife's designated successor. Philip was an even more bigoted Catholic than Mary and the persecutions and burnings of 'heretics' in Spain throughout his reign far exceeded anything seen in England.

As Mary's widower, Philip felt he had a claim on the English throne and in the 1580s began immense preparations for an invasion of England. The fleet which he prepared for this purpose, and arrogantly named the 'Invincible Armada', was thrown into disorder by a storm and completely destroyed by the English fire ships under the command of Sir Francis Drake.

Philip had moved the Spanish capital from Toledo to Madrid and he died after a long and painful illness, covered in boils and in a verminous condition, in the great monastery palace of El Escorial, which he had built, on 13 September 1598, aged 71. He was buried in the monastery, which was to become the last resting place of all future kings and queens of Spain.

ELIZABETH I   1558–1603

Born:	Greenwich Palace 7 September 1553
Acceded:	17 November 1558
Crowned:	Westminster Abbey 15 January 1559
Died:	Richmond Palace 24 March 1603
Buried:	Westminster Abbey

'This is the Lord's doing and it is marvellous in our eyes', quoted Elizabeth when the news was brought to her that her half-sister Mary was dead and she was now queen. By tradition, she received the news while sitting reading beneath a tree in the grounds of Hatfield House, where she was held in confinement. It seems unlikely that she would have been thus engaged in the middle of an English November.

Elizabeth's life before her succession had been chequered, to say the least. Her birth at Greenwich between three and four o'clock in the afternoon on Sunday 7 September 1533 was a bitter disappointment to her father, but he had her proclaimed heiress-presumptive to the Crown, displacing her elder half-sister Mary, and she was christened with great pomp in the Grey Friars Church at Greenwich. The Bishop of London officiated and the godparents were Cranmer, the Dowager Duchess of Norfolk and the Marchioness of Dorset. She was a strong, healthy child and escaped the taint of congenital syphilis which afflicted Henry VIII's other surviving children.

Anne Boleyn's disgrace and execution led to Elizabeth being declared illegitimate by Act of Parliament and deprived of her place in the succession before she was three years old. A later Act reinstated her and the kindness of her stepmother Queen Catherine brought her back to court where she shared the tutors of her half-brother Edward, becoming proficient in Latin, French, Italian and some Greek. She also had some leanings towards the Protestant faith, although by no means committed at this time.

In July 1553 Elizabeth entered London at Mary's side and attended her coronation in October. In the following year she refused to take part in Sir Thomas Wyatt's rebellion but was nevertheless, at the instigation of Gardiner, imprisoned in the Tower and later removed to Woodstock and thence to Hatfield. Mary's death brought her to the throne and her entry into London occasioned great popular rejoicing. Elizabeth was truly her father's daughter, but without his bad points. She loved display and magnificence of dress and could stir the people by her rhetoric and proud, masterful manner.

Elizabeth's coronation took place at Westminster Abbey on 15 January 1550. The see of Canterbury had been vacant since the death of Cardinal Pole and the only Bishop who could be found to perform the ceremony was Owen Oglethorpe, Bishop of Carlisle. At her annointing the Queen complained that the oil used was 'grease and smelled ill' and expressed further displeasure when the Bishop elevated the host at the consecration. She had decided to re-establish the Protestant faith, though she might as easily have decided the opposite, and set about doing so with dogged resolution. Successive Popes were to thunder against her to no avail and it was quite useless for Pius V to excommunicate her in 1570 and declare her subjects absolved of their allegiance to her.

To chronicle the events of Elizabeth's reign is not within the scope of this book. One deed which reflects poorly upon her is the execution of her cousin Mary, Queen of Scots, in 1587 after eighteen years'

imprisonment in England; but Mary did represent a threat and was the hope of the Catholic party which intrigued on her behalf.

Drake's defeat of the Spanish Armada was the crowning glory of Elizabeth's reign. This victory was made possible by the maritime experience of England's seamen, who had been encouraged by their Queen to seek new wealth overseas. The Elizabethan Age was one of adventure and discovery, Hawkins, Drake, Raleigh and the Gilberts all extending England's possessions in the Americas. The colony of Virginia was founded and named after the 'Virgin Queen' and the East India Company also had its beginnings. It was a flourishing age for literature, too, and produced Shakespeare, Spenser, Sidney, Bacon, Marlowe and many others.

Elizabeth was vain of her appearance and loved to dress richly with many jewels about her person. She refused to admit to ageing and in later life wore a huge red wig and employed many cosmetics. She loved dancing and the company of young men, who flattered her ego and dubbed her 'Gloriana'. Elizabeth shrewdly saw quite early on that her strength lay in her single state and she cleverly played her many suitors from home and abroad until she was well past middle age.

A portrait of Queen Elizabeth I by or after George Gower, Serjeant Painter to the Queen. The painting was probably made to commemorate the defeat of the Spanish Armada in 1588, and a naval battle scene can be discerned in the background.

Queen Elizabeth I towards the end of her life, a portrait by Marcus
Gheeraerts in the Burghley House collection.

Elizabeth was well served by her advisers the Cecils, Sir Nicholas Bacon and Francis Walsingham and was a loyal mistress to those who served her loyally. Her one weakness was her fondness for such unworthy favourites as the Earls of Leicester and Essex.

In the middle of January 1603, Elizabeth, who was now sixty-nine, a greater age than that reached by any of her predecessors, was suffering from a cold and removed from Whitehall to Richmond Palace. She recovered, but fell ill again at the end of February with severe tonsilitis which was relieved when a small abscess broke. She had no appetite, however, and complained of bad dreams. On 18 March she became very ill again, but refused to take to her bed, lying instead on a heap of pillows piled on the floor. When Cecil urged her to go to bed she showed a last flash of spirit in her reply, 'Little man,

little man, "must" is not a word to use to Princes.' Elizabeth died at 3 o'clock in the morning on Wednesday 24 March 1603. A messenger set out at once for Scotland to convey the news of his accession to the new King James.

Elizabeth was buried in Westminster Abbey in the same vault as her half-sister Mary. The tomb erected above it bears Elizabeth's effigy only but the following epitaph was inscribed by order of James I: *Regno Consortes et Urna. Hic obdormimus Elizabetha et Maria Sorores In Spe Resurrectionis* (Consorts both in Throne and Grave, here rest we two sisters, Elizabeth and Mary. In hope of our resurrection).

Elizabeth left an England which had become firmly established as a world power.

THE HOUSE OF STUART

The union of the crowns of England and Scotland which was effected in 1603 brought the whole of the British Isles under the rule of one sovereign for the first time and the Act of Union a little over one hundred years later was to create the Kingdom of Great Britain, a style which had been used unofficially by James I and his successors but had never been ratified.

The Kingdom of Scotland was of very respectable antiquity, antedating that of England by several hundred years.

Until 844 Scotland remained divided between the kings of the Scots (Dalriada) and the kings of the Picts, whose kingdom had been established even earlier. The Pictish Kingdom practised matrilineal succession, the crown passing from brother to brother, or from uncle to nephew and sometimes from cousin to cousin, always in the female line; whereas in the Scottish Kingdom the succession was reckoned in the male line and passed to the *tanistair* or appointed successor of the reigning king chosen from his brothers or cousins in the male line. Frequent marriages between Pictish princesses and descendants of Fergus led to the two kingdoms occasionally being united under one ruler, and a final union took place when Kenneth MacAlpin, who had become King of Dalriada in 841, succeeded as King of the Picts three years later and became the first King of Scots. The Kingdom of Strathclyde was annexed by Malcolm II (1005–1034) and the succession continued in the male line of Kenneth MacAlpin's descendants until the death of Alexander III in 1286.

Alexander was succeeded by his granddaughter Margaret, 'the Maid of Norway', whose death from seasickness at the age of seven, when on her voyage from Norway to Scotland in September 1290, was to be followed by the First Interregnum when thirteen competitors claimed the throne. Their claims were submitted to the arbitration of Edward I of England, who eagerly seized the opportunity of appointing a puppet king, who would acknowledge him as overlord, in the person of John Balliol. John proved an unsatisfactory vassal and was forced to abdicate in 1296, when the Second Interregnum ensued. Edward I took over the government and attempted to treat Scotland as a conquered country. A long struggle for independence led by Sir William Wallace and then by Robert Bruce, whose grandfather had been a competitor for the crown in 1290, was successful in 1306 when Robert ascended the throne as Robert I.

In 1371, on the death of Robert's son David II, the crown passed to the House of Stewart in the person of Robert II, whose mother was Robert I's daughter. The Stewarts were of Breton origin and had settled in Scotland in the eleventh century. They had long held the hereditary office of High Steward of Scotland, whence their name. The spelling Stuart which has become more familiar in England was a corruption of the French version Steuart and was widely adopted in the seventeenth century, doubtless being considered smarter.

The Scottish kings continued to be thorns in the flesh of the English monarchy in spite of the many marriage alliances which took place over the centuries. The culmination was James IV's invasion of England (taking advantage of his brother-in-law Henry VIII's absence in France), ending in an overwhelming defeat at Flodden Field in Northumberland on 9 September 1513, when the King and many of the Scots nobility were slain.

The Scottish monarchy was cursed with a long succession of minors, James II, James III, James IV, James V, Mary and James VI all being young children (the last three infants in arms) at their succession. James VI's claim to the English throne was through his great-grandmother Margaret, daughter of Henry VII, who had married James IV in 1503. When he succeeded Elizabeth on the English throne in 1603 James VI of Scotland and I of England achieved by peaceful means that which Edward I had failed to accomplish by force of arms.

JAMES I   1603–1625

Born:	Edinburgh Castle 19 June 1556	
Acceded in Scotland:	24 July 1567	
Crowned in Scotland:	Stirling 29 July 1567	
Acceded:	24 March 1603	
Crowned:	Westminster Abbey 25 July 1603	
Married:	(proxy) Kronborg 20 August 1589, (in person) Oslo 23 November 1589, and again Kronborg 21 January 1590, Anne, 2nd daughter of Frederick II, King of Denmark and Norway, and Sophia of Mecklenburg-Güstrow	
Children:	(1) Henry Frederick, Prince of Wales: *b.* Stirling Castle 19 February 1594; *d.* St James's Palace 6 November 1612	
	(2) Elizabeth: *b.* Dunfermline 19 August 1596; *d.* Leicester House, London 13 February 1662; *m.* Whitehall 14 February 1613, Frederick V, Elector Palatine of the Rhine, King of Bohemia 1619–20 ('the Winter King'), and had issue, of whom the youngest daughter, Sophia, became the mother of King George I	
	(3) Margaret: *b.* Dalkeith Palace 24 December 1598; *d.* Linlithgow March 1600	
	(4) Charles, later King Charles I	
	(5) Robert, Duke of Kintyre: *b.* Dunfermline 18 January 1602 *d.* there 27 May 1602	
	(6) A son: stillborn Stirling May 1603	
	(7) Mary: *b.* Greenwich Palace 8 April 1605; *d.* Stanwell Park, Middlesex 16 September 1607	
	(8) Sophia: *b.* Greenwich Palace 22 June; *d.* 23 June 1606	
Died:	Theobalds Park, Herts 27 March 1625	
Buried:	Westminster Abbey	

James I completely lacked the combination of charm and looks which was the hallmark of the House of Stuart and which assured the unswerving loyalties of the many adherents of this romatic but ill-starred dynasty. His mother, Mary, Queen of Scots, was pregnant with James when her Italian secretary David Riccio was torn from her side and murdered by her jealous husband Henry, Lord Darnley. The child was born at Edinburgh Castle on 19 June 1566 and we may safely discount the story that the Queen's baby was stillborn, or died at birth, and that a child of her illegitimate half-brother the Earl of Moray was substituted. At his baptism, the baby received the names of Charles James, in honour of his godfather King Charles IX of France (Mary's erstwhile brother-in-law), and his maternal grandfather King James V. He was to be the first British sovereign to bear more than one Christian name.

James was only eight months old when his father was murdered in the Kirk o' Field on 10 February 1567. Mary's suspected involvement and her marriage at Holyrood on 15 May to James Hepburn, Earl of Bothwell, led to her forced abdication on 24 July and James's proclamation as King James VI of Scots. The year-old child was solemnly crowned at Stirling on 29 July. He was consigned to the care of the Earl of Mar and later of Sir Alexander Erskine and received a good education from the historian and poet George Buchanan. During his reign in Scotland James was

A portrait of James I by John de Critz, painted about 1587 when he was still only James VI, King of Scots. The picture is in the Royal Collection and hangs at Hampton Court Palace.

James I in later life by an unknown artist.

James often employed the title of King of Great Britain (in the preamble to the Authorized Version of the Bible, for example), but his official style by which he was proclaimed was 'King of England, Scotland, France and Ireland, Defender of the Faith', and another hundred years would elapse before the words 'Great Britain' officially became part of the royal style and title.

Having escaped from the control of the Scottish lords and clergy, James was determined to exert his authority as ruler in his new kingdom. In order to do this he began to propound the theory of the 'divine right of kings', maintaining that the king was above the law and answerable only to God. He was enough of a statesman, however, not to press his claims too far. He did not confront Parliament head-on when they consistently refused to vote him extra funds, but turned to other ways of raising money. He instituted the order of Baronets, a new hereditary honour between knighthood and the peerage, and sold the dignity for £1,080.

In 1605 an attempt by Catholic sympathizers to blow up the King and Parliament at the state opening on 5 November was discovered and the conspirators, including Guido Fawkes who was to have fired the trail, were rounded up and executed. The plot brought a new wave of anti-Catholic feeling, and for a while Parliament felt amicable towards their Protestant King and voted him an extra subsidy. The extreme Puritans, however, pushed for further religious reforms, including the abolition of bishops. James, who had suffered under the rule of the extreme Protestants in Scotland, was determined to oppose this, believing that his power would be reduced, and was wont to say, 'No Bishop, no King'.

James's eldest son, Henry Frederick, Prince of Wales, a young man of great promise, died of typhoid in November 1612, at the age of eighteen, and his second son Charles became heir to the throne. The following year James's only surviving daughter Elizabeth was married to the Elector Palatine and left to live in Germany. Queen Anne died in 1619, but James was little moved by the event, his affections being entirely centred on George Villiers, whom he had first met in 1614 and advanced from honour to honour, culminating in the Dukedom of Buckingham in 1623. To James he was 'Steenie' from a fancied resemblance he saw to the central figure in a painting of the martyrdom of St Stephen.

James had always been self-indulgent where food and drink were concerned and early in 1625 he was stricken with many distressing symptoms. There was the usual suspicion of poison, but kidney failure seems to have been the immediate cause of the King's death, which took place at Theobald's Park, Hertfordshire on 27 March 1625.

James has aptly been called 'the wisest fool in

controlled by powerful nobles and the extreme Protestant clergy of the Kirk.

In 1589 James married Princess Anne of Denmark and this rather plain, characterless and somewhat masculine lady made an ideal consort for him. He had grown up with practically no female society and his affections tended to centre on his own sex, though whether he ever progressed beyond slobbering kisses and juvenile fumbling and fondling is debatable. His own appearance was unattractive, a large head with rheumy eyes topped an ungainly and ill-proportioned body. He suffered from the 'royal malady' porphyria, as had his mother. The disease takes its name from the dark purple hue which the urine of its sufferers acquires after standing a little while and James was to describe his own urine as resembling rich Alicante wine.

James was generally accepted as the heir to the English throne and Elizabeth, when dying, signified her assent that he should succeed her. A messenger, Sir Robert Carey, set off for Scotland to inform James of his accession. The new King set out for London immediately and he and his queen were crowned in Westminster Abbey on St James's Day 25 July 1603. As the first sovereign to reign over both England and Scotland,

Christendom'. He had many abilities and was a prolific author, penning, among other things, 'A Diatribe Against Tobacco' and a treatise on demonology and witchcraft, in which he was profoundly interested. He was also ill-mannered and coarse and a physical and moral coward, but with his upbringing this is hardly surprising. Although not a good king, there have been many far worse.

Anne of Denmark

Born: Skanderborg Castle, Jutland 14 October 1574
Married: (proxy) Kronborg 20 August 1589, (in person) Oslo 23 November 1589, and again Kronborg 21 January 1590
Crowned in Scotland: Holyrood 17 May 1590
Crowned in England: Westminster Abbey 25 July 1603
Died: Hampton Court Palace 4 March 1619
Buried: Westminster Abbey

The negotiations for James's marriage to Anne, the daughter of King Frederick II of Denmark and Norway, were commenced in 1585, but successfully blocked by Elizabeth, who held James's mother in captivity in England. It was only after Mary's execution in 1587 that James's advisers decided that the marriage should be concluded and it took a surprising number of ceremonies to do so. A proxy marriage at Kronborg on 20 August 1589 was followed up by James's arrival in Oslo, Norway,

where the second ceremony took place with the bride and bridegroom in person on 23 November 1589. A round of feasting and visits followed and for good measure there was another ceremony at Kronborg on 21 January 1590. The couple were still in no hurry to return to Scotland and did not land at Leith until 1 May 1590. Anne's coronation in the chapel at Holyrood House followed on 17 May.

In the course of the next twelve years five children were born, of whom three survived infancy. When the news of James's accession to the English throne arrived, Anne was again pregnant and he set out for England without her. In May 1603 she was delivered of a stillborn son at Stirling and as soon as she had recovered she set out to join James in England and was crowned with him in July. Her two youngest children were born in England and both died in infancy. Their memorials in Westminster Abbey have a strangely touching beauty.

Anne's portraits show a rather plain, masculine-looking woman. Her interests lay in court masques (the equivalent of amateur theatricals), in which she personally appeared, and in building, which ran her into debt. The Queen's House at Greenwich was created for her and is an exquisite example of Jacobean architecture.

The Queen also enjoyed travelling about the country and made a spectacular visit to Bath in 1613. She and James led more or less separate lives and ended up with little or no interest in each other. She died at Hampton Court Palace on 4 March 1619 and was buried in Westminster Abbey.

Anne of Denmark in hunting costume by Paul van Somer, a picture in the Royal Collection.

CHARLES I   1625–1649

Born:	Dunfermline 19 November 1600
Acceded:	27 March 1625
Crowned in England:	Westminster Abbey 2 February 1626
Crowned in Scotland:	Edinburgh 18 June 1633
Married:	(proxy) Paris 1 May 1625, (in person) Canterbury 13 June 1625, Henrietta Maria, 3rd and youngest daughter of Henry IV, King of France and Navarre, and his 2nd wife Marie de' Medici
Children:	(1) Charles James, Duke of Cornwall: b. and d. Greenwich Palace 13 May 1629
	(2) Charles, later King Charles II
	(3) Mary, Princess Royal (the first to bear that title): b. St James's Palace 4 November 1631; d. Whitehall Palace 24 December 1660; m. Whitehall 2 May 1641, William II, Prince of Orange, and had issue, her only son becoming King William III
	(4) James, later King James II

(5) Elizabeth: b. St James's Palace 29 December 1635; d. Carisbrooke Castle, Isle of Wight 8 September 1650

(6) Anne: b. St James's Palace 17 March 1637; d. Richmond Palace 5 November 1640

(7) Catherine: b. and d. Whitehall Palace 29 June 1639

(8) Henry, Duke of Gloucester: b. Oatlands, Surrey 8 July 1640; d. Whitehall Palace 13 September 1660

(9) Henrietta Anne: b. Bedford House, Exeter 16 June 1644; d. St Cloud 30 June 1670; m. Paris 31 March 1661, as his 1st wife, Philippe, Duke of Orleans, younger son of Louis XIII, King of France

Died:	Beheaded outside Whitehall Palace 30 January 1649
Buried:	St George's Chapel, Windsor

Charles I, 'the Martyr King', has inspired more intense feelings than any of our other sovereigns. The Stuart charm and charisma, lacking in his father, were present in him in full measure.

Charles was the second son of James I and Anne of Denmark and was born at Dunfermline Palace on 19 November 1600. He was a delicate backward child, still unable to walk or talk at the age of three, and was left behind in the care of nurses and servants when his parents went to London with his elder brother and sister. He was finally considered strong enough to make the journey south in July 1604 and proceeded in easy stages in a curtained litter. His parents met him at Northampton and placed him in the excellent hands of Lady Carey, whose husband had carried the news of James's accession to Scotland. This good woman patiently persevered with 'Baby Charles' and gradually he learned both to walk on his rickety legs and to talk with his stammering tongue.

Charles adored his elder brother Henry and longed to emulate him and when Henry died at the age of eighteen the twelve-year-old Charles felt it keenly. The separation from his sister Elizabeth on her marriage the following year was another blow and Charles now found himself virtually an only child.

Charles had been created Duke of Albany in the peerage of Scotland in 1603 and Duke of York in the peerage of England in 1605. Shortly before his sixteenth birthday he was created Prince of Wales and Earl of Chester.

James envisaged a marriage alliance for Charles with the Infanta Maria of Spain and in 1623 he was sent to Madrid accompanied by 'Steenie', the Duke of Buckingham, to pay court to her. They travelled incognito via Paris, where Charles had a first sighting of the French King's sister Henrietta Maria, who was eventually to become his bride, as she rehearsed a masque with the Queen and other members of the royal family. Charles and Buckingham were well received in Madrid, but the marriage negotiations foundered on the stumbling block of religion, and the travellers returned to England in October.

Charles succeeded his father in March 1625 and two months later was married by proxy to Henrietta Maria of France. The new Queen arrived in England in June and the marriage was solemnized at Canterbury on 13 June. Charles was crowned in Westminster Abbey on Candlemas Day 2 February 1626, but because of the religious difficulties the Queen was not crowned with him.

Charles encountered the same troubles with Parliament as his father, stubbornly refusing to accede to its requests. It was summoned and dissolved three times and in 1629 the King decided to govern without it, beginning an eleven year period of personal rule. To raise revenue Charles sold monopolies and levied the

A charming picture of Charles I, Henrietta Maria and the infant
Charles II by the Dutch artist Hendrik Gerritszoon Pot, who visited
London in 1632 when this picture was probably painted.

unpopular 'ship money' from seaports and later from
inland towns. After Parliament had finally been
summoned again, the King brought matters to a head by
entering the House of Commons with an armed guard
and demanding the arrest of five Members of Parliament,
who forewarned had made their escape. After this a civil
war became inevitable.

Charles raised his standard at Nottingham and the
long struggle between Cavaliers and Roundheads began
in earnest. The Royalist troops were finally over-
whelmed by Oliver Cromwell's New Model Army at
Naseby in 1645. Charles surrendered to the Scots in
1646 and was promptly handed over to the English.
After an imprisonment in Carisbrooke Castle in the Isle
of Wight, he was brought to trial in Westminster Hall
before a tribunal of 135 judges. Refusing to recognize the

legality of a court which could try a king, Charles
declined to plead and was found guilty by 68 votes to 67,
a majority of only one. A sentence of death was passed
and on 30 January 1649 Charles walked from St James's
Palace, where he was last confined, to Whitehall, where
a scaffold had been erected outside Inigo Jones's
elegantly proportioned Banqueting House. Charles wore
two shirts, for it was a cold day and he said if he were to
tremble from cold people might mistake it for fear. He
entered the Banqueting House and stepped onto the
scaffold from a first floor window. He was attended by
Bishop Juxon, to whom he spoke his last word,
'Remember'. When his head was severed from his body a
great groan went up from the assembled crowd and
people pressed forward to soak their handkerchiefs in the
royal blood. The cult of the Martyr King had begun.

Later that day Cromwell looked on the King's body as
it lay in its coffin at St James's Palace before being taken
to Windsor for burial. 'Cruel necessity!' he was heard to
utter. As the King's coffin was carried into St George's

An 18th century French engraving depicting the beheading of Charles I accords fairly accurately with contemporary descriptions of the scene. Bishop Juxon holds the Lesser George of the Order of the Garter which the King handed to him on the scaffold and Charles has just stretched out his hands as a pre-arranged signal to the headsman. The executioner and his assistant are both masked and hooded and the assistant is preparing to catch the King's head and hold it aloft. Note the artist sketching the scene.

Chapel, Windsor on 7 February 1649, a fall of snow turned the black velvet pall white. Heaven had declared his innocence, his supporters claimed.

Charles was one of England's most artistically cultured kings, and he delighted in collecting works of art and patronizing artists. The superb artistry of Van Dyck has made his face almost as familiar as the work of Holbein has made that of Henry VIII.

Henrietta Maria of France

Born: Hôtel du Louvre, Paris 26 November 1609
Married: (proxy) Paris 1 May 1625, (in person) Canterbury 13 June 1625
Died: Colombe, nr Paris 31 August 1669
Buried: St Denis

Henrietta Maria was a little over fourteen when negotiations for her marriage to Charles, Prince of Wales, were opened in 1624. By the time they were completed and the proxy marriage took place at Paris on 1 May 1625, Charles was king. The new Queen landed at Dover and the marriage was completed at Canterbury on 13 June 1625.

The early years of the marriage were unhappy. Charles had undertaken to relieve the penal laws imposed on English Catholics as part of the marriage treaty, but now found excuses not to do so. He was almost as much under the influence of Buckingham as his father had been, but the favourite's assassination at Portsmouth on 23 August 1628 removed a barrier, and the young couple soon developed a closer relationship which was to ripen into a deep and abiding love for each other.

In May 1629 the Queen was frightened by a mastiff which jumped at her while she was passing through a corridor of Greenwich Palace. She went into premature labour and her first child, Charles James, was born and died almost at once. Just over a year later the future Charles II was born and his birth was followed by those of six more children, of whom two died young.

Henrietta Maria (as she is known to us, though to her contemporaries in England she was Queen Mary) delighted in the court amusements of the time and, like her mother-in-law before her, enjoyed taking part in masques and dramatic entertainments. She took little interest in politics or religion until 1637 when she appointed an agent to reside at the papal court and received a papal agent accredited to her. This man, a Scotsman named George Cann, began making conversions among the nobility and gentry, causing alarm in Protestant circles.

The Queen gave the King her wholehearted support

in his struggles with the Commons and his schemes to raise money. On 3 April 1644, when seven months pregnant, she was compelled to leave the King at Oxford and made her way to Exeter where she gave birth to her youngest child, Henrietta, on 16 June 1644. Soon afterwards she escaped to France and was well received by her sister-in-law Anne of Austria, the Queen Regent for her son Louis XIV. Her years in exile were passed in caring for her children. Rumours that she had contracted a private marriage with her secretary Lord Jermyn were probably unfounded, but her close relationship with him led to her partial estrangement from her children.

After the Restoration, Henrietta Maria returned to England and received a Parliamentary grant of £30,000 a year as compensation for the loss of her dower-lands and a matching sum as a pension from the King. Pepys saw her at court on 22 November 1660 and described her as a 'very little plain old woman, and nothing more in her presence in any respect nor garb than any ordinary woman.' She was only fifty at this time, but her troubles had aged her.

The Queen Mother returned to France in January 1661 to attend the marriage of her daughter Henrietta to the Duke of Orleans. She came back in the summer of 1662 and resumed her residence at Somerset House, but found life in England uncongenial and the climate damaging to her health and returned to France again in June 1665. She settled at Colombes, near Paris, and died there on 31 August 1669. She was buried in the royal basilica of St Denis, where her tomb was despoiled in the French Revolution.

CHARLES II   1649 (1660)–1685

Born:	St James's Palace 29 May 1630
Acceded de jure:	30 January 1649
Crowned in Scotland:	Scone 1 January 1651
Restored:	29 May 1660
Crowned in England:	Westminster Abbey 23 April 1661
Married:	Portsmouth 21 May 1662, Catherine Henrietta, daughter of John IV, King of Portugal, and Luiza Maria de Guzman
Died:	Whitehall Palace 6 February 1685
Buried:	Westminster Abbey

Charles II is perhaps the most attractive of all our kings. He inherited his dark, romantic good looks from his mother's Italian ancestors; the Stuart charm in abundance from his father; and his strong sexuality from his maternal grandfather, Henry of Navarre.

Charles was born at St James's Palace on 29 May 1630, the second but first surviving child of Charles I and Henrietta Maria. He was declared Prince of Wales in 1638, but never formally created so by patent. His education was confided to the Earl (later Duke) of Newcastle and Dr Brian Duppa, Bishop of Chichester, who was later replaced by Dr John Earle. These wise men did not cram the boy's head full of learning as had been the fashion under the Tudors, but gave him a good grounding of general knowledge and plenty of sensible advice on everyday life.

As a boy of twelve, Charles, with his brother James, accompanied their father at the Battle of Edgehill, narrowly escaping capture by the Parliamentarians. He was at his father's side throughout most of the Civil War and towards the end of it escaped to France, later moving to Holland, where his sister Mary was married to the Prince of Orange. The execution of Charles I in January 1649 made Charles the *de jure* King Charles II and in 1650 he landed in Scotland, raised an army of 10,000 men and, after being crowned King of Scots at Scone on 1 January 1651, marched into England, only to suffer an overwhelming defeat by Cromwell's army at the Battle of Worcester. A price of £1000 was put on Charles's head and he became a fugitive for six weeks. The romantic story of his hiding in an oak tree belongs to this period.

Eventually Charles made his escape to France and the next eight years were spent in exile in France, Germany and Holland, engaged in plotting and planning. Cromwell, who had been installed as Lord Protector seated on the Coronation Chair, which was taken from the Abbey to Westminster Hall for that purpose, died on 3 September 1658 and was succeeded in that office by his son Richard. A new dynasty of hereditary Lord Protectors might have been envisaged, but Richard was not the man his father was and had no stomach for government. In May 1659 he was compelled to resign by the army, leaving the way open to negotiate Charles's restoration. The prime mover in the matter was General Monck (later Duke of Albemarle), and the satisfactory outcome was the return of Charles who entered London on his thirtieth birthday, 29 May 1660. He was crowned on St George's Day 1661 by William Juxon, Archbishop of Canterbury, the prelate who had attended his father on the scaffold. The old regalia had been broken up and sold under the Commonwealth and a completely new set had to be made. It has been used, at least in part, at all subsequent coronations.

Charles proved himself an astute ruler and the Earl of Rochester's well-known remark that 'he never said a foolish thing and never did a wise one' is largely untrue. His foreign policy, however, left much to be desired. He became very much the tool of France, concluding the Secret Treaty of Dover with Louis XIV in 1670.

Boscobel House, where Charles II spent a day hiding in an oak tree during his escape after the battle of Worcester. This painting by Robert Streeter is in the Royal Collection.

Shortage of money was a crucial problem as always and Dunkirk was sold to France for £400,000. In 1672 a Dutch fleet sailed up the Medway and fired British warships at Chatham, greatly damaging our prestige abroad, but peace was concluded in 1674.

In 1662 Charles had married the Portuguese Infanta Catherine of Braganza, who brought him a dowry of £300,000 and the naval bases of Tangier and Bombay. There were to be no children of the marriage, but Charles fathered a large progeny by his many mistresses. Most of them were recognized and ennobled by their father and the present Dukes of Buccleuch, Grafton, Richmond and St Albans derive their origin from Charles.

The Great Plague of London occurred in 1665 and was followed by the Great Fire in 1666, in which Charles himself helped to fight the flames and displayed great personal bravery. Charles was a great patron of the arts and sciences and the founder of the Royal Society. At the behest of his mistress Nell Gwynne he also founded the Royal Hospital in Chelsea as a home for army pensioners. The *Habeas Corpus* Act was passed in

Charles's reign and Parliamentary government began to develop the party system, Whigs and Tories emerging for the first time.

On 2 February 1685 Charles, who was fifty-four, suffered an apparent stroke at Whitehall. He rallied and lingered until 6 February, when he died after apologizing for having been 'an unconscionable time a-dying'. The real cause of his death appears to have been uraemia. He was received into the Roman Catholic Church on his deathbed, but was buried in Westminster Abbey with Anglican rites. He was the last sovereign to have an effigy carried at his funeral and the full-length wax figure, wearing the oldest known set of Garter robes in this country (there is an older set in Denmark), is still displayed in Westminster Abbey and may be said to convey more of the King's character than any other portrait.

Catherine of Braganza

Born:	Vila Viçosa, Lisbon 25 November 1638
Married:	Portsmouth 21 May 1662
Died:	Palace of Bemposta, Lisbon 31 December 1705
Buried:	Belém

When she was born at Vila Viçosa, near Lisbon, on 25 November 1638, Catherine of Braganza was merely the daughter of a Portuguese nobleman, but before she was two years old Portugal had thrown off the Spanish yoke under which it had chafed for sixty years, and her father had been called to the throne as King John IV.

Catherine's father first put her forward as a possible bride for the future Charles II in 1645, the proposals being renewed by her mother the Queen Regent after the Restoration in 1660. Rumours that she was barren had already begun to circulate, presumably she had some gynaecological problems, but the match went ahead as Charles was eager to secure the promised dowry of £300,000 with Tangier and Bombay thrown in. The marriage contract was signed on 23 June 1661 and Catherine sailed for England the following April, landing at Portsmouth on 13 May. The marriage took place privately on 21 May and Catherine was conducted to Hampton Court, where Charles, with uncharacteristic insensitivity, compelled her to receive his mistress Lady Castlemaine, causing a great emotional outburst from the new Queen. In August the court moved to Whitehall and Pepys reported in his diary on seeing her for the first time, 'though she be not very charming, yet she hath a good, modest, and innocent look, which is pleasing.'

Sadly the reports of Catherine's barrenness were to be proved true, although she did become pregnant and miscarry more than once. On 9 October 1662 Pepys reported: 'It is believed the Queen is with child, for that the coaches are ordered to ride very easily through the streets.' No more was heard of this, however. On 19 February 1666 Pepys wrote of Catherine that 'it is confessed by all that she miscarryed lately; Dr Clerke telling me yesterday at White Hall that he had the membranes and other vessels in his hands which she voided, and were perfect as ever woman's was that bore a child.' Again on 9 May 1668 he reported: 'I . . . hear that the Queene hath miscarryed of a perfect child, being gone about ten weeks, which do show that she can conceive, though it be unfortunate that she cannot bring forth.' Nor was this apparently Catherine's last attempt at maternity, for on 19 May 1669 Pepys 'waited upon the King and Queen all dinner-time, in the Queen's lodgings, she being in her white pinner and apron, like a woman with child; and she seemed handsomer plain so, than dressed.' Obviously Catherine was wearing the fashionable maternity dress of the day. There is another reference to her 'being supposed with child' on 26 May, but after that we hear no more.

Catherine chose to live at Somerset House rather than at Whitehall and her chapel there became a fashionable rendezvous, giving cause for complaint. Probably the music was good and the unaccustomed ceremonial had its appeal. Attempts by the Whigs to implicate the Queen in the Popish Plot in 1678 were refuted by Charles.

When Charles was dying Catherine was ill and sent a message begging his forgiveness for not being able to come to him. 'Alas, poor woman', said Charles, 'It is I who should be begging her forgiveness.' After her initial shock at the presentation of Lady Castlemaine, Catherine had maintained a dignified attitude towards Charles's mistresses and shown many acts of kindness to his illegitimate children.

Catherine continued to reside at Somerset House after Charles's death and in 1688 was present at the birth of James II's son, later giving evidence as to his legitimacy to the Council. She remained in London after James II fled but, finding she did not get on well with William and Mary, decided to return to her native Portugal. She made a leisurely journey through France and Spain and arrived in Lisbon in January 1693. In the last year of her life she acted as Regent of Portugal for her brother King Pedro II, who had grown weary of government. She died at the Palace of Bemposta in Lisbon on 31 December 1705 and was buried in the monastery of Belém.

Catherine of Braganza, by Jacob Huysmans, a portrait in the Royal Collection.

JAMES II   1685–1688

Born: St James's Palace 14 October 1633
Acceded: 6 February 1685
Crowned: Westminster Abbey 23 April 1685
Married: 1st (secretly), Breda 24 November 1659,
           (publicly) Worcester House, London
           3 September 1660, Anne (b. Cranbourne
           Lodge, nr Windsor 12 March 1638; d. St
           James's Palace 31 March 1671) eldest
           daughter of Edward Hyde, 1st Earl of
           Clarendon, Lord High Chancellor of
           England, and his 2nd wife Frances
           Aylesbury
Children: (1) Charles, Duke of Cambridge:
               b. Worcester House, London
               22 October 1660; d. Whitehall
               5 May 1661
           (2) Mary, later Queen Mary II
           (3) James, Duke of Cambridge: b. St
               James's Palace 12 July 1663; d. St
               James's Palace 22 May 1667
           (4) Anne, later Queen Anne
           (5) Charles, Duke of Kendal: b. St
               James's Palace 4 July 1666;
               d. Richmond Palace 20 June 1667
           (6) Edgar, Duke of Cambridge: b. St
               James's Palace, 14 September 1667;
               d. Richmond Palace 15 November
               1669
           (7) Henrietta: b. Whitehall 13 January
               1669; d. St James's Palace 15
               November 1669
           (8) Catherine: b. Whitehall 9 February
               1671; d. St James's Palace 5 December
               1671
Married: 2nd, (by proxy) Modena 30 September
           1673, (in person) Dover 21 November
           1673, Mary Beatrice Eleanora, only
           daughter of Alfonso IV (d'Este), Duke of
           Modena, and Laura Mortinozzi
Children: (9) Catherine Laura: b. St James's Palace
               10 January; d. there 3 October 1675
           (10) Isabella: b. St James's Palace 18
                August 1676; d. St James's Palace
                2 March 1681
           (11) Charles, Duke of Cambridge: b. St
                James's Palace 7 November; d. there
                12 December 1677
           (12) Charlotte Maria: b. St James's Palace
                16 August; d. there 6 October 1682
           (13) James Francis Edward, Prince of
                Wales, later the Jacobite James III,

known to posterity as 'The Old
Pretender': b. St James's Palace 10
June 1688; d. Rome 1 January 1766;
m. (by proxy) Bologna 19 May 1719,
(in person) Monte Fiascone 3
September 1719, Maria Casimire
Clementina (b. 18 July 1702; d. Rome
18 January 1735), daughter of Prince
James Louis Sobieski, and
granddaughter of John III, King of
Poland

Children: (a) Charles Edward Louis
              John Casimir Silvester
              Maria, later the
              Jacobite Charles III,
              known to posterity as
              'The Young Pretender'
              and 'Bonnie Prince
              Charlie': b. Rome 31
              December 1720;
              d. Rome 31 January
              1788; m. Macerata 17
              April 1772, Louise
              Maximilienne
              Caroline Emanuele
              (b. Mons 20 September
              1752; d. Florence 29
              January 1824),
              daughter of Gustavus
              Adolphus, Prince of
              Stolberg-Gedern; no
              legitimate issue
          (b) Henry Benedict
              Thomas Edward Maria
              Clement Francis
              Xavier, styled Duke of
              York, later a Cardinal
              and the Jacobite Henry
              IX: b. Rome 6 March
              1725; d. Frascati 13
              July 1807

(14) Louisa Maria Theresa: b. St Germain-
     en-Laye 28 June 1692; d. St Germain-
     en-Laye 8 April 1712

Left the   11 December 1688 and was declared by
country: Parliament (28 January 1689) to have
              abdicated on that day. However, he
              remained de facto King of Ireland until his
              defeat at the Battle of the Boyne 1 July
              1690
Died: St Germain-en-Laye, France 6 September
              1701
Buried: Church of the English Benedictines, Paris;
              later transferred to St Germain-en-Laye

James II, a portrait by an unknown artist painted during his exile in France about 1690.

James II possessed much less of the Stuart charm than his elder brother Charles, and also lacked his sense of humour. He was good looking but his looks were spoiled in later life by a cynical sneer which is apparent in almost all his portraits. He looks as if he has a bad smell under his nose.

Charles I's second surviving son was born at St James's Palace on 14 October 1633. He was designated Duke of York from his birth, but not formally created so until January 1643. With his brother Charles he accompanied their father in the campaigns of the Civil War and was handed over to Parliament on the surrender of Oxford in 1646. He managed to escape to Holland in 1648 and, after Charles II's defeat at Worcester in 1651, volunteered for the French army and later for the Spanish. He was a brave soldier and a good commander and gave loyal service to those for whom he fought.

James shared his brother's strong sexuality, but his penchant was for ugly women and Charles was wont to say jokingly of some of James's mistresses that his confessor must have given them to him as a penance. While still in exile he fell in love with 'ugly Anne Hyde', a maid of honour to his sister the Princess of Orange, and the daughter of Edward Hyde (later Earl of Clarendon and Lord Chancellor), one of Charles's most ardent supporters. The girl was far below James in situation but he pledged himself to her in secret at Breda in a ceremony later held to have been a marriage on 24 November 1659. Anne became pregnant in 1660 and on discovery by her father the story of the 'secret marriage' at Breda came out. The King was consulted and James and Anne were married publicly at Worcester House, London on 3 September 1660, seven weeks before the birth of their first child, a boy who lived less than a year.

On the Restoration James was created Lord High Admiral of England, Ireland and Wales, and of the town and marches of Calais, Normandy, Gascony and Aquitaine, a position which he held until the passing of the Test Act in 1673 compelled him to relinquish it as a Roman Catholic. James had long had leanings towards the Roman Catholic Church and in 1670 both he and his wife were secretly received into it. Like many converts he was to become an ardent fanatic in his zeal for his faith. James distinguished himself as a naval commander, winning victories over the Dutch in 1665 and 1672.

Anne died of complications following the birth of her eighth child Catherine in 1671 and James found a second wife in the person of the charming Italian Princess Mary Beatrice of Modena, whom he married in 1673.

In the next few years James was gradually rehabilitated in the offices he had been forced to resign because of his Catholicism and after serving as Lord High Commissioner to the Parliament of Scotland in 1681,

was reappointed Lord High Admiral in 1684. All attempts to exclude him from the succession in favour of his daughter Mary, a staunch Protestant married to her cousin the Prince of Orange, were thwarted by Charles II, on whose death in February 1685 James ascended the throne.

Although he openly acknowledged his Catholicism, James opened his reign well by summoning a Parliament, appointing his Protestant brother-in-law Laurence Hyde, Earl of Rochester as Lord High Treasurer, and banishing Charles II's French mistress the Duchess of Portsmouth, an agent of Louis XIV. James and Mary were crowned on St George's Day 1685 with Anglican rites (but omitting the communion), having been privately crowned and anointed with Catholic rites in their chapel at Whitehall the previous day.

On 11 June 1685, James, Duke of Monmouth, the eldest of Charles II's many illegitimate children, landed at Lyme Regis, claiming the throne as the Protestant champion, and was proclaimed king at Taunton on 20 June. James's forces were sent against him and Monmouth's army was defeated at Sedgemoor on 5 July. Monmouth was discovered cowering under a hedge and taken to London, where he threw himself on James's mercy to no avail. On 17 July he was beheaded in the Tower, the executioner bungling the job and causing him undue suffering before his head was finally hacked from his shoulders. The other rebels were dealt with by the 'Bloody Assize' of Judge Jeffreys, 230 being executed and several hundred more transported for life, imprisoned, fined or flogged.

James was now determined on a course of bringing England back to Catholicism and as a first step issued a Declaration of Indulgence removing restrictions imposed on those who did not conform to the established Church of England. Seven Bishops who protested against this were imprisoned in the Tower and tried for seditious libel but were acquitted on 30 June 1688.

The country might have tolerated James, knowing that his heirs were his daughters the Protestant Mary and Anne, but on Trinity Sunday 10 June 1688, the Queen, who had no surviving children, gave birth to a son at St James's Palace. Rumours were at once circulated to the effect that the child was supposititious and had been smuggled into the Queen's bed hidden in a warming-pan. They were, of course, completely false, but many people believed them. James's son-in-law (who was also his nephew) William, Prince of Orange, landed at Brixham on 5 November 1688 with the vowed intent of safeguarding the Protestant interest and gathered many supporters on his march to London. Deserted on all sides, James panicked. He sent his wife and baby son to France and followed himself on 11 December, dropping the great seal of England into the Thames as he was ferried to the boat which was to take him to France. He was recognized at Sheerness and brought back to Faversham, but managed (or was allowed) to make good his escape a few days later, accompanied by his natural son the Duke of Berwick. Parliament meeting on 28 January 1689 was to declare that James had abdicated the throne on 11 December, the day he first attempted to leave the country.

The exiled King with his wife and baby son settled down at the palace of St Germain-en-Laye near Paris, made over to their use by Louis XIV, and a court in exile was soon set up. James was determined to regain his throne and landed in Ireland with a French force in 1689. He held a Parliament in Dublin and remained *de facto* King of Ireland until defeated by William at the Battle of the Boyne on 1 July 1690, when he was forced to withdraw again to France. An interesting reminder of these times is the 'gun money' which James struck from melted down brass cannon to pay his troops. The coins are dated by month as well as by year and are now much sought after collectors' items.

James spent the rest of his life in France, planning further invasions which did not come off and devoting himself to religious observances. He found great consolation in the little daughter the Queen bore him in 1692 and was also comforted by correspondence with his daughter Anne, who could never quite reconcile her conscience with the betrayal of her father.

The exiled King died at St Germain from a cerebral haemorrhage on 6 September 1701, and was first buried in the Church of the English Benedictines in Paris, but later removed to the parish church of St Germain, where his tomb was despoiled during the French Revolution.

Mary of Modena

Born: Modena 25 September 1658
Married: (by proxy) Modena 30 September 1673, (in person) Dover 21 November 1673
Crowned: Westminster Abbey 23 April 1685
Died: St Germain-en-Laye 7 May 1718
Buried: Convent of Chaillot

England's only Italian queen, the only daughter of Alfonso IV, Duke of Modena, of the great House of Este, and his wife Laura Martinozzi, a niece of the famous Cardinal Mazarin, was born at Modena on 25 September 1658. As a girl Mary had the intention of becoming a nun, having had a strict religious upbringing, but largely through the influence of Louis XIV she was proposed as a possible second wife for James, Duke of York. The negotiations being successfully completed she set out for England after a proxy marriage at Modena on 30 September 1673. She visited the French court *en route*, where her charm, beauty and air of distinction gained

A charming portrait of our only Italian Queen, Mary of Modena, by W. Wissing.

much approval, and was married to James on arrival at Dover on 21 November 1673.

'I have brought you a new playmate', said James to his daughters Mary and Anne on presenting their stepmother to them. There was less than four years between the two Marys and the three teenage girls got on well together and formed a warm friendship. In the first nine years of her marriage the Duchess of York gave birth to four children, of whom only one, the Princess Isabella, survived more than a few months, and she died in her fifth year.

At the death of Charles II Mary became Queen Consort and she was crowned with James. It was noted that she joined in the responses in the Anglican service, whereas James remained tight-lipped. As a 'cradle catholic', the Queen did not share his bigotry.

In 1687 Mary announced that she was again pregnant after a gap of five years and the outcome was the birth of her son James Francis Edward on 10 June 1688. The story of her flight to France with the baby has already been told. The exiled Queen of England was greatly admired at the French court and when she gave birth to a daughter, Princess Louisa Maria, on 28 June 1692, the French ladies were astonished to see the tiny baby dressed in little shoes and stockings for her baptism.

Doubtless there was a rush to emulate this example of English *chic*.

After James II's death his widow, who received an annual pension of 100,000 francs from Louis XIV, was regarded as Queen Regent until the coming of age of her son 'James III'. She frequently retreated to the convent of Chaillot where the nuns became the recipients of her confidences and recorded many of her reminiscences. In 1712 Queen Mary had the great sorrow of losing her only surviving daughter, an attractive girl of twenty, who succumbed to smallpox. She lived on another six years and died of cancer at St Germain-en-Laye on 7 May 1718, aged fifty-nine. She was buried in the convent of Chaillot among her beloved nuns.

Mary of Modena was a sweet, gentle character as well as being one of our more beautiful queens and it is a tragedy that her life was ruined by the bigotries of religion.

William III, a portrait after W. Wissing in the National Portrait Gallery.

Mary II, the Queen who reigned as joint-sovereign with her husband.

WILLIAM III AND MARY II	1689–1694
WILLIAM III (ALONE)	1694–1702

WILLIAM III
Born:	The Hague 4 November 1650
Proclaimed:	13 February 1689 (joint sovereign with his wife)
Crowned:	Westminster Abbey 11 April 1689
Married:	St James's Palace 4 November 1677, Mary, eldest daughter of King James II
Died:	Kensington Palace 8 March 1702
Buried:	Westminster Abbey

MARY II
Born:	St James's Palace 30 April 1662
Proclaimed:	13 February 1689 (joint sovereign with her husband)
Crowned:	Westminster Abbey 11 April 1689
Married:	St James's Palace 4 November 1677
Died:	Kensington Palace 28 December 1694
Buried:	Westminster Abbey

William and Mary are always spoken of as though they were one person, although their joint reign (the only one in our history if one discounts the rather dubious precedent of Mary I and Philip of Spain) only lasted a little under six years and William continued to reign alone for nearly another eight.

William, who was born at The Hague on 4 November 1650, was the only child of William II, Prince of Orange, and Charles I's eldest daughter Mary, the first to bear the title of Princess Royal. He was educated at Leyden and at the age of seventeen was admitted to the

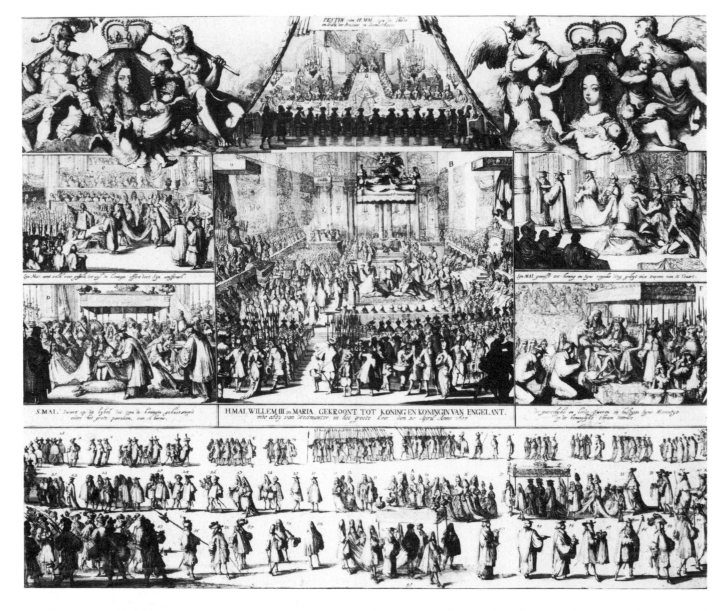

A Dutch print depicting the coronation of William and Mary in
April 1689. Various stages of the ceremony are shown in this
elaborate composition.

Council of State of the Dutch Provinces. He paid his
first visit to England in 1670, meeting the eight-year-old
cousin who was later to become his wife. Returning to
Holland he was appointed Captain General of the Dutch
Forces and a little later *Stadhouder* of the United
Provinces of the Netherlands, an office which had
practically become hereditary in his family

William returned to England and was married to Mary
at St James's Palace on 4 November 1677. William was a
most unprepossessing individual, undersized, asthmatic,
hook-nosed and with a penchant for the society of young
men similar to that of his great-grandfather James I. The
statuesque Mary towered above him. She was a
handsome, though not pretty, woman inclined to
plumpness, although never reaching the proportions of
her sister Anne. If the couple were ill matched
physically, they were ideally suited in other ways, and
William adored his rather formidable wife. There were
no children although Mary appears to have miscarried
twice during her residence in Holland.

The story of William's landing at Brixham and march
to London has already been told. William refused to
accept the crown by right of conquest, yet was unwilling
to play second fiddle to his wife, fond of her though he
was. The solution was the offer of the throne to William
and Mary jointly. They were proclaimed on 13 February
1689 and crowned on 11 April 1689. A duplicate
Coronation Chair and a duplicate set of regalia for Mary
had to be hastily provided for the ceremony. To his
everlasting credit, Archbishop Sancroft, who had
crowned James II, declined to officiate in spite of having
been one of the 'Seven Bishops' tried for seditious libel
the year before, and the ceremony was performed by
Henry Compton, Bishop of London.

Mary had behaved very badly on her arrival in England, running through the palace recently vacated by her father and stepmother and bouncing on the beds in triumph. Her sister Anne adopted a very different attitude. Mary played no part in public affairs except during William's absences abroad when she was left in charge. She was not particularly intelligent or well-educated and leaned towards Puritanism in religion, doubtless influenced by her encounter with Calvinism during her early married life in Holland. To this end, she abolished the sung services in the Chapel Royal at Whitehall. Her preferred residences were Hampton Court and Kensington Palace and she was largely responsible for the construction of the ornamental water known as the Serpentine in Kensington Gardens.

Mary died of smallpox on 28 December 1694 at the age of thirty-two. William had a succession of fainting fits on hearing of her death. Her funeral at Westminster Abbey was attended by both Houses of Parliament, a unique occurrence as up till then Parliament had always been dissolved on the death of a sovereign.

William continued to reign alone for the remainder of his life, unloved by his English subjects who found him too cold and serious. One of the last acts of his reign was the passing of the Act of Settlement to secure the Protestant succession to the crown after Mary's sister Anne.

In February 1702 William was riding at Hampton Court when his horse stumbled on a mole hill and threw him, breaking his collar bone. After it had been set, he insisted on returning to Kensington Palace by coach, which aggravated his condition. He became feverish some days later and was put to bed but died of pleuro-pneumonia a few days later on 8 March 1702. The Jabobites toasted the 'little gentleman in black velvet' (the mole) who had brought about the death of their enemy.

ANNE   1702–1714

Born:	St James's Palace 6 February 1665
Acceded:	8 March 1702
Crowned:	Westminster Abbey 23 April 1702
Married:	Chapel Royal, St James's 28 July 1683, Prince George of Denmark (b. Copenhagen 2 April 1653; d. Kensington Palace 28 October 1708), younger son of Frederick III King of Denmark and Sophia Amelia of Brunswick-Lüneburg
Children:	(1) A daughter: stillborn 12 May 1684
	(2) Mary: b. Whitehall 2 June 1685; d. Windsor Castle 8 February 1687
	(3) Anne Sophia: b. Windsor Castle 12 May 1686; d. Windsor Castle 2 February 1687
	(4) A son: stillborn 22 October 1687
	(5) William, Duke of Gloucester: b. Hampton Court Palace 24 July 1689; d. Windsor Castle 30 July 1700
	(6) Mary: b. and d. St James's Palace 14 October 1690
	(7) George: b. and d. Syon House, Brentford, Middlesex 17 April 1692
	(8) A daughter: stillborn Berkeley House 23 March 1693
	(9) A daughter: stillborn 18 February 1696
	(10) A son: stillborn Windsor 20 September 1696
	(11) A son: stillborn 15 September 1698
	(12) A daughter: stillborn 25 January 1700
	Plus at least six other stillbirths or miscarriages of unknown or unrecorded sex
Died:	Kensington Palace 1 August 1714
Buried:	Westminster Abbey

When Bishop Burnet arrived to give Anne the news of her accession she was at a loss for words and fell back on the usual English opening gambit of the weather. Looking out of the window she remarked, 'It is a fine day.' 'The finest day that ever dawned for England, ma'am', the courtly Bishop responded.

Anne was the second daughter of James II and his first wife Anne Hyde and she and her elder sister Mary were the only two of their eight children to survive infancy. She was born at St James's Palace on 6 February 1665 and brought up in the Protestant faith of the Church of England from which she never swerved. A suggestion that she might marry Prince George Louis of Brunswick-Lüneburg (who was later to succeed her as George I) came to nought when the young people developed an antipathy to each other, and instead Anne was married at the Chapel Royal, St James's on 28 July 1683, to her second cousin once removed Prince George of Denmark. He was a solid, stolid uninteresting young man, but he suited Anne very well and the marriage was a happy one from the beginning. Charles II was to say of George that he had 'tried him drunk and tried him sober and there

Queen Anne presiding at the opening of Parliament, by Peter Tillemans. Compare this with the picture of Edward I's Parliament. When Queen Anne made her first opening speech, her melodious voice is said to have thrilled all who heard it.

was nothing in him either way.' The great tragedy of Anne's life was her appalling maternity record, eighteen pregnancies in sixteen years producing only five living children, the longest-lived of whom was the engaging little Duke of Gloucester, who got overheated dancing on his eleventh birthday and died as a result. His brief life was minutely detailed by his Welsh servant and makes pathetic reading.

Anne was kindly, warm-hearted and not very bright. She never felt happy about supporting William and Mary against her father and taking the place of her half-brother, and worked hard behind the scenes to try to secure his succession after her. She formed an intense (perhaps slightly lesbian) attachment for the masculine-minded Sarah Churchill, Lady Marlborough, whose husband's victories abroad in the course of the War of the Spanish Succession were to be the glory of her reign. Sarah gained a great ascendancy over Anne while she was still Princess and the two were in the habit of addressing each other as 'Mrs Freeman' (Sarah) and 'Mrs Morley' (Anne) to avoid the formality that would otherwise have been inevitable.

Anne's health was always precarious and at her coronation on St George's Day 1702 she was suffering so badly from gout that she had to be carried in a chair, unable to stand on her two feet. Her husband, who had been created Duke of Cumberland by William and Mary soon after their accession, and made Lord High Admiral of England by Anne, paid homage to her. He was the first husband of a reigning queen to do so, and the ceremony was not to be repeated until Prince Philip paid homage to Queen Elizabeth II in 1953.

On 6 March 1707 the Act of Union between England and Scotland was passed and Great Britain officially came into being. Anne's title was changed from 'Queen of England, Scotland, France and Ireland' to 'Queen of Great Britain, France and Ireland'. The following year she lost her husband Prince George, who died at Kensington Palace on 28 October, aged fifty-five. Queen Victoria was later to refer to him as 'the very stupid and insignificant husband of Queen Anne'.

In 1711 the Duchess of Marlborough (as she had become) was dismissed as Keeper of the Queen's Privy Purse, her place in Anne's affections having been usurped by her first cousin Abigail Masham, whom she herself had introduced to the Queen. Lady Masham remained in the royal favour until the Queen's death.

Anne was a High Church Protestant with a great interest in religious affairs. She founded Queen Anne's Bounty to increase the stipends of the poorer clergy, and several London churches were built at her instance, including St John's, Smith Square, the architecture of which is said to have been suggested by the Queen's kicked-over footstool.

Anne's health was not helped by her addiction to brandy and it was obvious that she was not going to live very long. She became ill in the summer of 1714 and, after suffering a series of strokes, died on 1 August, aged forty-nine. She had become so stout that her massive coffin was almost square.

THE HOUSE OF HANOVER

The House of Hanover, which by virtue of the Act of Settlement inherited the throne of Great Britain in 1714, is always thought of as being thoroughly German. It was, however, of Italian origin, sharing a common male line of descent with the great House of Este, to which James II's queen belonged, from Adalbert of Este, who lived early in the tenth century. In 1055 Azzo II, Marquess of Este, married Kunigunde (or Chuniza), daughter and heiress of Welf II, Count of Altdorf, thus acquiring the Welf (or Guelf) possessions in Germany. Later generations also acquired Bavaria, Saxony and Brunswick, and one of the line, Henry the Lion, was to marry Matilda, the eldest daughter of our Henry II, in 1168. George I was their direct descendant in the male line, but his claim to the throne was derived through his maternal grandmother Elizabeth, the daughter of James I.

Like most German sovereign families, the House of Brunswick divided and sub-divided many times. The branch which acquired the British throne so fortuitously was the ultimate junior line of Brunswick-Celle, which obtained the Electoral dignity in 1692. They also held the proud title of Arch-Treasurer of the Holy Roman Empire, which in abbreviated form was to appear on the coins of our Hanoverian kings for many years.

GEORGE I   1714–1727

		Children:	(1) George Augustus, later King George II
Born:	Leineschloss, Hanover 28 May (7 June) 1660		(2) Sophia Dorothea: *b*. Hanover 16/26 March 1687; *d*. Monbijou Palace, Berlin 28 June 1757; *m*. proxy Hanover 3/14 November 1706, in person Berlin 17/28 November 1706, Frederick William I, King of Prussia (*d*. Berlin 31 May 1740)
Acceded:	1 August 1714		
Crowned:	Westminster Abbey 20 October 1714		
Married:	Celle 22 November 1682 (divorced by a specially constituted tribunal Hanover 28 December 1694), Sophia Dorothea, only surviving daughter of George William, Duke of Brunswick-Lüneburg-Celle, and Eléonore Desmiers d'Olbreuse		
		Died:	Osnabrück 22 June 1727
		Buried:	Leineschloss Church, Hanover; removed to Herrenhausen 1957

On the day before King Charles II was restored to his throne, his cousin Sophia, wife of Duke Ernest Augustus of Brunswick-Lüneburg, gave birth to her first son in Hanover. Fifty-four years later that baby was to ascend the same throne, a possibility so remote that it must have been entirely uncontemplated when he was born. George's mother was to describe him as 'beautiful as an angel', and sturdy, strong and healthy he was to remain all his life, although his heavy features and slightly disagreeable expression, apparent in all his portraits, do not give us the impression of a handsome man.

The law of primogeniture had not been established in the Duchy of Brunswick-Lüneburg, and George's father was the youngest of four brothers between whom complicated exchanges of various portions of their inheritance were continually taking place. Ernest Augustus first achieved ruling status a year after his eldest son's birth when he became Prince-Bishop of Osnabrück, an office which had been secularized in 1648, since when Catholic and Protestant 'bishops' alternated. In 1679, by a rearrangement following the death of one of his elder brothers, he became reigning Duke of Brunswick-Lüneberg-Calenberg, and finally, in 1692, acquired the much coveted title of Elector from the Emperor, being known thereafter as Elector of Hanover.

George Louis had five younger brothers and one sister. Their loving mother, whose own childhood had been unhappy, took great care with their education and in providing a happy home atmosphere. George displayed an early bent for a military career and campaigned in the Dutch and Turkish wars. In 1680 he paid his first visit to his future kingdom, where it was suggested he might become a suitor for the hand of his second cousin Princess Anne. The young couple developed a mutual antipathy, however, and Anne's later opposition to the Hanoverian succession has been attributed in part to her memories of an unhappy encounter when George made it plain that she held no attractions for him.

On his return to Hanover, the question of George's marriage was settled by his father, who betrothed him to his cousin Sophia Dorothea, the only surviving daughter and heiress of Duke George William of Brunswick-

George I in Garter robes, a portrait painted by Sir Godfrey Kneller in 1716.

Lüneburg-Celle. The marriage took place in 1682 and was reasonably happy at first, but after the births of two children the affections of both husband and wife became engaged elsewhere. George fell in love with one of his mother's ladies-in-waiting, Melusine von der Schulenburg (later to be ennobled in England as Duchess of Kendal), who bore him three daughters, never publicly acknowledged as such. Sophia Dorothea, for her part, fell in love with Count Philip Christopher von Königsmarck, a young officer in the Hanoverian army. Königsmarck disappeared under mysterious circumstances, and a hastily convened tribunal of jurists and Lutheran Church officials declared the marriage dissolved on the grounds of the wife's refusal to cohabit with her husband. The right to remarry was reserved to George alone and, although there is no proof, it seems highly likely that he did contract a secret marriage with Melusine, whom Robert Walpole later described as being 'as much Queen of England as anyone ever was.'

The Elector Ernest Augustus died in 1698 and George Louis succeeded him as Elector of Hanover. Three years later the Act of Settlement made his mother heiress-presumptive to the throne of Great Britain and George Louis received the Order of the Garter. In 1705 he was naturalized by Act of Parliament. The old Electress Sophia, who said it was her ambition to have the words 'Queen of Great Britain and Ireland' inscribed on her tombstone, was within two months of its achievement when she died. George Louis became heir-presumptive in her place and in August 1714 the death of Queen Anne made him King.

George lost no time in repairing to England and made his state entry into London on 20 September 1714. He was accompanied by Melusine von der Schulenburg, who was soon to be nicknamed 'the Maypole' became of her tall, thin appearance. The amply proportioned Sophie Charlotte, Baroness von Kielmansegg, later to be created Countess of Darlington, was also prominent at court. She was nicknamed 'the Elephant' and was popularly believed to be another of George's mistresses but was, in fact, his illegitimate half-sister.

It has often been stated that George knew no English, but the researches of a recent biographer have shown that he did have a limited knowledge of the language. He opened his first Parliament with an English sentence (which might, of course, have been learnt by heart): 'My Lords and Gentlemen, I have ordered my Lord Chancellor to declare to you in my name the causes of calling this Parliament.' A memorandum of 1723, annotated in English by the King's own hand, is in the Public Record Office, and there is evidence that he often used English words and phrases and sometimes whole sentences in his conversation, although his preferred language was French, which was the language of polite society throughout Europe at the time. George's

coronation service in October 1714 was conducted in Latin to overcome the language difficulties.

In 1715 the Jacobite rising in Scotland in favour of the Stuart claimant 'James III and VIII' was soon put down and several of its leaders were executed. The new King was tolerated rather than popular and the Whigs, with a view to strengthening his support, introduced septennial Parliaments. George himself presided over cabinet meetings throughout his reign, the Prince of Wales acting as interpreter where necessary until the rift between father and son in 1717.

George frequently visited his German dominions, where he was happiest, and in 1719 these were increased by the cession of the secularized bishoprics of Bremen and Verden. George set out for Hanover for the last time on 3 June 1727. He embarked on his yacht at Greenwich and sailed for Holland, landing st Schoonhaven on 18 June. His coach was waiting for him and, although he had been seasick, he set out on the road at once. The next evening he reached Delden, where he had supper and unwisely gorged himself on melons (or in some accounts strawberries and oranges) afterwards. In the morning he set out early after breakfasting on a cup of chocolate. A violent attack of diarrhoea forced a halt, and when the King returned to his coach it was noticed that his face was distorted and his right hand hung limply at his side. He fainted almost immediately and a surgeon was fetched from another coach. George recovered consciousness on being bled and at once demanded that the journey should continue, crying out 'Osnabrück, Osnabrück!' in slurred tones. He soon lost consciousness again, but it was decided to complete the journey. The party reached Osnabrück late in the evening and George rallied sufficiently to be able to raise his hat with his left hand as a sign of greeting before being carried from his coach to his bed, where he again lapsed into unconsciousness. Death came at 1.30 a.m. on 22 June 1727. In modern terms, George died of a cerebral haemorrhage, precipitated by the stomach upset. He had left a request that his body was not to be opened or embalmed, and on George II's instructions he was buried in the Leineschloss Church at Hanover near his mother the Electress Sophia. The church was severely damaged during the Second World War and in 1957 George's sarcophagus and that of his mother were moved to the mausoleum in the grounds of Herrenhausen, where they still repose.

George I was plain and simple in his tastes and appearance. The general impression is of a dull, rather humourless man and an uninspiring monarch, but it is said that he could be lighthearted and amusing with his intimates. His family relations were marred by the quarrel with his son and daughter-in-law. He had little interest in intellectual pursuits, but appreciated music, especially opera, and was the patron of Handel.

Sophia Dorothea of Celle

Born: Celle 10 September 1666
Married: Celle 22 November 1682
Divorced: Hanover 28 December 1694
Died: Ahlden 2/13 November 1726
Buried: Celle

Sophia Dorothea is often referred to as 'the uncrowned Queen' and whether she was Queen of Great Britain or not is debatable; if she was, she was by no means the first to be uncrowned in the literal sense. The divorce pronounced at Hanover in 1694 is generally thought to have been ineffective as far as this country was concerned and, had Sophia Dorothea survived George I, she would almost certainly have been recognized as Queen Mother and brought to England by her son George II, who believed in her innocence.

Sophia Dorothea started life at a great disadvantage, for although her father Duke George William of Brunswick-Lüneburg-Celle was of royal birth her mother Eléonore Desmiers d'Olbreuse was but a French Huguenot lady of a noble but untitled family. She was of such inferior rank to her husband that she had originally been known as Frau von Harburg when the Duke entered into a 'marriage of conscience' with her in 1665. Sophia Dorothea was born in September 1666, but it was not until 1674 that her mother was raised to the rank of a Countess of the Empire, finally becoming Duchess of Celle in 1675 on the legalization of her marriage. All this meant that Sophia Dorothea was regarded as unmarriageable by most of the ruling houses of Germany. In spite of being the only child of loving parents and having an upbringing surrounded with every comfort and luxury, she must continually have been aware of a terrible sense of inferiority. Her marriage to her cousin George Louis was arranged by their respective fathers and received some opposition from George's mother on account of the bride's maternal ancestry. However, it was solemnized on 22 November 1682, when Sophia Dorothea was sixteen and George Louis twenty-two.

Having got over her initial objections, Sophia proved a kind mother-in-law and Sophia Dorothea fitted well into her new family. She was an attractive, high-spirited girl. In December 1683, she gave birth to her first child, the future George II, and in 1687 a daughter, named after her mother, completed the family.

One day in 1689, Sophia Dorothea's brother-in-law Charles Philip brought a friend to meet her, a Count Philip Christopher von Königsmarck. One year older than Sophia Dorothea, he was an officer in the Hanoverian service, handsome, dashing and debonair, a complete contrast to George Louis. By now the marriage which had started so well was beginning to come apart.

George Louis had come under the spell of his Melusine and was frequently away on campaigns, and it did not take long for Sophia Dorothea to become infatuated with Königsmarck. Opinions are still divided as to whether they actually became lovers in the physical sense and Sophia Dorothea was to maintain to the end of her life that they were not, though the letters they exchanged tend to show that they were. The affair became an open scandal and the couple ignored the warnings of their friends and relations to bring it to an end. Matters came to a head in 1694 when rumours that the lovers planned to elope became rife. On the night of 11 July, while George Louis was away visiting his sister in Berlin, Königsmarck was seen to enter the palace in Hanover and head for the Princess's apartments. He was never seen again and the generally accepted story is that he was intercepted and murdered by a group of zealous young officers, anxious to safeguard the reputation of the Electoral House. His body, weighted with stones, was sunk in the Leine.

The following day Sophia Dorothea was ordered to be confined to her apartments, where incriminating letters from Königsmarck were found hidden in curtain linings. The Elector Ernest Augustus and his brother Duke George William of Celle agreed, when confronted with the evidence, that a divorce must be arranged on the safe grounds of Sophia Dorothea's refusal to continue to cohabit with George Louis. A specially convened tribunal of jurists and Lutheran Church officials obligingly declared the marriage dissolved on 28 December 1694.

Meanwhile, Sophia Dorothea had been removed to Ahlden, a castle in her father's territory of Celle, where she lived in hope of being allowed to rejoin Königsmarck, of whose fate she was kept ignorant, after the divorce was completed. She was soon to be dis-illusioned. The terms of the divorce provided that she, as the guilty party, was not to be allowed to remarry and furthermore was to be denied access to her children. Her father refused to see her and she was destined to remain a virtual prisoner at Ahlden for the rest of her life.

The poor woman's long captivity of over thirty years, arduous though it must have been, was never an excessively harsh one and many of the conditions were relaxed as time passed. She enjoyed an adequate income, enabling her to live in a style befitting her rank, and was even allowed to drive out in her coach for short distances under escort. She could receive visitors, including her mother, who constantly sought to procure her release, even asking Queen Anne to intercede on the grounds that her daughter's situation was unfitting for the mother of a future King of Great Britain. It was all to no avail. Her days of boredom and loneliness were only ended when she died at the age of sixty in November 1726. She was buried with her parents at Celle.

GEORGE II — 1727–1760

Born:	Herrenhausen 30 October 1683
Acceded:	22 June 1727
Crowned:	Westminster Abbey 11 October 1727
Married:	Herrenhausen 22 August/1 September 1705, (Wilhelmina Dorothea) Caroline, daughter of John Frederick, Margrave of Brandenburg-Ansbach, and Eleonore Erdmuthe Louise of Saxe-Eisenach
Children:	(1) Frederick Louis, Prince of Wales: b. Hanover 20/31 January 1707; d. Leicester House, London 20/31 March 1751; m. Chapel Royal, St James's 8 May 1736, Augusta (b. Gotha 19/30 November 1719, d. Carlton House, London 8 February 1772), youngest daughter of Frederick II, Duke of Saxe-Gotha, and Magdalena Augusta of Anhalt-Zerbst

Children:

(a) Augusta: b. St James's Palace 31 July/12 August 1737; d. London 23 March 1813; m. St James's Palace 16 January 1764, Charles II, Duke of Brunswick; had issue, of whom Caroline m. King George IV

(b) George William Frederick, later King George III

(c) Edward Augustus, Duke of York: b. Norfolk House 14/25 March 1739; d. Monaco 17 September 1767

(d) Elizabeth Caroline: b. Norfolk House 30 December 1740/10 January 1741; d. Kew Palace 4 September 1759

(e) William Henry, Duke of Gloucester: b. Leicester House 14/25 November 1743; d. Gloucester House 25 August 1805; m. London 6 September 1766, Maria (b. Westminster 3 July 1736; d. Gloucester Lodge, Brompton 22 August 1807), widow of James Waldegrave, 2nd Earl Waldegrave, and natural daughter of Hon. Sir Edward Walpole, KB, and Dorothy Clement; left issue, of whom William Frederick, 2nd Duke of Gloucester, m. Princess Mary, fourth daughter of King George III

(f) Henry Frederick, Duke of Cumberland: b. Leicester House 27 October/7 November 1745; d. London 18 September 1790; m. London 2 October 1771, Anne (b. London 24 January 1743; d. Trieste 28 December 1808), widow of Christopher Horton, and daughter of Simon Luttrell, 1st Earl of Carhampton, and Judith Maria Lawes; no issue

(g) Louisa Anne: b. Leicester House 8/19 March 1749; d. Carlton House 13 May 1768

(h) Frederick William: b. Leicester House 13/24 May 1750; d. Leicester House 29 December 1765

(i) Caroline Matilda: b. (posthumously) Leicester House 11/22 July 1751; d. Celle 10 May 1775; m. proxy London 1 October, in person Christiansborg 8 November 1766 (divorced 6 April 1772), Christian VII, King of Denmark and Norway

(2) Anne, Princess Royal: b. Herrenhausen 2 November 1709; d. The Hague 12 January 1759; m. French Chapel, St James's 25 March 1734, William IV, Prince of Orange

(3) Amelia Sophia Eleanor: b. Herrenhausen 10 July 1711; d. Cavendish Square, London 31 October 1786

(4) Caroline Elizabeth: b. Herrenhausen 10/21 June 1713; d. St James's Palace 28 December 1757

(5) A son: stillborn St James's Palace 9/20 November 1716

(6) George William: b. St James's Palace 2/13 November 1717; d. Kensington Palace 6/17 February 1718

(7) William Augustus, Duke of Cumberland: b. Leicester House 15/26 April 1721; d. London 31 October 1765

(8) Mary: b. Leicester House 22 February/5 March 1723; d. Hanau 14 January 1772; m. proxy St James's Palace 8/19 May, in person Cassel 28 June 1740, Frederick II, Landgrave of Hesse-Cassel

(9) Louisa: b. Leicester House 7/18 December 1724; d. Christiansborg 8/19 December 1751; m. proxy Hanover 30 October/10 November, in person Christiansborg 11 December 1743, Frederick V, King of Denmark and Norway

Died:	Kensington Palace 25 October 1760
Buried:	Westminster Abbey

George II in coronation robes, from the studio of C. Jervas.

Act of Settlement. George Augustus learnt to speak English fluently but he never lost his guttural accent and must have seemed very foreign to his English subjects. However, he was a courteous and courtly man, although hasty tempered, and these qualities were greatly appreciated by his ministers.

Deprived of their mother's care when George Augustus was eleven and his sister Sophia Dorothea seven, the children were brought up with loving kindness by their grandmother, the Electress Sophia, and in the charge of her *Oberhofmeisterin* (Mistress of the Robes), Frau von Harling, who had similarly looked after their father.

In 1705, the year in which George Augustus was naturalized a British subject, a marriage was arranged for him with Caroline of Brandenburg-Ansbach, and in the following year Queen Anne rather begrudgingly created him Duke and Marquess of Cambridge, Earl of Milford Haven, Viscount Northallerton and Baron Tewkesbury, and sent the Earl of Halifax to Hanover to invest him with the Order of the Garter on her behalf. George became Duke of Cornwall and Rothesay on his father's accession and was created Prince of Wales and Earl of Chester on 22 September 1714, two days after the state entry into London. The Prince and Princess of Wales took part in the coronation, and George Augustus wore

A revealing caricature of George II by George, 1st Marquess Townshend, who was noted for his witty satirical drawings of the leading figures of the day.

'Dat is vun big lie!' So bawled King George II in his heavily accented English when the news that his father was dead and that he had ascended the throne was first brought to him. After years of being at loggerheads with his disagreeable father, the disagreeable son could not believe that he was free of parental oppression at last. Strangely enough, the bad relations which had existed between him and his father were to be repeated in the next generation, as George and his son Frederick were equally antagonistic towards each other.

George Augustus, who ascended the throne as George II in his forty-fourth year, was almost as much an alien in this country as his father had been. His grandmother, the old Electress Sophia, was careful to engage English tutors for her grandchildren and great-grandchildren as soon as she had been declared heiress-presumptive by the

Mary of Modena's crown adapted for his use by the removal of one of the arches.

For the first three years of the new reign the Prince of Wales attended cabinet and Privy Council meetings, acting as his father's interpreter where necessary, but in 1717 a rift occurred between the King and the Prince and Princess of Wales, who withdrew themselves from court early in 1718. The quarrel was precipitated by a disagreement over the choice of godparents for the Prince and Princess's short-lived son George William, and soon grew out of proportion. The Prince and Princess moved out of St James's Palace into Leicester House, Leicester Square, which became their chief residence until their succession. Relations between the two courts thus established remained uneasy for the rest of George I's reign.

George II's reign was a time of great prosperity for the country both at home and abroad. Peace with Spain was concluded in 1729, but infractions of the Treaty of Seville and encroachments on foreign trade led to war being declared again in 1739. Admiral Vernon was sent with a squadron to the West Indies and demolished Portobello but failed to take Cartagena. In 1743, George himself took the field, the last British monarch to do so, and led his army on the Continent, where the French were beaten in the battle of Dettingen. In the Jacobite rising of 1745, 'Bonnie Prince Charlie', a more forceful and attractive character than his father 'The Old Pretender', marched as far south as Derby. This rebellion was put down with great severity by George's son, the Duke of Cumberland, who thereby earned himself the unenviable nickname of 'Butcher Cumberland'. The Continental war was ended by the Treaty of Aix-la-Chapelle in 1748. War with France broke out again in 1755 and did not go well until William Pitt (later Earl of Chatham) took over the administration and concluded treaties with Prussia. A series of victories in 1759 destroyed French power in the East Indies and led to the conquest of Canada and the capture of Guadaloupe and Senegal. The British Empire was beginning to take shape.

By now the House of Hanover had gained a measure of popularity and support and the earliest version of what was to become our national anthem, 'God Save Great George Our King', was first heard when George attended a gala performance of the theatre to celebrate one of Britain's victories.

George had lost his queen in 1737 and his eldest son, Frederick, Prince of Wales in 1751. On 25 October 1760 he rose as usual and breakfasted on the inevitable cup of chocolate. After enquiring about the direction of the wind, being anxious for the arrival of his overseas mail, he entered his water-closet. A few minutes later his valet heard a crash and found the King lying on the floor. He was lifted on to his bed and asked 'in a faint voice' for his favourite daughter, Princess Amelia, but before she reached him he was dead. A post mortem revealed the cause of death as a ruptured aneurism of the aorta.

George II was a small man of delicate build and majestic carriage. He was inordinately proud of his 'fine foot', which we can see him showing off in the coronation portrait from the studio of Charles Jervas now in the National Portrait Gallery. He had the protuberant blue eyes and pink and white complexion which were characteristic of the House of Hanover. Like his father, he had little interest in the arts and deprecated all 'boets and bainters', but he had a taste for music and continued the royal patronage of Handel. Indeed, he is said to have been so moved on hearing the 'Hallelujah Chorus' in *The Messiah* that he spontaneously rose to his feet, starting the custom which has been observed ever since whenever that great work is performed.

Caroline of Ansbach

Born:	Ansbach 1 March 1683
Married:	Herrenhausen 22 August/1 September 1705
Crowned:	Westminster Abbey 11 October 1727
Died:	St James's Palace 25 November/ 1 December 1737
Buried:	Westminster Abbey

The child who was to become our most politically astute queen consort was born into the small German court of Ansbach on 1 March 1683. Caroline's father died when she was only three and in 1692 her widowed mother married the Elector of Saxony and took her with her to Dresden. There were some plans for her to marry Duke Frederick II of Saxe-Gotha, whose daughter Augusta was later to become Caroline's daughter-in-law, but nothing came of them. After her mother's death in September 1696 Caroline became a ward of the King and Queen of Prussia and went to live in Berlin. There she became acquainted with the Queen's Hanoverian family, including her mother the Electress Sophia.

A grandiose scheme for Caroline's marriage to the future Emperor Charles VI came to nought because of her staunch Protestantism – Vienna was not worth a mass to Caroline. She returned to Ansbach in 1704. The Electress Sophia had marked her down as a suitable wife for her grandson George Augustus and, the necessary negotiations being satisfactorily concluded, they were married at Herrenhausen in 1705. The young couple were very well suited in every way and the marriage was a happy one from the start. In anticipation of being called to the British throne Caroline began to learn English, and was to become fluent in the language although she always preferred to write in French.

Caroline of Ansbach as Princess of Wales, after Kneller. This portrait depicts her as she would have appeared at the coronation of her father-in-law George I. The single-arched crown on which she rests her hand must have been made for her for the occasion as her husband wore Mary of Modena's crown, suitably adapted.

When George I ascended the throne in 1714, Caroline accompanied her husband and father-in-law to England and, in the absence of a queen, occupied the position of first lady of the land as Princess of Wales. Four children had been born to her in Hanover and the stillbirth of her fifth child at St James's Palace in November 1716 was attributed by Caroline and her German ladies to the insistence of the English doctors on using instruments contrary to the natural childbirth methods in vogue in Germany. Four more children were to be born in England. Caroline loyally supported her husband in his quarrel with his father, which resulted in their withdrawal from the King's court and the setting up of a separate establishment at Leicester House and Richmond Lodge.

The death of the King in 1727 brought George and Caroline to the throne, and, although she remained more German than English in outlook and temperament all her life, she was to play a greater role in affairs of state than any other queen consort since the Middle Ages. She gave her unqualified support to Robert Walpole and was to find a great mentor in all political matters in the person of Lord Hervey, who sat as Whig MP for Bury St Edmunds for eight years and held the office of Vice-Chamberlain of the Household for ten.

Caroline's control of affairs was acknowledged by the witty couplet:

You may strut, dapper George, but 't'will all be in vain,
We know 'tis Queen Caroline, not you, that reign.

The Music Party, by Philip Mercier, painted in 1733. A delightful group depicting Frederick, Prince of Wales and his sisters, the Princesses Anne, Caroline and Amelia in the grounds of Kew Palace, which can be seen in the background.

The Queen wisely flattered George's vanity and connived at his affairs, particularly that with her Bedchamber Woman, Mrs Howard, later Countess of Suffolk, with whom she remained on the best possible terms. George was well content to allow Caroline to run things and she acted as regent during his absences in Hanover.

Caroline had sustained an umbilical rupture at the birth of her last child in 1724 and, doubtless fearing the crude medical practices of the day, made light of the matter for many years until the condition became acute in 1737 and surgical intervention of some sort became imperative. There was of course no anaesthetic, and while the surgeons prodded and probed the Queen's body she had to beg them to desist for a moment when she was overcome with laughter at the sight of a smouldering wig on the head of a surgeon who had bent over her in too close proximity to a candle. The operation was hopeless, gangrene set in and all hope of saving the Queen's life was abandoned.

As Caroline lay dying she begged her weeping husband to marry again after her death. 'Never, never',

he sobbed, 'I shall only have mistresses.' He was true to his word. Caroline was the love of his life and he left instructions that on his own death the side boards of their coffins were to be removed and the two joined together so that their bones might mingle. These orders were carried out and, years later, those whose business it was to enter the royal vault beneath Henry VII's Chapel were to describe the two discarded coffin sides neatly leaning against a wall.

The only flaw in Caroline's character seems to have been her complete detestation of her eldest son, whom she was to describe as 'the greatest ass, and the greatest liar' that ever lived. In this matter George and Caroline repeated the pattern of George I's behaviour towards them, continuing a trend which was to last in greater or lesser degree for two centuries.

GEORGE III   1760–1820

Born:	Norfolk House, St James's Square, London 4 June 1738
Acceded:	25 October 1760
Crowned:	Westminster Abbey 22 September 1761
Married:	St James's Palace 8 September 1761, (Sophia) Charlotte, fifth and youngest daughter of Duke Charles Louis Frederick of Mecklenburg-Strelitz and Elizabeth Albertine of Saxe- Hildburghausen

Children:

(1) George Augustus Frederick, later King George IV

(2) Frederick, Duke of York: *b.* St James's Palace 16 August 1763; *d.* Rutland House, Arlington Street, London 5 January 1827; *m.* Berlin 29 September and London 24 November 1791, Frederica Charlotte Ulrica Catherine (*b.* Charlottenburg 7 May 1767; *d.* Oatlands Park, Weybridge, Surrey 6 August 1820), daughter of Frederick William II, King of Prussia, and his first wife Elizabeth Christina of Brunswick-Wolfenbüttel; no issue

(3) William Henry, later King William IV

(4) Charlotte Augusta Matilda, Princess Royal: *b.* Buckingham House, St James's Park, London 29 September 1766; *d.* Ludwigsburg 6 October 1828; *m.* Chapel Royal, St James's Palace 18 May 1797, Frederick I, King of Württemberg

(5) Edward, Duke of Kent: *b.* Buckingham House 2 November 1767; *d.* Sidmouth, Devon 23 January 1820; *m.* Coburg 29 May and Kew Palace 11 July 1818, Victoria Mary Louisa (*b.* Coburg 17 August 1786; *d.* Frogmore House, Windsor 16 March 1861), widow of Emich Charles, 2nd Prince of Leiningen, and fourth daughter of Francis Frederick Anthony, Duke of Saxe-Coburg-Saalfeld, and Augusta Reuss-Ebersdorf
Child: Alexandrina Victoria, later Queen Victoria

(6) Augusta Sophia: *b.* Buckingham House 8 November 1768; *d.* Clarence House, St James's 22 September 1840

(7) Elizabeth: *b.* Buckingham House 22 May 1770; *d.* Frankfurt-am-Main 10 January 1840; *m.* Buckingham House 7 April 1818, Frederick VI, Landgrave of Hesse-Homburg

(8) Ernest Augustus, Duke of Cumberland, later (1837) King of Hanover: *b.* Buckingham House 5 June 1771; *d.* Herrenhausen 18 November 1851; *m.* Neustrelitz 29 May and Carlton House, London 29 August 1815, Frederica Caroline Sophia Alexandrina (*b.* Hanover 2 March 1778; *d.* there 29 June 1841), widow of Prince Frederick William of Solms-Braunfels and previously of Prince Louis of Prussia, and fifth daughter of Charles, Grand Duke of Mecklenburg-Strelitz and his first wife Frederica of Hesse-Darmstadt; had issue

(9) Augustus Frederick, Duke of Sussex: *b.* Buckingham House 27 January 1773; *d.* Kensington Palace 21 April 1843; *m.* twice in contravention of the Royal Marriages Act

(10) Adolphus Frederick, Duke of Cambridge: *b.* Buckingham House 24 February 1774; *d.* Cambridge House, Piccadilly, London 8 July 1850; *m.* Cassel 7 May and Buckingham House 1 June 1818, Augusta Wilhelmina Louisa (*b.* Rumpenheim 25 July 1797; *d.* St James's Palace, 6 April 1889), third daughter of Landgrave Frederick of Hesse-Cassel and Caroline Polyxene of Nassau-Üsingen; had issue

(11) Mary: *b.* Buckingham House 25 April 1776; *d.* Gloucester House, Piccadilly, London 30 April 1857; *m.* Buckingham House 22 July 1816, Prince William Frederick, 2nd Duke of Gloucester

(12) Sophia: *b.* Buckingham House 3 November 1777; *d.* Vicarage Place, Kensington 27 May 1848

(13) Octavius: *b.* Buckingham House 23 February 1779; *d.* Kew Palace 3 May 1783

(14) Alfred: *b.* Windsor Castle 22 September 1780; *d.* there 20 August 1782

(15) Amelia: *b.* Royal Lodge, Windsor 7 August 1783; *d.* Augusta Lodge, Windsor 2 November 1810

Died:	Windsor Castle 29 January 1820
Buried:	St George's Chapel, Windsor

George III, Queen Charlotte and their six eldest children painted by John Zoffany in 1770. The future George IV and Frederick, Duke of York stand together to the left, while the future William IV plays with a cockatoo. This picture is in the Royal Collection.

George III was to declare at his first opening of Parliament that he 'gloried in the name of Briton', referring to his birth as the first British-born monarch since Anne. In spite of his German antecedents he was the epitome of all that we consider British and a living example of the triumph of environment over heredity.

George was born at Norfolk House, St James's, on 4 June 1738, at a time when his parents were estranged from King George II. On the death of his father Frederick, Prince of Wales, in 1751, George's education was entrusted to Lord Harcourt and the Bishop of Norwich, though his mother Augusta was to play a big part in the formation of his mind and character. He succeeded his grandfather George II in October 1760 at a time when the country was enjoying a high peak of prosperity. An early event of the reign was the appointment of the Earl of Bute, a favourite of the King's mother, as Prime Minister.

The young King possessed the strong sex drive common to many of the House of Hanover, but he also had strong moral principles which inhibited him from finding relief with a mistress, so he was determined to marry as soon as possible. His interest was aroused by Lady Sarah Lennox, but realizing the unsuitability of the match he set his sights elsewhere and finally decided on an obscure little German Princess, Charlotte of Mecklenburg-Strelitz. It was to prove an excellent choice. The Princess arrived in time to marry the King and be crowned with him. This was to be the last coronation of a British sovereign who also claimed to be

King of France and, in accordance with an established custom, two actors were hired to personate the Dukes of Normandy and Aquitaine at the ceremony. An eye-witness was much amused by the jaunty way in which these two gentlemen clapped on their caps of maintenance at the moment when the King was crowned and the peers donned their coronets. On leaving the Abbey a large jewel fell from its setting in George's crown and the superstitious were later to point to this as an omen foretelling of the loss of the American colonies.

George was a man of very simple habits and tastes and he and Queen Charlotte adopted a lifestyle far more akin to that of the rising middle class than to that of the nobility and gentry. This way of life has been largely maintained by the royal family ever since, with one or two notable exceptions. Their preferred residences were Kew or Windsor, and in 1762 George bought Buckingham House in St James's Park for £21,000 from Sir Charles Sheffield. Buckingham House, sometimes referred to as the Queen's House, was to become Buckingham Palace.

Early in 1764 the King suffered the first attack of an illness which we now know to have been porphyria, the 'royal malady' to which reference has already been made several times. On recovering from this attack he proposed that Parliament should legislate an act enabling him to appoint the Queen, or some other member of the royal family, guardian to the heir apparent and regent of the kingdom if the necessity arose. The bill was passed but met with a considerable amount of opposition leading to a change of ministry.

The King was anxious to break the power of the Whig oligarchy which ruled the country under the first two Georges and created his own party of 'King's Friends'. Through them he was able to manipulate affairs and effected frequent changes of ministry. He finally appointed his own minister, Lord North, in 1770.

The marriages of two of the King's brothers to ladies he considered entirely unsuitable led to the passing of the Royal Marriages Act in 1772. This provided that no descendant of King George II under the age of twenty-five (with the exception of the descendants of princesses married into foreign families) might contract matrimony without first obtaining the consent of the sovereign in council. Over the age of twenty-five, those wishing to marry without obtaining this consent were obliged to give notice of their intention to do so to the Privy Council. They would then be free to marry after a year had elapsed provided no objection had been raised by either House of Parliament. The Act was to give rise to some strange situations affecting George's sons and grandsons. It is still in force but it can be legally argued that it is no longer operative as there are no persons now covered by its provisions, the loose wording of the Act ensuring that there are now no persons to whom it might apply who are not exempted by descent from a princess married into a foreign family.

The American War of Independence was a great blow to the King and in 1789 he suffered a second attack of porphyria. This time it was more serious and he was badly deranged from November to the following February. Fanny Burney has left a graphic account of some of his delusions and on one memorable occasion she was chased by him at Windsor. A characteristic of the illness was that the King would become extremely agitated, uttering staccato shouts of 'What! What! What!' He made a full recovery, however, and on St George's Day 1790 went in state with the Queen and royal family to St Paul's to return thanks for his deliverance.

The French Revolution was a further cause for concern, and in the 1790s there were several attempts on the King's life. On 15 May 1798 he was attending a review in Hyde Park when a gentleman standing by him was wounded by a musket-ball, whether by accident or by design there is no knowing. The incident caused the King's attendants to try to dissuade him from visiting Drury Lane Theatre that evening. He refused to listen to them and, accompanied by the Queen and some of their daughters, went to the theatre. A moment after he had entered the royal box a man in the pit fired at him but a person near the would-be assassin was able to deflect his aim so that the bullet missed the King and lodged in the roof of the box. George remained quite calm and turned to the Queen and Princesses who were just entering the box, saying 'Keep back, keep back; they are firing squibs for diversion, and perhaps there may be more.' The loyalty of the audience at this display of firmness was manifested by prolonged cheering and the singing of 'God Save the King!' three times, with the addition of an impromptu verse hastily penned by Sheridan:

> From every latent foe,
> From the assassin's blow,
> God Save the King!
> O'er him thine arm extend,
> For Britain's sake defend,
> Our father, prince and friend;
> God Save the King!

The would-be assassin was indicted for high treason but found to be of unsound mind and committed to Bedlam.

The last ten years of George's active reign were dominated by the Napoleonic wars in Europe and the threat of invasion. The King entered the fiftieth year of his reign on 25 October 1809 and a Jubilee was held. His eyesight was beginning to fail and the death of his youngest daughter Princess Amelia from consumption at the end of 1810 precipitated his last attack of insanity. This time there was to be no recovery. The Regency Act was passed and on 11 February 1811 the Prince of Wales was proclaimed Prince Regent of the United Kingdom. George passed the last years of his life at Windsor, blind, deaf and mad. His beard was allowed to grow and the patriarchal figure was sometimes to be glimpsed staring with sightless eyes from a window of the Castle. He was unaware of the death of the Queen in November 1818 and under the care of his second son, the Duke of York, lived on until 29 January 1820, when he died, having lived longer than any previous sovereign.

There is something very engaging about George's character. He inherited the family love of music and was also a patron of the arts and sciences, his books forming the nucleus of the future British Library. He had, however, a healthy contempt for Shakespeare ('Was there ever such *stuff* as this Shakespeare, Miss Burney? Only one must not say so, what! what!'). He took a keen interest in agriculture and his creation of model farms at Windsor earned him the nickname of 'Farmer George', which he greatly relished.

Charlotte of Mecklenburg-Strelitz

Born: Mirow 19 May 1744
Married: St James's Palace 8 September 1761
Crowned: Westminster Abbey 22 September 1761
Died: Kew Palace 17 November 1818
Buried: St George's Chapel, Windsor

The monkey-faced little Princess who was to become George III's queen had the distinction of belonging to the only German reigning family to possess a non-German origin. The Ducal House of Mecklenburg was descended from the Slavonic Niklot, Prince of the Obotrites, who died in 1160 and whose descendants obtained Mecklenburg and other territories in northern Germany from the Holy Roman Emperors. Charlotte's father was a brother of the reigning Duke of Mecklenburg-Strelitz and she was born at Mirow on 19 May 1744. The story of her writing to Frederick the Great of Prussia and the publication of the letter first bringing her to the notice of George III has been proved apocryphal. George began to cast around for a suitable bride very soon after his accession and it was after his initial overtures to Lady Sarah Lennox had been set aside that his choice fell on the Mecklenburg Princess. It seems highly probable that his mother had a good deal to do with the choice.

Once the marriage had been agreed the Princess set out for England. On the voyage she practised playing 'God Save the King!' on her harpsichord while most of her attendants were prostrate with seasickness. The marriage took place at St James's Palace on 8 September 1761 and the coronation followed a fortnight later. It

Queen Charlotte painted at Frogmore in 1796 by Sir William Beechey. Her resemblance to her great-granddaughter Queen Mary is apparent in this portrait.

says a lot for the character of the seventeen-year-old girl that she was able to conduct herself with perfect equanimity in the exalted position in which she found herself, far from home and surrounded by strangers.

George and Charlotte settled down to a comfortable married life and were quite content with each other. George, if not handsome, was tolerably good-looking and had the fresh complexion and blue eyes characteristic of the Hanoverians, while Charlotte's monkey face had a certain appeal which is apparent in her portraits. The couple produced fifteen handsome children, only two of whom died young, and Gainsborough's portraits of them together show them to be a family of which their parents could be justly proud.

The life led by the King and Queen was simple in the extreme and almost the only disruptions in their routine were caused by George's attacks of illness, which sorely worried poor Charlotte. The Queen's life was tranquil and uneventful although she lived through stirring times. She exercised little political influence and was only interested in domestic matters.

When the King finally lapsed into insanity the Queen was given the custody of his person but could seldom bring herself to see him. The death of her grand-daughter, Princess Charlotte, a year before her own was a great blow to her, especially as she was staying in Bath when it occurred and received some criticism for not being on the spot, though how her presence could have helped matters it is difficult to see. She became immensely stout in her old age, which caused an unkind observer to remark that she looked as if she were carrying all her fifteen children at once.

The Queen was able to preside at the weddings of her sons at Kew Palace during the last year of her life, but her health was failing fast and she died on 17 November 1818, seated in a small armchair (still to be seen in Kew Palace), with her hand in that of her son, the Regent.

GEORGE IV   1820–1830

Born:	St James's Palace 12 August 1762
Prince Regent:	5 February 1811
Acceded:	29 January 1820
Crowned:	Westminster Abbey 19 July 1821
Married:	Chapel Royal, St James's 8 April 1795, Caroline Amelia Elizabeth, daughter of Charles William Ferdinand, Duke of Brunswick, and Princess Augusta, eldest daughter of Frederick, Prince of Wales
Child:	Charlotte Augusta: *b.* Carlton House 7 January 1796; *d.* Claremont House, Esher, Surrey 6 November 1817; *m.* Carlton House 2 May 1816, Prince Leopold George Frederick of Saxe-Coburg-Saalfeld, later Leopold I, King of the Belgians; no live issue
Died:	Windsor Castle 26 June 1830
Buried:	St George's Chapel, Windsor

George IV was a cross between Nero and Toad of Toad Hall. He possessed Nero's flair for showmanship without his viciousness and all Toad's affability and amiable egocentricity. To compare him thus to real and fictional characters is very apposite, for George was often to indulge in flights of fancy which left the real world far behind. A good instance is the way in which he was able to delude himself that he had actually been present and led a charge at the Battle of Waterloo. He was wont to describe his imaginary exploits in graphic detail at the annual Waterloo Banquet held at Apsley House. On one such occasion, perceiving that his listeners appeared to doubt his word, he called to the Duke of Wellington for confirmation: 'Is that not so, Duke?' 'I have often heard Your Majesty say so', was the tactful reply.

The first child of King George III and Queen Charlotte was born at St James's Palace on 12 August 1762 and created Prince of Wales and Earl of Chester five days later. Like all his parents' children he was endowed with outstanding good looks, fair hair, blue eyes and a pink and white complexion, although a tendency to corpulence was to become more pronounced in later life, aided by indulgence in food and drink and lack of exercise. George was very close to his next brother Frederick, and the two boys shared an upbringing and education in the privacy of Kew Palace. Their preceptor was Dr William Markham (later Archbishop of York), assisted as sub-preceptor by Dr Cyril Jackson (later Dean of Christ Church, Oxford). In 1776 these gentlemen were replaced by Dr Richard Hurd, Bishop of Lichfield and Coventry (and later of Worcester) and Mr Arnold, of St John's College, Cambridge. George learnt easily and acquired a good grounding in literature and science. As he grew up, his good looks, high spirits and agreeable manners were to

George IV striking an heroic pose, from the studio of Thomas Lawrence.

The coronation banquet of George IV by George Jones.

earn him considerable popularity and make him the darling of the fashionable world.

Up to his eighteenth year the Prince met few people apart from his family circle and his tutors, but he then began to associate with the members of the Whig nobility and formed political connections with Lord Moira, Fox, Sheridan, and others. He also possessed the strong sex drive of the Hanoverians and developed a penchant for amply proportioned ladies somewhat older than himself. His first mistress was the actress Mrs Robinson, whom he first saw in the role of Perdita in Shakespeare's *Winter's Tale* in 1778, when she was twenty and he sixteen. She was very beautiful, as her portraits by Reynolds, Gainsborough, Romney and other artists testify, but George soon deserted her and embarked on a series of love affairs.

On coming of age in 1783, George set up his own establishment at Carlton House, was voted £30,000 by Parliament to pay his debts, and received an annual allowance of £50,000 from his father. About this time he met and fell in love with a respectable Roman Catholic widow of twenty-seven. Mary Anne (or Maria, as she was usually known) was the daughter of Mr Walter Smythe of Brambridge in Hampshire, the scion of a baronet's family, and had been married successively to Edward Weld of Lulworth Castle, Dorset, and Thomas Fitzherbert of Norbury, Derbyshire, and Swynnerton, Staffordshire, both of whom had died leaving her childless. George's passion for her knew no bounds, but the only way he could get her was by marriage. Consequently, on 21 December 1785, a ceremony was performed at the lady's house in London. The marriage was null and void in law as it contravened the terms of the Royal Marriages Act. Had it not been illegal, George, as the husband of a Roman Catholic, would have lost his position as heir to the throne under the terms of the Act of Settlement. Rumours of the Prince's marriage were soon all over London, and he took the step of getting his friend Charles James Fox to deny it in the House of Commons.

His lavish outlay in the building and furbishing of Carlton House had again involved him in debts, this time amounting to more than £250,000, and, after several fruitless attempts to raise funds, he applied to the King, who refused him any aid. There was nothing for it but for George to adopt a system of retrenchment, and he sold off his stud of race horses, dismissed many of his servants, and announced his intention of living in retirement until he had liquidated his debt. The good impression this created paid off. The King agreed to add £10,000 per annum to his son's income out of the civil list and Parliament voted a further sum of £161,000 to satisfy his creditors and £20,000 for the completion of Carlton House. George's immediate reaction was to plunge into a new round of extravagance. He began the construction of the Brighton Pavilion at the watering-place on the south coast which he had made fashionable by his visits. This fantastic palace, Indian in style on the outside and an extravaganza of Chinoiserie within, still delights the thousands who pass through it annually to gaze on the splendours created at the behest of England's most artistically gifted sovereign.

George III's first prolonged attack of madness in 1788

This section takes us from Georgian days to the present. Among the pictures included we see George III in his coronation robes, Queen Elizabeth II riding on an elephant, and the investiture and marriage of the Prince of Wales.

Allan Ramsay's magnificent coronation portrait of the young George III (**facing page, top left**) contrasts strangely with the gross Gillray caricature of his son the Prince Regent (**top right**), who could, however, cut an equally regal figure when occasion demanded as can be seen from the contemporary print (**below**) of his coronation procession in 1821. Here the newly crowned King is walking under a canopy of cloth of gold from the Abbey to Westminster Hall for the coronation banquet.

George IV's coronation was probably the most magnificent ever staged in this country and the King gave full reign to his love of splendour and sense of showmanship. It was the last occasion on which this foot procession took place, headed by the 'King's Herb-woman' and her attendants strewing sweet-smelling herbs in the royal path. The King walked slightly ahead of the canopy in order that he might be seen by as many people as possible and was at his most graciously affable. Earlier in the day the pathetic attempts of Queen Caroline to gain admittance to the Abbey had threatened to mar the arrangements, but she was finally induced to give them up. The King's Champion made his last appearance as such at George's coronation and his horse created an amusing diversion by insisting on entering Westminster Hall backwards instead of backing away from the royal presence as it had been trained to do. The cost of the ceremony was so great that rigid economies were called for at the next coronation and the banquet was omitted, never to be revived subsequently.

A VOLUPTUARY under the horrors of Digestion.

Above, Queen Victoria passing beneath a triumphal arch during a visit to Brighton made early in her reign.

Right, Balmoral Castle, Queen Victoria's beloved 'home in the Highlands', which she and the Prince Consort created together, completely rebuilding the castle after buying the estate in 1852. Everything was in high Victorian taste and tartan carpets, curtains and upholstery adorned many of the rooms. After her widowhood, Queen Victoria used to spend a third of each year at the castle and it has remained the favourite summer residence of the Royal Family.

Opposite
Above, the King's bedroom in the Royal Pavilion at Brighton, a good example of the Chinese taste which prevails throughout George IV's exotic marine palace.
Below, Kensington Palace as it was in the early nineteenth century. Queen Victoria was born here and it was her principal residence until she ascended the throne. Its later division into apartments for the accommodation of sundry members of the Royal Family led the Duke of Windsor, when Prince of Wales, to christen it 'the aunt heap'. Above, Queen Victoria passing under a triumphal arch.

Left, King George VI working in his study at Buckingham Palace. **Below,** Queen Elizabeth II's coronation procession passing through Hyde Park. The richly carved and gilded state coach, which weighs four tons and needs eight horses to pull, was built for King George III and first used by him at the opening of Parliament in 1765. The allegorical panels were painted by Giovanni Battista Cipriani. It has been used at all coronations from that of George IV onwards and until the Second World War for state openings of Parliament. It was last used by the Queen when she drove to St Paul's Cathedral for her Silver Jubilee Service in 1977.

Above, the Royal Family on the balcony of Buckingham Palace watching the fly past following the annual parade on the Queen's official birthday in June. Left to right, Prince Philip, the Queen, Princess Michael of Kent, the Prince of Wales and the Princess of Wales. In front, Peter Phillips (son of Princess Anne) and Lord Frederick Windsor (son of Prince and Princess Michael of Kent).

Left, the Queen and Prince Philip descending the steps of St George's Chapel, Windsor after a service of the Order of the Garter. They are followed by Queen Elizabeth the Queen Mother (obscured) and the Prince of Wales and the steps are lined by the Knights Companion in their kingfisher blue mantles.

Below, the Queen and Prince Philip driving to the state opening of Parliament in the Irish State Coach, built for Queen Victoria's visit to Dublin in 1900. It is now used for state openings, royal weddings, and occasionally for state visits by foreign heads of state.

The Investiture of the Prince of Wales at Caernarvon Castle on 1 July 1969. Prince Charles is here seen rendering homage to his mother the Queen. Those peers who attended the ceremony in an official capacity wore their parliamentary robes and the late Duke of Norfolk can be discerned at the bottom right hand corner.

The Queen riding on an elephant during one of her visits to India.

Group taken at Buckingham Palace to mark the 80th birthday celebrations of HM Queen Elizabeth the Queen Mother in 1980. Seated (left to right), Princess Margaret, the Queen, the Queen Mother, Princess Anne. Standing (left to right), Lord Linley, Lady Sarah Armstrong-Jones, Prince Andrew, Prince Philip, the Prince of Wales, Prince Edward, Captain Mark Phillips.

The Prince and Princess of Wales begin the march down the aisle after their wedding in St Paul's Cathedral on 29 July 1981. They are followed by the chief bridesmaid, Lady Sarah Armstrong-Jones, and the other bridal attendants await them below the steps leading to the choir.

The Queen leaving St George's Chapel, Windsor after the Garter Service. The Garter Service is usually held in June on the Monday of Ascot Week. The Knights of the Order in their robes precede their sovereign on foot in the procession to St George's, and are themselves preceded by the Military Knights of Windsor (originally the "Poor Knights", who were paid to attend mass on behalf of the Knights who were absent for some reason), the Honourable Corps of Gentlemen-at-Arms and the members of the College of Arms in their tabards. It is an impressive sight. Any new Knights who have been appointed to the Order are installed in the course of the service and at its conclusion the Queen and Prince Philip with other members of the Royal Family return to the Castle in small open carriages drawn by the famous Windsor Greys. This photograph affords a fine view of the west end of St George's Chapel which was built in the reign of Edward IV, who is buried in the Chapel together with many other Kings and Queens.

brought the question of the Prince of Wales's possible regency to the fore, and caused him to intrigue with the Lord Chancellor Thurlow and Lord Loughborough against the Queen and Pitt. The King's recovery in 1789 put an end to the matter.

Pressures were now being put on George to marry. He had temporarily deserted Mrs Fitzherbert for the Countess of Jersey, 'the worst and most dangerous of profligate women', as she was to be described in an anonymous letter sent to the Duchess of Brunswick. She was the most mature of his mistresses to date, nine years his senior and already a grandmother at forty-one. In 1794 George's creditors were pressing again and the conditional promise of a settlement, together with an increase of income, led him to announce that he was ready to marry his cousin Princess Caroline of Brunswick. The Earl of Malmesbury was despatched to Brunswick to negotiate with the ducal family and escort the Princess back to England. They arrived on 5 April 1795 but the first meeting between George and Caroline was disastrous. George was a fastidious man and the first encounter with this badly groomed girl, who was not over-fond of washing, revolted him. 'Harris, I am not well; pray get me a glass of brandy', was the Prince's first utterance to Malmesbury, whereupon he promptly left the room. 'Mon dieu!', said Caroline, 'Is the Prince always like that? I find him very fat, and nothing like as handsome as his portrait.' Nevertheless the marriage took place at the Chapel Royal, St James's on 8 April 1795 and George only got through the ceremony by being drunk. In fact he was so far gone that at one stage he rose from his knees and began to wander about, having to be led back to his place by the King. He spent his wedding-night lying drunk in the grate, as Caroline was to relate later, but he had managed to consummate the marriage and from that one act of intercourse (for they were never to sleep together again) Caroline conceived and bore Princess Charlotte nine months later.

The Princess of Wales had been obliged to accept Lady Jersey as a Lady of the Bedchamber and was soon to learn of the circumstances which had led to her unhappy marriage. After Princess Charlotte's birth George sent her proposals for a separation, to which she readily acceded. In 1804 there was a dispute over the custody of Princess Charlotte which was settled by the King undertaking her guardianship. George now returned to Mrs Fitzherbert, but continued to be distracted by the mature charms of other ladies from time to time.

The threat of invasion by Napoleon led George, then only the colonel of a regiment of dragoons while the Duke of York was Commander-in-Chief and some of his other brothers were generals, to demand to be given a higher position in the army but the ministry coolly declined his request.

The deterioration in the King's mental health now led

to new proposals for a regency and, after negotiations with the Whigs, George was persuaded by his current mistress, Lady Hertford, to agree to a restricted regency, being proclaimed Prince Regent of the United Kingdom on 5 February 1811. The Regency saw the final defeat of Napoleon and gave George a chance to indulge his love of display by lavishly entertaining the Emperor of Russia, the King of Prussia, and other allied sovereigns when they visited England in the course of their triumphant victory progress.

George's only daughter, Princess Charlotte, was married in May 1816 to Prince Leopold of Saxe-Coburg-Saalfeld. The young couple were blissfully happy and were given Claremont House near Esher in Surrey as a residence. Charlotte suffered two miscarriages but a third pregnancy lasted the full term. The Princess had a long and difficult labour ending in the delivery of a stillborn son, 'as like the royal family as could be', on 5 November 1817. The mismanagement of the accouchement by the Princess's physician (who subsequently committed suicide) led to her death from haemorrhage and shock the following morning. She had been liberally dosed with brandy and almost her last words were 'They have made me tipsy.' His daughter's death plunged George into a paroxysm of grief, partly occasioned by a guilty conscience, no doubt, as he had not always treated her with kindness or consideration, his violent dislike of her mother being extended in some measure to his child. He was not by nature an unkind man and his treatment of both Caroline and Charlotte was uncharacteristic. The Princess's death meant that there were now no legitimate heirs to the throne in the second generation, and George's unmarried brothers, the Dukes of Clarence, Kent, and Cambridge, hastily sought brides to provide for the succession.

The general unrest felt throughout the country in the aftermath of the Napoleonic wars caused the outbreak of very serious riots in the large manufacturing towns. In London a few desperate men, later to be known as the Cato Street Conspirators, were tried and executed for plotting to assassinate the Regent and the leading members of the administration.

The death of George III on 29 January 1820 brought the Regent to the throne as George IV. Almost his first concern was to find a way to prevent his estranged wife, who had been living abroad for some years, from returning to England to take up her position as Queen. Failing in this, he forced his ministers to introduce a 'Bill of Pains and Penalities' to deprive her of the title of Queen and effectively dissolved the marriage. The so-called 'trial of Queen Caroline' followed in the House of Lords, ending with the Bill being dropped after its third reading on 10 November 1820.

George, as was only to be expected, spent much time and thought in planning the details of his coronation.

As a result it was probably the most magnificent ever staged in this country, and it was the last at which the sovereign proceeded on foot from Westminster Hall to the Abbey and then back again for the banquet. The ceremony was marred by the pathetic attempts of Queen Caroline to gain entrance to the Abbey, no provision having been made for her to be crowned or even to witness the spectacle. For her it was the last straw and she died a few weeks later.

In August 1821 the King visited Ireland; in September he went to Hanover; and in 1822 he went to Scotland, the first Hanoverian monarch to set foot there. The event was largely stage-managed by Sir Walter Scott and was a great success. George wore the kilt and displayed the graciousness and affability for which he was never at a loss. The reign was to see many changes of ministry, and the most important events towards its end was the Catholic Emancipation Act, passed in April 1829 after George had done his best to block it.

The King suffered a great deal from gout in his later years and divided his time between Brighton and Windsor, living very quietly with his last mistress, Lady Conyngham. His final illness began in January 1830 with a severe cough, and although there was a slight improvement in March, respiratory trouble persisted, complicated by pain in the urinary tract and faintness. He rode in Windsor Great Park for the last time on April 12 and thereafter attacks of biliousness and difficulty in breathing became increasingly frequently. At 3.15 on the morning of 26 June he died peacefully, murmuring 'This is death' to his attendants.

Mrs Fitzherbert, whom George acknowledged as his wife in his will, refused the offer of a dukedom from William IV but proudly accepted permission to dress her servants in the royal livery colours. She died in 1837 and was buried in the Roman Catholic church in Brighton, where the figure on her monument clearly displays her three wedding rings.

Caroline of Brunswick

Born: Brunswick 17 May 1768
Married: Chapel Royal, St James's 8 April 1795
Died: Brandenburg House, Hammersmith
            7 August 1821
Buried: Brunswick

The high-spirited, ill-educated young woman who became the bride of her first cousin George, Prince of Wales, in 1795 could not have been a worse choice for him. Caroline was born at Brunswick and grew up in her parents' uncultured court. Her mother, George III's eldest sister, spent her time 'in knitting, netting, embroidery, and even the homely occupation of knitting stockings' with her ladies at her palace outside Brunswick, while the Duke lived happily in the capital, with his mistress Frau Hertzfeldt installed in the palace.

Caroline was brought up without religion, as were many princesses of that day, so that she might adopt that of her future husband. She was vivacious, wilful and witty, always seeking to gain attention and raise a laugh with her sallies, which it must be admitted were often cruelly barbed. At the age of sixteen she was forbidden to attend a ball on which she had set her heart. She retired to bed, announcing that she was pregnant, and made such a fuss that her parents sent for a midwife, whereupon Caroline jumped up crying: 'Now will you forbid me to go to a ball again?'

Caroline's elder sister had married a Duke of Württemberg (who was later to marry George III's eldest daughter) and had mysteriously disappeared in Russia, where her husband had been serving in the army. She had been unfaithful, it was rumoured, with the Grand Duke Paul, and her husband and children returned to Germany without her. Catherine the Great had her imprisoned in the Castle of Lode in the Baltic and after two years the bare news of her death was reported. The circumstances were never explained. Caroline dwelt

Queen Caroline, a portrait by Sir Thomas Lawrence painted when she was still Princess of Wales in 1804.

A contemporary print depicting Queen Caroline returning in
triumph from the House of Lords after the outcome of her 'trial'.

much on this story and years later was to relate it to her ladies-in-waiting with obvious signs of relish.

Although unfeminine in many respects and careless of her appearance and personal hygiene, Caroline had an eye for men and was alleged to have had at least one serious affair before George, Prince of Wales, asked for her hand in 1794. George's then-current mistress, Lady Jersey, became a Lady of the Bedchamber to Caroline, who on learning of the relationship indulged in a number of coarse jokes at her expense, a thing in which she excelled.

Queen Charlotte was no friend to her new daughter-in-law, whose reputation had travelled ahead of her, and almost her only friend at court was her uncle the King. Caroline was to recount many stories of the early days of her marriage, most of them grossly exaggerated or polished up for the sake of a laugh. She had become pregnant on her wedding night when, in her own words, the Prince 'passed the greatest part of his bridal night under the grate, where he fell, and where I left him.' Queen Charlotte took the keenest possible interest in the arrangements for the lying-in, supervising every

minute detail. As the mother of fifteen, she knew what she was saying when she referred to herself as 'an experienced woman in such matters'. Caroline was in labour for nine hours and gave birth to 'an *immense girl*', as George was to write, at Carlton House on the morning of 7 January 1796. The news of the birth was received with mixed feelings but the King was delighted.

Lady Jersey had become a great thorn in Caroline's flesh. Her poise, elegance and general air of sophistication contrasted with the Princess's gaucheness and probably irritated her by making her aware of her shortcomings. An acrimonious correspondence between the Prince and Princess was at its height when Lady Jersey resigned, temporarily solving the problem. In the long run, however, the situation was little eased, and in August 1797 Caroline left Carlton House and went to live at Blackheath. She rented Montague House and occupied herself by running an orphanage for nine children. She took such an interest in one of these,

William Austin, that rumours began to circulate that he was her own child. This became the subject of a 'Delicate Investigation', which completely cleared the Princess, whose spirited remark when asked outright if the boy was hers was 'Prove it, and he shall be your King!'

Caroline was denied any part in her daughter Princess Charlotte's upbringing and was only allowed to see her at infrequent intervals. In 1807 her mother, now a widow, arrived in England as a refugee from Napoleon, who had overrun the Duchy of Brunswick. Caroline let her have Montague House for a time, herself moving into apartments in Kensington Palace. In 1810 the Duchess moved to a house in Hanover Square and Caroline moved back to Blackheath, where she stayed until 1813 when, forced to economize, she moved to Connaught Place, Bayswater. Her way of life was becoming more and more eccentric and her appearance increasingly odd. This contributed to her deliberate exclusion from the celebrations surrounding the visit of the allied sovereigns, at which her daughter shone.

With the Napoleonic wars nearly at an end, Caroline sought permission to travel abroad and it was granted. She then began several years of wandering, visiting Germany, Switzerland, Italy, Tunis and Palestine. When in Milan she engaged as courier one Bartolomeo Pergami, an attractive rogue with pretensions to nobility. Very soon Caroline had appointed him her Chamberlain and accorded him the style of baron, which was attached to a small estate she bought for him in Sicily. It is clear that she was quite infatuated with him, but whether they actually became lovers is open to doubt. There are many women who enjoy the close company of a man without actually entering into a sexual relationship; Queen Victoria and John Brown are a case in point. Caroline loved to tease and to keep people guessing and once, when the question of her adultery came up, stated that she had only committed adultery once – with Mrs Fitzherbert's husband! Pergami was a married man and had Caroline taken him as her lover she would certainly have been committing adultery on that score.

While in Jerusalem Caroline amused herself by founding an order of chivalry, a thing she had no right to do. It was called the Order of St Caroline of Jerusalem and the insignia consisted of a red cross inscribed with the motto of the Order of the Garter, *Honi soit qui mal y pense*, suspended from a lilac and silver ribbon. Pergami was appointed Grand Master of the Order and the rest of her entourage, including William Austin, became Knights.

The travellers eventually returned to Italy, where Caroline bought the Villa d'Este on Lake Como and set up house. Her daughter Charlotte had been forbidden to write to her by her father, but once married was able to please herself and entered into a friendly correspondence with her mother. The news of Charlotte's death affected Caroline greatly. 'This is not only my last hope gone, but what has England lost?' she exclaimed.

On the death of George III in January 1820, Caroline suddenly found herself queen and determined to return to England to assert her rights. She was on her way to Calais when she received a proposition from the King offering her an income of £50,000 a year for life if she would agree to continue to reside abroad. She indignantly rejected this proposal and returned to England, receiving an enthusiastic reception from the majority of the people. Her arrival was stage-managed to a large extent by Sir Matthew Wood, a radical City Alderman, who saw an opportunity to further his own interests by supporting the Queen. Caroline landed at Dover on 6 June and was greeted by a royal salute of twenty-one guns from Dover Castle. Her drive to London the following day was a triumphal progress all the way. Alderman Wood was in attendance and gave many manifestations of the utmost vulgarity and bad taste.

The Bill of Pains and Penalties to enquire into Caroline's conduct and deprive her of her title was introduced in August and the Queen appeared in the House of Lords for what amounted to, and has come to be known as, her trial. She was ably defended by Mr (later Lord) Brougham, her Attorney-General, and Thomas Denman, her Solicitor-General. Caroline was treated with the utmost courtesy throughout the proceedings, which lasted until 10 November, when the vote following the third reading of the Bill resulted in a majority of only nine in favour and the Government thought it prudent to withdraw it.

Scenes of wild rejoicing lasted for three days and nights and Caroline returned to Brandenburg House, Hammersmith, loaned to her by the Margravine of Ansbach (formerly Lady Craven). On 29 November she attended a public thanksgiving service at St Paul's Cathedral, being escorted by 150 horsemen and received at Temple Bar by the Lord Mayor and Sheriffs. Her disgruntled husband was skulking in Brighton while all this went on.

George's coronation was to take place on 19 July 1821, but no provision was made for the Queen's coronation or for her participation in any part of the ceremony. Undeterred, she drove to the Abbey and demanded admittance, only to find her way barred at every door until she gave up in despair and drove back to Hammersmith. She still had enough spirit to write to the King demanding that he should agree to her being crowned 'next Monday', and having done so set off for the theatre at Drury Lane.

Caroline had suffered intermittently from bowel trouble (probably a form of colitis) for several years and was in the habit of dosing herself with calomel and laudanum to ease her pains. She felt unwell while at the theatre on the coronation evening and in a day or two had taken to her bed and sent for her physician Henry Holland, who diagnosed 'acute inflammation of the bowels', bled her and administered calomel and castor oil in 'a quantity . . . that would have turned the stomach of a horse.' Caroline rallied to receive Brougham and sign her will and almost her last words to him were: 'I am going to die, Mr Brougham, but it does not signify.' The end came on 7 August 1821 after a long night of pain.

The Queen had expressed a wish that she should not be buried in England, but in Brunswick. The funeral procession through London was the scene of a violent conflict between the Life Guards, who had been instructed to escort it through the side streets, and the people, who insisted on it passing through the main thoroughfares, and in the end they had their way.

nursemaid had to be dismissed for losing her temper with Prince William and banging his head against the wall. As his immediate elder brother Prince Frederick was destined for an army career, so William's future was to be a naval one. He went to sea at the age of fourteen, serving under Captain (later Admiral) Robert Digby on board the *Prince George*, a 98-gun ship, as an ordinary able seaman at the relief of Gibraltar in 1779. In the following year he became a midshipman but, on his father's orders, received no privileges and was treated in every respect the same as his fellows. He was present with Admiral Rodney at Cape St Vincent and was stationed in the West Indies and off Nova Scotia. He later transferred to HMS *Warwick* under the command of Captain Elphinstone (later Admiral Viscount Keith) with whom he saw action off the Delaware in 1782. He next joined Lord Hood in quest of the French fleet and became friendly with Nelson. Lord Hood's squadron

WILLIAM IV	1830–1837

Born:	Buckingham House 21 August 1765
Acceded:	26 June 1830
Crowned:	Westminster Abbey 8 September 1831
Married:	Kew Palace 11 July 1818, Adelaide Louisa Theresa Caroline Amelia, elder daughter of George I, Duke of Saxe-Meiningen and Princess Louisa Eleonora of Hohenlohe-Langenburg
Child:	(1) Charlotte Augusta Louisa: *b* (prematurely) and *d.* at the Fürstenhof, Hanover 27 March 1819
	(2) Elizabeth Georgiana Adelaide: *b.* St James's Palace 10 December 1820; *d.* there 4 March 1821
	(3) and (4) Male twins, stillborn at Bushy Park 23 April 1822
Died:	Windsor Castle 20 June 1837
Buried:	St George's Chapel, Windsor

It would be difficult not to warm to the character of a man whose first remark on being roused with the news that he had just become King was to say that he would go straight back to bed because he had never been in bed with a queen before. Such homeliness was to be the keynote of the new reign and William's down-to-earth bluffness and heartiness, tempered by Queen Adelaide's moderating influence and sweetness of character, were to mark the end of the Georgian era and set the stage for the Victorian age to come.

As the third son of King George III and Queen Charlotte, there seemed little likelihood that Prince William Henry would ever be more than a royal duke. The fast filling royal nursery was a lively place and the three noisy little boys must have been very trying; a

William IV in Garter robes, by Sir William Archer Shee.

returned to England in June 1783 and in the summer of 1785 the Prince was appointed third lieutenant of the frigate *Hebe*. In 1786, as Captain of the *Pegasus* (28 guns), he sailed for Nova Scotia and thence to the Leeward Islands station, where he remained for several months under Nelson's command. The friendship between the two deepened, and on 22 March 1787 Prince William undertook the pleasant duty of giving away the bride when Nelson married Mrs Frances Nisbet, a doctor's widow. The following December the Prince returned to England and was appointed to command the frigate *Andromeda*, in which he returned for a short time to the West Indies. Fanny Burney gives a delightful account of him at this time, describing a visit he made to his sisters when he got rather drunk and told Queen Charlotte's formidable waiting woman, Miss Schwellenberg, 'hold your potato jaw, my dear', when she remonstrated with him about his louche conduct.

Prince William had received the Order of the Garter in 1782. On 20 May 1789 he was created Duke of Clarence and St Andrews and Earl of Munster by his father and subsequently took his seat in the House of Lords. The following year he was appointed Rear Admiral of the Blue and commanded HMS *Valiant* in home waters. He was to see no more active service afloat.

It was at about this time that he formed a deep attachment for an actress called Dorothea Bland, but known professionally as 'Mrs Jordan'. Over the next twenty years she had ten children by him, whom he acknowledged and ennobled after his accession to the throne. They bore the surname FitzClarence and the eldest boy was eventually created Earl of Munster.

In 1811 William, who had been promoted to Vice Admiral in 1794 and Admiral in 1799, became Admiral of the Fleet in succession to Sir Peter Parker, and in that capacity hoisted his flag for the last time to escort Louis XVIII back to France and to receive the Emperor Alexander I of Russia and King Frederick William III of Prussia on board HMS *Impregnable*.

His happy life with Mrs Jordan ended abruptly in 1811 for reasons which have never been clear. Dorothea certainly had what would today be described as 'a drink problem' and this may well have been a contributory factor. She received an annual allowance of £4000 for the maintenance of herself and her daughters with the proviso that, should she resume her stage career, the cost of the care of the four youngest daughters and £1500 allowed for them should revert to the Duke. The shock of the separation was a great blow to Dorothea and, after an unsuccessful attempt to make a come-back on the stage, she went to France, where she suffered a complete physical and mental breakdown and died in a state of abject misery at St Cloud on 3 July 1816. William's behaviour in this matter seems little in keeping with his kindly and generous nature, although it was the sort of conduct which might have been expected from almost any of his brothers.

In November 1817 the untimely death of Princess Charlotte plunged the nation into mourning and the ageing progeny of George III into a frantic scramble to find brides and beget heirs to the throne. The Prince Regent was still married to his unloved and now childless Caroline and the Duke of York to his unloved and childless Frederica, so William, at fifty-two and the unmarried father of ten children, suddenly became one of the most eligible bachelors in Europe. For a time he assiduously courted an English heiress, Miss Sophia Elizabeth Wykeham, of Thame Park, Oxfordshire, but the Regent would not give his consent to the marriage. His eventual choice of bride was a happy one for both himself and the nation and, although the object – to provide an heir – was sadly unfulfilled, Britain gained one of the most sympathetic queens ever to wear the crown. William fell touchingly in love with his young wife, who was less than three years older than his eldest daughter, and she became devoted to him and, strangely, to her illegitimate stepchildren.

The death of George III made William second in line to the throne, and on the death of the Duke of York in 1827 he became heir-presumptive and received a parliamentary grant raising his income to £40,000 a year. He was also appointed Lord High Admiral of England, a post specially revived for him, but resigned the office after the Duke of Wellington raised objections to the expenses of William's progresses.

On 26 June 1830 George IV died and William became king. He wished at first to reign as Henry IX, but after it was pointed out to him that this style had been adopted by the Jacobite Cardinal Duke of York, who had died as recently as 1807, he agreed to become William IV. The coronation was subjected to so many government economies that it soon became lampooned and caricatured as the 'half-crownation'. The traditional processions on the raised footway from Westminster Hall to the Abbey and back again were abolished as also was the coronation banquet with the challenge by the King's Champion, never to be revived again. Queen Adelaide was obliged to provide the jewels for her own crown and other jewels had to be hired. Nevertheless, the coronation took place on 8 September 1831, almost exactly seventy years after that of the King's parents, the last king and queen to be crowned together.

William had become a garrulous old body, given to impetuous outbursts, yet he possessed some shrewd, statesmanlike instincts. The political position was fraught with difficulties. Wellington's administration was followed by that of Earl Grey, who brought in the Reform Bill. After its first rejection by the House of Lords, the King resolutely refused to create new peers to form a Whig majority but sent round a circular letter to the Tory peers, as a result of which a hundred of them abstained from voting so that the Bill became law.

The King's personal tastes were simple and he retained many of the ways and habits of an old serving officer. From time to time the newspapers published rumours that the Queen was pregnant, dismissed by the King, perhaps a little regretfully, as 'stuff and nonsense'. His heiress-presumptive was his niece Victoria, the only child of the Duke of Kent. The King was fond of her but loathed her mother, the Duchess of Kent, whom he publicly insulted in a speech he made in August 1836 at a dinner to celebrate his seventy-first birthday. He replied after his health had been drunk by saying:

I trust in God that my life may be spared for nine months longer, after which period, in the event of my death, no regency would take place. I should then have the satisfaction of leaving the royal authority to the personal exercise of that young lady [pointing to the Princess Victoria], the Heiress Presumptive of the Crown, and not in the hands of a person now near me, who is surrounded by evil advisers and who is herself incompetent to act with propriety in the station in which she would be placed. I have no hesitation in saying that I have been insulted – grossly and continually insulted – by that person, but I am now determined to endure no longer a course of behaviour so disrespectful to me. Among many other things I have particularly to complain of the manner in which that young lady has been kept away from my court: she has been repeatedly kept from my drawing-rooms at which she ought always to have been present, but I am fully resolved that this shall not happen again. I would have her know that I am King, and that I am determined to make my authority respected, and for the future I shall insist and command that the Princess do upon all occasions appear at my court, as it is her duty to do.

Consternation followed this outburst and it was only with the greatest difficulty that the Duchess of Kent was dissuaded from immediately ordering her carriage. The King's wish that his life might be spared for another nine months was granted.

In May 1837 William was reported to be suffering from asthma or hay fever, in a day or two pneumonia ensued and he died peacefully at 2.15 in the morning of 20 June 1837. A detailed description of the post-mortem findings was published in *The Lancet* and revealed cirrhosis of the liver and heart disease as contributory causes of death.

Lord Grey gave an eloquent summing-up of William's character:

A man more sincerely devoted to the interests of his country, and better understanding what was necessary for the attainment of that object, there never did exist; and if ever there was a sovereign entitled to the character, His Majesty may truly be styled a Patriot King.

Adelaide of Saxe-Meiningen

Born:	Meiningen 13 August 1792
Married:	Kew Palace 11 July 1818
Crowned:	Westminster Abbey 8 September 1831
Died:	Bentley Priory, near Stanmore, Middlesex 2 December 1849
Buried:	St George's Chapel, Windsor

Queen Adelaide has been called 'the first of the Victorians' and the designation is singularly apt for she exemplified all the best qualities which later generations have come to associate with the Victorian age.

Princess Adelaide of Saxe-Meiningen was brought up in one of the many minor German courts which existed until 1918. Her father, the reigning Duke George I, died in 1803 when she was only eleven, leaving his duchy and three young children in the very capable hands of his widow. The Duchess Louise Eleonore, who acted as regent until 1821, steered her son's heritage through the difficult times of the Napoleonic wars and ensured that her children received a good education. Adelaide was the eldest and there was a strong bond of affection between her and her sister Ida (b. 1794) and brother Bernhard (b. 1800). They led a happy but very secluded life and the family was not broken up until Ida's marriage to Prince Bernhard of Saxe-Weimar in 1816. Negotiations for Adelaide's marriage to the Duke of Clarence, in which Queen Charlotte was largely instrumental, having been successfully accomplished, some two years later she set out for England.

For a young woman who had led such a sheltered life to suddenly attain a prominent position in one of the major courts of Europe must have been a daunting experience. The wedding took place in the Queen's drawing-room at Kew Palace in the presence of Queen Charlotte, whose health was failing rapidly, and the Duke and Duchess of Kent, who had already been married in Germany, were remarried at the same time according to the Anglican rite.

The domestic life of the Duke and Duchess of Clarence was little different from that of any upper middle class couple and closely followed the pattern set by King George III and Queen Charlotte. The only remarkable thing about their household was that it was also 'home' for William's children by Mrs Jordan and later their children also. Unfortunately, Adelaide's hopes of maternity were doomed to failure. Her first baby was born prematurely in Hanover and lived but a few

Queen Adelaide, when Duchess of Clarence, a watercolour miniature by Mrs James Green, probably painted soon after Adelaide's marriage in 1818.

lived for nearly three months and then succumbed, the victim of a strangulated hernia for which there was then no surgical remedy. A further pregnancy ended in the premature birth of twin boys and no more were to follow. Adelaide's maternal instincts found an outlet in the close and loving relationships she established and maintained throughout her life with her stepchildren and stepgrandchildren, with her niece and nephew Prince Edward and Princess Louise of Saxe-Weimar (children of her sister Ida), and with William's niece Victoria, the future Queen.

After William had become King, Adelaide went through a period of personal unpopularity occasioned by her Tory sympathies and the completely unjustified belief that she interfered in politics during the agitation surrounding the passing of the Reform Bill. She also had to contend with scurrilous rumours that her Chamberlain, Lord Howe, was her lover.

On William IV's death in 1837, Adelaide became Queen Dowager, the first to bear that title since Catherine of Braganza. She received Marlborough House as her official residence with an income of £100,000 a year. Following her natural inclinations, she resumed the retired life which she preferred. Now immensely popular with the people as well as with the royal family, she made few public appearances, although she was present at Queen Victoria's wedding and also stood as godmother to the Princess Royal, who received her second name in the Queen Dowager's honour. In 1841 she saw her beloved nephew Prince Edward of Saxe-Weimar enter the British army and embark on the lifelong career which was to be crowned with the award of a Field Marshal's baton in 1897.

The strain of the years of living with such an unpredictable, if lovable, eccentric as William had taken their toll and Adelaide's health was extremely poor, her chief ailment being a weakness of the chest. For this reason she took to wintering abroad and paid visits to Malta and Madeira, in both of which islands she spent several months. No lasting cure was effected, however, and in December 1849, the gentle Queen died aged fifty-seven, sincerely mourned by the royal family and the nation.

Her contemporaries described Queen Adelaide as plain, but her portraits tend to show otherwise. Her expression concords well with the sweetness of her character. Undoubtedly she was sallow, had a poor complexion, and was far too thin to suit the tastes of the day, but by today's standards she was a pretty woman.

It is to be hoped that Adelaide's private diary, written in German and charmingly illustrated with her own sketches, will one day be translated and published. It passed, together with her writing desk and some other personal effects, to her sister Ida and was still in the possession of her descendants until very recently.

hours. She became pregnant again the same year and the Duke, wishing the child to be born in England, set out to bring his wife home, taking the reigns of the carriage horses himself to ensure a smooth ride. It was of no avail and poor Adelaide miscarried when they reached Dunkirk in September 1819. The following year, however, things went better and a healthy daughter was born at St James's Palace in December. The little girl

VICTORIA	1837–1901

Born:	Kensington Palace 24 May 1819	Castle 5 July 1866, Prince (Frederick)
Acceded:	20 June 1837	Christian Charles Augustus of
Crowned:	Westminster Abbey 28 June 1938	Schleswig-Holstein
Married:	Chapel Royal, St James's Palace,	(6) Louise Caroline Alberta:
	10 February 1840, (Francis) Albert	*b.* Buckingham Palace 18 March 1848;
	Augustus Charles Emmanuel (Prince	*d.* Kensington Palace, 3 December
	Consort from 26 June 1857) (*b.* Schloss	1939; *m.* St George's Chapel, Windsor
	Rosenau, near Coburg 26 August 1819,	21 March 1871, John Campbell, 9th
	d. Windsor Castle 14 December 1861),	Duke of Argyll
	younger son of Ernest I, Duke of Saxe-	(7) Arthur William Patrick Albert, Duke
	Coburg and Gotha, and his first wife	of Connaught and Strathearn:
	Louise of Saxe-Gotha-Altenburg	*b.* Buckingham Palace 1 May 1850;
Children:	(1) Victoria Adelaide Mary Louisa,	*d.* Bagshot Park, Surrey 16 January
	Princess Royal: *b.* Buckingham Palace	1942; *m.* St George's Chapel, Windsor
	21 November 1840; *d.* Friedrichshof	13 March 1879, Louise Margaret
	5 August 1901; *m.* St James's Palace	(Alexandra Victoria Agnes)
	25 January 1858, Frederick III,	(*b.* Potsdam 25 June 1860; *d.* Clarence
	German Emperor and King of Prussia	House, London 14 March 1917), third
	(2) Albert Edward, later King	daughter of Prince Frederick Charles
	Edward VII	of Prussia and Maria Anna of Anhalt; had issue
	(3) Alice Maud Mary: *b.* Buckingham	(8) Leopold George Duncan Albert, Duke
	Palace 25 April 1843; *d.* Darmstadt	of Albany: *b.* Buckingham Palace
	14 December 1878; *m.* Osborne	7 April 1853; *d.* Cannes 28 March
	House, Isle of Wight 1 July 1862,	1884; *m.* St George's Chapel, Windsor
	Louis IV, Grand Duke of Hesse and	27 April 1882, Helena Frederica
	Rhine	Augusta (*b.* Arolsen 17 February 1861;
	(4) Alfred Ernest Albert, Duke of	*d.* Hinterriss, Tyrol 1 September
	Edinburgh, reigning Duke of Saxe-	1922), fifth daughter of George
	Coburg and Gotha from 1893:	Victor, Prince of Waldeck and
	b. Windsor Castle 6 August 1844;	Pyrmont and Helena Wilhelmina
	d. Schloss Rosenau, near Coburg	Henrietta Pauline Marianne of
	30 July 1900; *m.* St Petersburg 23	Nassau, had issue
	January 1874, Marie (*b.* St Petersburg	(9) Beatrice Mary Victoria Feodore:
	17 October 1853; *d.* Zürich 25 October	*b.* Buckingham Palace 14 April 1857;
	1920), daughter of Alexander II,	*d.* Brantridge Park, Balcombe, Sussex
	Emperor of Russia, and his first wife	26 October 1944; *m.* Whippingham,
	Marie of Hesse; had issue	Isle of Wight 23 July 1885, Prince
	(5) Helena Augusta Victoria:	Henry Maurice of Battenberg
	b. Buckingham Palace 25 May 1846;	Died: Osborne House, Isle of Wight
	d. Schomberg House, Pall Mall,	22 January 1901
	London 9 June 1923; *m.* Windsor	Buried: Royal Mausoleum, Frogmore

With Queen Victoria we reach a period where so much is known and so much has been published that to attempt a sketch of her life and those of her successors on the same lines as those of their predecessors would be futile. Much more can be conveyed by selecting a few incidents from the crowded lives of those sovereigns and their consorts which highlight their characters and place them in historical perspective.

We know today that Queen Victoria very often *was* amused. The delightful reminiscences of two of her granddaughters leave no doubt about this. Indeed, one of them, HRH the late Princess Alice, Countess of

Athlone, when interviewed on television a few years ago said that she once asked her grandmother if she had ever really said 'We are not amused', and received a categorical denial. 'Wasn't it a pity?' was the Princess's chuckling comment. Queen Victoria did, however, employ the royal 'we' on several occasions and this usage is explained by the fact that she always wished to associate her beloved husband Albert in every statement of opinion she uttered, this being one way in which she felt she was keeping his memory alive after his death.

Victoria never knew her father, who died when she was only a few months old. The father-figure in her life

A photograph of Queen Victoria gazing mournfully at a bust of the Prince Consort while her son and daughter-in-law, Bertie and Alexandra, direct their attention elsewhere.

was to be her mother's brother Leopold, the widower of Princess Charlotte. 'Uncle Leopold', who became first King of the Belgians in 1831, remained her chief mentor and adviser until the end of his life in 1865 and there was an almost daily correspondence between them.

The little Princess was brought up in ignorance of her closeness to the throne, which was finally revealed to her by the clever insertion of a genealogical table into one of her history books. Her childhood was a somewhat lonely one as she had no children of her own age to play with and was restricted to the society of her mother and her household, her much older half-brother and half-sister Charles and Feodora of Leiningen (children of the Duchess of Kent's first marriage), and her devoted and much loved governess, Fräulein Lehzen, later created a Hanoverian baroness. Victoria greatly resented the influence of her mother's comptroller, Sir John Conroy, an insensitive boor reputed to be the Duchess's

lover, and this resentment greatly contributed to a breach between the young Queen and her mother which lasted for many years.

Victoria was fortunate in finding another father-figure in her first prime minister, Lord Melbourne, upon whom she came to rely almost as much as she did on Uncle Leopold. However, from 1840 onwards the greatest influence in her life was that of her cousin and husband, Prince Albert of Saxe-Coburg. The Prince was a man of culture and taste, a true polymath, and he moulded and shaped the character and tastes of his young wife completely. Victoria had inherited much of the temperament of her father and uncles, including a strong sexuality which Albert was to satisfy. He, strangely enough, has always been considered something of a prude, but his high moral standards precluded any extramarital activity of the kind heavily indulged in by his father and brother, both notorious womanizers. In any case, marriage to Victoria was a full-time occupation, exacting both physically and mentally. When the Prince died at the age of forty-two he had the appearance of a much older man. The cause of his death was attributed by his doctors to typhoid, but in recent years there has been some medical speculation as to whether he suffered from cancer or some other wasting disease.

The effect of the Prince's death on the Queen and her almost complete withdrawal from public life for the remaining nearly forty years of her reign are well known. She found some comfort in her large and ever growing family of children, grandchildren and great-grand-children, and later in travel to the south of France, where she enjoyed the Mediterranean sunshine.

Victoria always preferred the company of men to that of women and her partiality for her Highland servant John Brown was a matter of concern to her family and household. He treated the Queen in a rough and familiar yet kindly manner which she greatly relished, and in return he was allowed many privileges which infuriated the other members of the household. After Brown's death the Queen was only dissuaded with the greatest difficulty from writing and publishing a personal memoir of him.

Almost as great an influence on the Queen in her later years, and even more resented, was her Indian secretary, known as 'the Munshi', who claimed to be the son of a Surgeon-General in the Indian Army. Victoria's favourite son, Prince Arthur, Duke of Connaught, made some investigations into the Munshi's origins when he was in India and discovered that he was in reality the son of a very lowly apothecary. The Queen was so affronted when given this information that she would not speak to her son for several days. The Munshi was given a house which he soon filled with a number of Indian ladies, euphemistically described as his 'sisters, aunts and cousins', and a succession of pretty young 'nephews' with whom he was often photographed. Some of the photographs still hang in the corridors of Osborne House, the elegant Italianate palace on the Isle of Wight created by the Prince Consort and now (apart from being the repository of the many elaborate presents received by the Queen from the Indian princes on the occasion of her Golden Jubilee) a convalescent home for naval officers.

The Queen's proclamation as Empress of India in 1877 marked the apogee of the British Empire and was a source of great pride and satisfaction to Victoria herself, as she could now feel herself on a par with the Emperors of Russia and Austria and the recently proclaimed German Emperor, to all of whom she considered herself vastly superior anyway.

Victoria's relationship with her Prime Ministers was not always a smooth one. She disliked and distrusted the Liberals, and Gladstone, whom she termed a 'half-mad firebrand', was particularly scorned by her both in public and in private. At a royal wedding he once inadvertently entered the marquee where the Queen was sitting and she was heard to ask in a loud voice, 'Does Mr Gladstone think this is a public tent?' On the other hand, the wily, Conservative flatterer Disraeli could do no wrong in the Queen's eyes. She offered to visit him on his deathbed but he declined the honour, remarking to his attendants with a last summoning up of his ready wit that she would probably want to give him a message for Albert and he would find the visit too tiring.

After fifty years on the throne the Queen had become the most politically astute person in the kingdom and was able to advise and influence her ministers to a considerable extent. On one occasion the Secretary of State for War, Campbell-Bannerman (later Prime Minister under Edward VII) brought what he claimed to be some entirely new army schemes for the Queen's approval. 'No, Mr Bannerman', she said, 'Lord Palmerston proposed exactly the same thing to me in '52, and Lord Palmerston was wrong.' Lord Palmerston, of course, was another Prime Minister whom Victoria much disliked.

At Victoria's succession the throne was far from secure, there was a strong republican movement and the Queen was hissed at Ascot on one occasion. By the end of the reign 'the widow of Windsor' had acquired a popularity greater than that enjoyed by any other sovereign and her death at Osborne House was an occasion of real and heartfelt grief to the majority of her subjects, most of whom had grown up in her reign and could remember no other. The sixty-three year span linked the age of the stage-coach, highwaymen and public executions (abolished in 1868) to the age of the motor-car and the eve of the conquest of the air.

The Queen had been greatly impressed, when visiting Germany in the early days of her marriage, by the mausoleum which was used as the burial place of the ducal family at Coburg, and determined that she herself would not be buried in the Royal Tombhouse at Windsor constructed by George III. Accordingly, on the Prince Consort's death, the construction of an impressive mausoleum at Frogmore was begun and there the Queen and her husband now rest side by side in a great sarcophagus surmounted by their effigies. A smaller mausoleum nearby houses the remains of Victoria's mother, the Duchess of Kent, while the grounds surrounding the Royal Mausoleum have been laid out as a burial ground for many of Victoria's descendants.

THE HOUSE OF WETTIN

It is not always realized that Queen Victoria was the last sovereign of the House of Hanover and King Edward VII was the first of the House of Wettin or the House of Saxony. Queen Victoria was most particular that all her children should be aware of their parental heritage and the titles of Duke or Duchess of Saxony were added immediately after those of Prince or Princess of Great Britain and Ireland in all official documents and works of reference. These also bore the Saxon arms crossed with the rue crown as an inescutcheon of pretence on their coats-of-arms.

The family to which Victoria's beloved Albert belonged descended from one Burkhard, Count in the Grabfeld, who died in 908. His descendant Count Dedi I received grants of land from the Holy Roman Emperor Otto III in 997 and further territories were acquired by purchase, cession, or marriage through the succeeding centuries. The family divided into two main branches, the Ernestine and the Albertine. The senior line obtained the Electoral dignity but was forced to transfer it to the junior after siding with the Protestant reformers, although the title of Duke of Saxony and many territories were retained. The Duchy went into several divisions and its branches have provided Britain with a Princess of Wales (Augusta of Saxe-Gotha), a Queen (Adelaide), a Duchess of Kent (Victoria), and a Prince Consort (Albert). The son of the last ascended the British throne in 1901 and it was his son who, in an outburst of anti-German feeling engendered by the First World War, was to change the name of his 'House and Family' from Wettin to Windsor in 1917.

EDWARD VII	1901–1910

Born: Buckingham Palace 9 November 1841
Acceded: 22 January 1901
Crowned: Westminster Abbey 9 August 1902
Married: St George's Chapel, Windsor 10 March 1863, Alexandra Caroline Mary Charlotte Louisa Julia, eldest daughter of Christian IX, King of Denmark and Princess Louise of Hesse-Cassel
Children: (1) Albert Victor Christian Edward, Duke of Clarence: b. Frogmore House, Windsor 8 January 1864; d. Sandringham House, Norfolk 14 January 1892
(2) George Frederick Ernest Albert, later King George V
(3) Louise Victoria Alexandra Dagmar, Princess Royal: b. Marlborough House, London 20 February 1867; d. 15 Portman Square, London 4 January 1931; m. Buckingham Palace 27 July 1889; Alexander William George Duff, 1st Duke (and 6th Earl) of Fife
(4) Victoria Alexandra Olga Mary: b. Marlborough House, London 6 July 1868; d. Coppins, Iver, Bucks 3 December 1935
(5) Maud Charlotte Mary Victoria: b. Marlborough House, London 26 November 1869; d. London 20 November 1938; m. Buckingham Palace 22 July 1896, Haakon VII, King of Norway
(6) (Alexander) John Charles Albert: b. Sandringham House 6 April; d. 7 April 1871
Died: Buckingham Palace 6 May 1910
Buried: St George's Chapel, Windsor

It seems scarcely credible that Queen Victoria's eldest son was an unwanted child. The young Queen strongly resented a second pregnancy coming so soon after the birth of the Princess Royal and curtailing her activities, especially dancing, for which she had a passion. This resentment was to mar the relationship between mother and son for the rest of her life. In a milder form it was a continuation of the feud waged by the first three Georges against their sons and heirs.

Albert Edward was the first to be born heir apparent for 101 years and received the traditional titles of Prince of Wales and Earl of Chester just one month after his birth. His father, Prince Albert, devised a careful plan for his education, but it soon became evident that he was not a brilliant scholar and was also lacking in diligence. He was denied the companionship of any children of his own age apart from his brothers and sisters, and the tutors chosen by his father were for the most part gravely austere and humourless. It was a sad environment for a high-spirited, affectionate boy, but he managed not to be crushed by it.

The Prince had inherited all the strong sexuality of his Georgian great-uncles, as well as that of his paternal grandfather and uncle, and his parents soon became well aware of this. Victoria was to attribute the Prince Consort's untimely death in part to a journey he made to Oxford to sort out some of Albert Edward's early sexual adventures at a time when he was in a weakened state of health. This further exacerbated the uneasy relations between mother and son.

Bertie's sister Princess Frederick William of Prussia played a large part in finding a bride for him when the time came. The choice fell on Princess Alexandra, a frigid beauty and, as Queen Victoria and her new family were soon to discover, 'sadly deaf'. Bertie and Alix were married at St George's Chapel, Windsor, with the recently widowed Queen gazing mournfully down upon them from the Royal Closet, the small latticed gallery on the north side of the sanctuary. Six children were born in fairly quick succession and then marital relations probably ceased, although the couple remained on friendly, even deeply affectionate, terms for the rest of their lives together. Bertie found satisfaction in the society of warmer-natured ladies. He was a *bon viveur* in every sense, loving good food, good wine, good cigars and good company. His mother excluded him completely from any participation in affairs of state so that he had all the time in the world to indulge his sybaritic tastes. Many happy times were spent in Europe visiting the fashionable spots, and at the Café de Paris in Monte Carlo the Prince of Wales was credited with naming 'crêpes suzette'. The inventor of the dish begged leave to name it after His Royal Highness, who pooh-poohed the idea with an expansive wave of the royal cigar, saying, 'No, no, don't name it after me. Name it after that pretty girl over there instead.'

The Prince of Wales also visited Canada and India, where his mother would have loved to go had such a thing been feasible in those days. He shot tigers from the backs of elephants and was fêted by the maharajas, most of whom recognized a kindred spirit.

The old Queen's death in January 1901 brought Bertie

A photograph of three Kings, Edward VII with his son and grandson the future George V and Edward VIII, taken on board the royal yacht about 1908.

to the throne at last, in his sixtieth year, and he chose to reign as Edward VII. The coronation was arranged for 26 June 1902 and London filled with visitors from all over the world, including many of the maharajas with whom the King had gone tiger hunting in India. A day or two before the date the King was struck down with an illness diagnosed as acute appendicitis and an emergency operation was performed at Buckingham Palace. It was entirely successful and the King's recovery was so rapid that the coronation was held, with slightly curtailed ceremonial, on 9 August 1902. Most of the souvenir china prepared for the event carried the June date, but some items have the postponement date added and these have now become much sought after.

The great achievement of Edward's reign was the conclusion of the *Entente Cordiale* with France, largely brought about by his own diplomacy and earning him the name of 'Edward the Peacemaker'.

'King Teddy' enjoyed immense popularity with all classes and his ebullience and bonhomie came as a welcome relief after the rather drab years of the latter half of his mother's reign. The years of self-indulgent good living, however, had inevitably undermined his heath and he was a martyr to chronic bronchitis. His death came peacefully and quite suddenly after a short illness in May 1910, not long after he had returned from an enjoyable stay at Biarritz. The nation grieved sincerely. Many realized that the King's influence had maintained peace in Europe and that it would now be only a matter of time before that peace was broken.

Alexandra of Denmark

Born:	Yellow Palace, Copenhagen 1 December 1844
Married:	St George's Chapel, Windsor 10 March 1863
Crowned:	Westminster Abbey 9 August 1902
Died:	Sandringham House, Norfolk 20 November 1925
Buried:	St George's Chapel, Windsor

The 'Sea-King's Daughter from over the sea' was to become the most beautiful of all Britain's queens. She was also one of the most superficial and self-centred.

Alexandra was brought up very simply in Copenhagen, sharing an attic bedroom with her sister Dagmar (known in the family as 'Minnie') and making and mending many of her own clothes. Her father became heir to the Danish throne in 1853, but did not actually succeed as King Christian IX until eight months after his eldest daughter had become Princess of Wales.

Alexandra won all hearts with her beauty and elegance, although greatly handicapped by progressive deafness (a hereditary defect). She also had a limp, which fashionable ladies soon copied so that it became known as the 'Alexandra glide'. Sexually frigid, she became a violently possessive mother, demanding the complete devotion of her children, who were brought up always to address her as 'Mother dear'.

The effect on her eldest son, Prince Albert Victor (known as 'Eddy'), later Duke of Clarence, was disastrous. He was of limited intellect, almost ineducable, and when he reached young manhood his dandyism earned him the nickname of 'Prince Collar and Cuffs'. His sexual proclivities were doubtful and he was believed to frequent a male brothel in Cleveland Street. However, he also fell madly in love with the statuesque Princess Hélène of Orleans, whose parents lived in exile in England. He wished to marry her, but the religious difficulties were insuperable and instead he was induced to become engaged to Princess May of Teck, a 'safe' choice. Before the marriage could take place, however, he succumbed to typhoid, to his mother's inexpressible grief, but to the relief of those who were aware of his shortcomings. Princess May was passed on as fiancée to his younger brother George, a far more stable character, and was to become in fullness of time the stately Queen Mary.

Alexandra's three daughters were all excessively plain, travesties of their beautiful mother. She was as possessive with them as with their brothers, but the eldest and the youngest managed to escape into marriage, the middle one, Victoria, becoming her mother's constant companion and living out her spinsterly existence until Alexandra's death at last enabled her to set up her own establishment for the last ten years of her life.

Both as Princess and as Queen, Alexandra was notoriously unpunctual – to such an extent that the King had to tell her she would not be crowned if she was not ready in time on their coronation day. As Queen Mother she threw the cat among the pigeons by trying to insist that she should take precedence over her daughter-in-law the Queen Consort. In this she was encouraged by her sister Minnie, now the Dowager Empress Maria Feodorovna of Russia, who assured her (truly, as it happened) that this was the protocol of the Russian

Queen Alexandra. A photograph taken of her as Queen Mother in 1913.

court. King George V had to be quite firm with 'Mother dear' for once.

Queen Alexandra was the first Queen Consort since the Middle Ages to be made a Lady of the Order of the Garter. George III had contemplated conferring it on Queen Charlotte, but for some reason had never done so. Now its conferment on Alexandra created a precedent which has been followed ever since.

Towards the end of her life the Queen became almost completely deaf and suffered from mild senile dementia. She resided chiefly at Sandringham House, Norfolk, which Edward VII had purchased as Prince of Wales, and in her drives about the countryside would graciously wave and bow to the cows in the fields, the faithful Princess Victoria always in attendance.

When Alexandra died she had reached a greater age than that attained by any other Queen Consort with the possible exception of Eleanor of Aquitaine.

THE HOUSE OF WINDSOR

The House of Windsor came into being on 17 July 1917 when King George V, by an Order in Council, adopted the name of Windsor for himself and his descendants. The change was occasioned by the anti-German fever, almost amounting to hysteria, which swept the country in the middle of the First World War. The King's cousin and enemy, the German Emperor, received the news with amusement and said that he would arrange for a performance of 'The Merry Wives of Saxe-Coburg' to be staged at his court theatre. In his view a leopard could not change its spots.

King George V's decision proved a wise one. The House of Windsor has a good, solid British sound to it, and the present Queen's decision early in her reign that it was to continue as the name of her descendants was a popular one, although it has since been slightly modified by Her Majesty's decision on 8 February 1960 that the third generation of her male descendants should bear the surname of Mountbatten-Windsor. It seems a pity that the sturdy name of Windsor should not be allowed to stand alone without any addition, however worthy that addition might be.

| GEORGE V | 1910–1936 |

Born: Marlborough House, London 3 June 1865
Acceded: 6 May 1910
Crowned: Westminster Abbey 22 June 1911
Married: Chapel Royal, St James's Palace, 6 July 1893, Victoria Mary Augusta Louisa Olga Pauline Claudine Agnes, only daughter of Francis, Prince and Duke of Teck, and Princess Mary Adelaide, younger daughter of Prince Adolphus Frederick, Duke of Cambridge, 7th son of King George III

Children:
(1) Edward Albert Christian George Andrew Patrick David, later King Edward VIII
(2) Albert Frederick Arthur George, later King George VI
(3) (Victoria Alexandra Alice) Mary, Princess Royal (from 1 January 1932): b. York Cottage, Sandringham, Norfolk 25 April 1897; d. Harewood House, near Leeds 28 March 1965; m. Westminster Abbey 28 February 1922, Henry George Charles Lascelles, 6th Earl of Harewood
(4) Henry William Frederick Albert, Duke of Gloucester: b. York Cottage, Sandringham 31 March 1900; d. Barnwell Manor, Northants 10 June 6 November 1935, Lady Alice Christabel Montagu-Douglas-Scott (b. London 25 December 1901), third daughter of 7th Duke of Buccleuch and (9th Duke of) Queensberry, and Lady Margaret Alice Bridgeman, second daughter of 4th Earl of Bradford; had issue (see Table 21)
(5) George Edward Alexander Edmund, Duke of Kent: b. Sandringham House 20 December 1902; d. (killed in a flying accident on active service at Morven, Scotland) 25 August 1942; m. Westminster Abbey 29 November 1934, Marina (b. Athens 30 November 1906), youngest daughter of Prince Nicholas of Greece and Denmark, and Grand Duchess Helen Vladimirovna of Russia; had issue (see Table 21)
(6) John Charles Francis: b. York Cottage, Sandringham 12 July 1905; d. Wood Farm, Wolferton, Norfolk, 18 January 1919

Died: Sandringham 20 January 1936
Buried: St George's Chapel, Windsor

A group at Abergeldie in 1906. From left to right:- Lady Katherine Coke, Prince Albert of Wales (later King George VI), the Princess of Wales (later Queen Mary), Princess Mary of Wales (later Princess Royal), Prince Edward of Wales (later King Edward VIII and Duke of Windsor), the Prince of Wales (later King George V, note the cigarette), and Mr H. P. Hansell.

Windsor Castle.

King George V, being the second son of the heir apparent, was able to embark on a naval career, his prospects of succeeding to the throne being considered remote. He was therefore able to see more of life at an ordinary level than many princes and the rough and ready manners of the quarterdeck were to remain with him to a large extent throughout his life. In this he resembled King William IV, though without that King's eccentricity. His brusque heartiness was to endear him to his subjects, so that by the end of his reign he had become one of the best loved and respected of all our kings. He was very touched by the warmth of the reception accorded to him by the crowds when he drove through the streets of London on the occasion of his Silver Jubilee in 1935, recording in his diary 'They must love me for myself alone.'

George grew up a devoted son to both his parents and a devoted brother to his brother and sisters. He had a simple, straightforward mind and was completely incapable of deviousness in any form. His relations with his father were particularly good, unlike those which had persisted between the sovereign and the heir apparent

since the time of George I. This may surprise us as no two men could have been more different in temperament, outlook and general lifestyle than George and his father. Unfortunately, the same cordial relations were not to extend into the next generation, and George and his eldest son grew increasingly irritated with each other, although their differences never reached the proportions of those which had obtained in the eighteenth century.

In marrying the fiancée of his deceased elder brother Eddy in 1893, George found a wife who was ideally suited to him. It is safe to say that he never looked at another woman, although he and his sister Princess Victoria, both notoriously philistine, were often to scoff at Mary's artistic pretensions. The King, who once said that his favourite opera was *La Bohème* 'because it is the shortest', was interested in sailing and racing and little else. Lord Tweedsmuir relates an amusing story recounted to him by his father, the novelist John Buchan, who was received in audience by the King on being appointed Governor-General of Canada in 1935. In the course of conversation the King remarked how much he enjoyed reading Buchan's books. After making appropriately gratified noises the author was passed on to

King George V riding with his cousin the German Emperor Wilhelm II at Potsdam in 1913.

The Delhi Durbar, 12 December 1911. This photograph shows the arena with the thrones awaiting the arrival of the King-Emperor and Queen-Empress to receive the homage of the Indian Princes.

King George V and Queen Mary (rather apprehensively) riding on a miniature railway at the Wembley Exhibition in 1924.

Queen Mary who also said how much she enjoyed his books, but added 'the King only reads the most dreadful rubbish.'

George's reign commenced with the great Delhi Durbar, a triumph of Empire, when he and the Queen visited India as Emperor and Empress to receive the homage of the Indian princes and show themselves in imperial splendour to their Indian subjects. It was a unique occasion, and it must have seemed then that the British Empire was one not only on which the sun never set, but on which the sun never would set. Three years later the world was plunged into the First World War, which was to bring about the biggest change in the old

order of things since the Napoleonic wars a century before. Britain weathered the storm and the Empire survived, although it was clear that the days of colonialism were now numbered. It is doubtful if King George ever accepted this, however, and among the last words attributed to him as he lay dying at Sandringham was the question, 'How is the Empire?' Did he sense that it was dying with him? At any rate it is more edifying to believe that these were his last words rather than the prosaic though characteristic 'Bugger Bognor!', said to be uttered in response to the suggestion by a well-meaning attendant that the King would recover his health at Bognor again, as he had done after being gravely ill with septicaemia in 1928. Both these stories of the King's last words are now considered apocryphal, and it seems most likely that his last coherent utterance was an apology for his inability to concentrate when called upon to sign the deed appointing counsellors of state to act for him during his illness.

King George V was the first king to make use of wireless to broadcast a message to his people and established the custom of an annual Christmas message which has been continued by his successors. It is also interesting to note that he revived the custom of distributing the Royal Maundy money in person on the Thursday before Easter, a function which had long been delegated to the Lord High Almoner. The King's interest in the matter was stimulated by his cousin Princess Marie Louise, who had formed the habit of attending the service at Westminster Abbey and felt it would be appropriate for the sovereign to resume this pleasant custom, whereby gifts of money are distributed to as many men and women as the years of the sovereign's age.

Mary of Teck

Born: Kensington Palace 26 May 1867
Married: Chapel Royal, St James's Palace, 6 July 1893
Crowned: Westminster Abbey 22 June 1911
Died: Marlborough House 24 March 1953
Buried: St George's Chapel, Windsor

Few who saw the stately, regal figure of Queen Mary in later life could have imagined that in her childhood she had been something of a tomboy. As the only sister of three lively brothers, she climbed trees and played cricket with them and the children of the gamekeepers and lodgekeepers of Richmond Park, where her parents resided at White Lodge. Princess May, as she was then known, was the daughter of Francis, Duke of Teck, a morganatic scion of the Royal House of Württemberg, and the immensely popular Princess Mary Adelaide of Cambridge, a first cousin of Queen Victoria. The Duchess of Teck, known behind her back to the Queen and other members of the royal family as 'Fat Mary', was a large, jolly, generous lady, who often found herself in pecuniary difficulties. At one time, in order to economize, she moved to Florence with her family, and it was there that Mary acquired the interest in art which was to remain with her all her life, although it must be admitted that her taste was far from impeccable. In later life she was to acquire 'art treasures' in magpie fashion and many stories are told of the unscrupulous way in which she would cajole friends and even casual acquaintances into donating to her collection objects to which she had taken a fancy. After her death the Victoria and Albert Museum arranged an exhibition of

some of her possessions, and precious jewelled objets and bibelots by Fabergé and others were displayed cheek-by-jowl with sentimental watercolours of rustic cottages with hollyhocks clustering round the door.

Princess May became the unprotesting fiancée of the rather unsavoury Prince Eddy, and on his death was passed on, as it were, to his younger brother George, a much more suitable match. She was a young woman of great tact and well able to handle the rather difficult mother-in-law she acquired in 'mother dear'.

As Queen Mary, May, who was never a beauty (she herself was to say that she was far too like her great-grandmother Queen Charlotte ever to be considered good-looking), acquired a regal bearing and dignity of carriage surpassing any other queen. She could wear jewels superbly and in profusion, and on her they never looked vulgar as they would on other women. On her death in 1953 Sir Winston Churchill, paying tribute in the House of Commons, was to say, 'She looked like a Queen and she acted like a Queen', and indeed she did.

As Queen Mother, Queen Mary spent the years of the Second World War in the safety of Badminton House, the Gloucestershire seat of the Duke of Beaufort who had married her niece Lady Mary Cambridge. Years later the Duchess was to be asked which part of the house Queen Mary had occupied. 'All of it', was the laconic reply. At Badminton the old Queen was photographed in her inevitable toque and caped coat 'helping' the woodmen to cut down trees in a series of artlessly posed photographs. She found the drawing-room rather too distant from the 'usual offices' for her comfort and had a commode installed behind a screen at one end of the room. She would retire behind this whenever she felt the need, regardless of the assembled company who had to continue making embarrassed and loud conversation until she reappeared.

Queen Mary loved the theatre and the cinema, and both before and after the Second World War her distinctive Daimler motor-car was to be seen parked outside various suburban cinemas, where she had ventured to see a particular film which had been recommended to her, thus avoiding the fuss which would have surrounded her attendance at a West End performance.

One of Queen Mary's failings was her inability to express her feelings for her children in any outward form. She did care for them deeply and had the great sorrow of seeing three of her five sons die before her. Prince John, the youngest, was an epileptic and his mother was able to regard his death as a 'happy release', but the deaths of the Duke of Kent on active service and of King George VI were an added burden in her old age. The defection, as she saw it, of her eldest son David also grieved her deeply although she never ceased to love him as much as ever.

EDWARD VIII   JANUARY–DECEMBER 1936

Born:	White Lodge, Richmond Park, Surrey 23 June 1894
Acceded:	20 January 1936
Abdicated:	10 December 1936 (confirmed by Declaration of Abdication Act 11 December 1936)
Created Duke of Windsor:	8 March 1937
Married:	Château de Candé, Monts, France 3 June 1937, (Bessie) Wallis Warfield (which name she resumed by Deed Poll after her second divorce) *d.* Paris 24 April 1986, formerly wife of Ernest Aldrich Simpson, previously of Captain Earl Winfield Spencer, Jr, and only child of Teackle Wallis Warfield of Baltimore, Maryland, USA, and Alice Montague
Died:	Paris 28 May 1972
Buried:	Frogmore

It is tempting to say of Edward VIII that if ever a man failed to fulfil his early promise it was he; but that poses the question whether there was really any early promise to fulfil.

The Prince was always known in his family circle by his last name of David. At his birth he occupied the unique position of being the third male heir in direct line to the throne. His good looks and boyish charm were to be his undoing. He was wilful and irresponsible and as he grew up it became obvious that he was almost as much addicted to worldly pleasure as his grandfather King Edward VII had been, but without that monarch's sagacity and sense of *comme il faut*. Things might have been improved had David been allowed to see active service in the front line in the First World War, a thing he very much wished to do but which was categorically forbidden by his father, in spite of David pointing out quite reasonably that as he had three younger brothers his life could be risked. The sense of frustration he felt was to be recalled throughout his life.

David chafed at all royal ceremonial and protocol. At the sensitive age of seventeen he was made to dress up in what he considered a ridiculous fancy dress and take part in a ceremony, largely devised by Lloyd George, formally to invest him as Prince of Wales at Caernarvon Castle. It is easy to imagine how he shrank from the insensitive jibes of his fellow-students at the Royal Naval College (where he was being educated), when they saw the photographs of him in this theatrical garb.

In the twenties and thirties David made several successful overseas tours, where his charm stood him in

good stead. He had a great following at home and abroad, being considered something of an arbiter of fashion, admired for his fashionable style of dress and ease of manner. He showed no sign of wanting to marry and settle down, however, much to his father's annoyance, and it soon became obvious that his taste, like that of an earlier Prince of Wales (George IV), was for mature married ladies, although whereas 'Prinny' had liked them to be well-rounded, David preferred them to have thin, boyish figures in the prevailing fashion. A succession of ladies occupied his attention and by the mid 1930s it became evident in court circles that his affections had been permanently engaged by an American lady, Mrs Ernest Simpson, who resided in London with her businessman husband. The Simpsons were frequent guests at David's house Fort Belvedere, near Windsor, and Wallis acted as his hostess and queened it there in spite of the presence of her complacent husband.

Matters were swiftly coming to a head when King George V died and David found himself King Edward VIII. He was now completely besotted with Wallis and with almost incredible naïvety was convinced that once

Edward, Prince of Wales as 'Chief Morning Star', the title bestowed on him by the Stoney-Creek Indians at Alberta during his visit to Canada in 1919.

King Edward VIII leaving the House of Lords after his first (and only)
State Opening of Parliament in 1936. The Lord Great Chamberlain
with his wand of office faces the King while heralds look on.

An example of the popular feeling for King Edward VIII during the abdication crisis. It soon faded away to nothing after the accession of King George VI.

she was freed of her marriage he would be able to marry her and make her his queen. For the sovereign head of the Church of England to marry a twice divorced woman was unthinkable, and the King's insistence on going ahead with his plans in spite of all advice provoked a government crisis. Compromise was impossible, and after a reign of nearly eleven months the King abdicated in favour of his brother the Duke of York, leaving the country after making a touching farewell broadcast, the words of which were drafted for him by Winston Churchill.

Wallis's divorce from Ernest Simpson was later made final and in June 1937 she and the former King were married in France. In March David had been created Duke of Windsor by his brother and successor King George VI, and in May had received 'reconferment' of the qualification of Royal Highness by Letters Patent, which expressly stated that this style was reserved to him alone and could not extend to any wife or children he might acquire. The legality of this was extremely doubtful. As the son of a sovereign, David was naturally entitled to the qualification, which should have reverted to him automatically on his renunciation of the throne, while the limitation imposed by the new Letters Patent was completely unconstitutional. David was to chafe for the rest of his life at this injustice, but out of deference to his brother never made an open issue of it, although within his own household the Duchess was always addressed as 'Royal Highness'.

Apart from a short wartime tour of duty as Governor and Commander-in-Chief of the Bahamas from 1940 to 1945, the rest of David's life was lived out in the obscurity of a self-imposed exile in France, participating with his wife in an endless social round. He produced a volume of memoirs, A King's Story, and two other books of royal reminiscence, while his wife produced her version, The Heart has its Reasons.

Tired, old and ill, the Duke was dying of cancer at his residence in the Bois de Boulogne when he was cheered by a visit from his beloved niece Queen Elizabeth II with her husband and eldest son, and was able to muster up the last vestiges of his strength to receive them. Within a matter of days he was dead. His body was flown back to Britain and lay in state in St George's Chapel, Windsor, where thousands flocked to pay their respects to their one-time monarch before he was taken to the royal burial ground at Frogmore, where he rests beneath a simple memorial. His widow lived on for nearly fourteen years in an increasing state of senile dementia until she too died in the Paris home they had shared on 24 April 1986. Her body was flown to England and buried beside her husband in the royal burial ground at Frogmore.

GEORGE VI   1936–1952

Born:	York Cottage, Sandringham, Norfolk 14 December 1895
Acceded:	10 December 1936
Crowned:	Westminster Abbey 12 May 1937
Married:	Westminster Abbey 26 April 1923, Lady Elizabeth Angela Marguerite Bowes-Lyon, youngest daughter of Claude George Bowes-Lyon, 14th Earl of Strathmore and Kinghorne, and Nina Cecilia Cavendish-Bentinck
Children:	(1) Elizabeth Alexandra Mary, later Queen Elizabeth II
	(2) Margaret Rose: b. Glamis Castle, Angus 21 August 1930; m. Westminster Abbey 6 May 1960 (divorced 1978), Anthony Charles Robert Armstrong-Jones, 1st Earl of Snowdon
Died:	Sandringham House, Norfolk 6 February 1952
Buried:	King George VI Memorial Chapel, St George's Chapel, Windsor

King George V's second son grew up, as his father had done, without any specific training for the throne, which it seemed unlikely he would ever occupy. Following the tradition for second sons in the royal family, Prince Albert (known in the family as Bertie) entered the Royal Navy as a midshipman in 1913. Unlike his elder brother, he was allowed to see active service during the First World War with the Grand Fleet and distinguished himself at the Battle of Jutland in 1916, being mentioned in despatches. He was promoted Lieutenant in 1918 and Commander in 1920. His health was always delicate, however, and apart from a speech impediment which he fought hard to overcome, he had a severe attack of appendicitis, necessitating an operation in August 1914. This was followed by recurring attacks of gastric trouble for several years, eventually diagnosed as a duodenal ulcer, which was successfully operated on in November 1917. His active naval career came to an end and in 1920 he was created Duke of York, the traditional title for the sovereign's second son. He wrote ingenuously to his father, 'I must ... thank you again ever so very much for having made me Duke of York. I'm

King George VI and Queen Elizabeth standing among the ruins after Buckingham Palace had been bombed in 1941.

very proud to bear the name you did for many years and I hope I shall live up to it in every way.'

In the early twenties Bertie started the Duke of York's Camps, a scheme for bringing together public schoolboys and working boys in seaside summer holiday camps. They were a great success, being held annually until 1939. The Duke himself attended the camps and enjoyed participating in the nightly sing-songs around the camp fire.

At about this time, the Duke began to develop his friendship with Lady Elizabeth Bowes-Lyon who, as a Girl Guide District Commissioner, had become a close friend of his sister Princess Mary, at whose wedding in 1922 she was a bridesmaid. The engagement of the Duke of York and Lady Elizabeth was announced in January 1923 and the wedding took place at Westminster Abbey in April. The romance fired the popular imagination from the start. King George and Queen Mary were delighted with their new daughter-in-law and with the two little granddaughters who appeared in the course of the next seven years. It seemed that the Duke and Duchess of York were destined to fulfil a supporting role in the royal family far into the foreseeable future, but the abdication of King Edward VIII suddenly called them to the throne. The King chose to reign as George VI, using his last Christian name.

The new King and Queen and their daughters were tremendously popular and the country soon recovered from the blow of the abdication. The coronation took place on the day already appointed for that of Edward VIII (in whose name many coronation souvenirs had already been made and marketed), and for the first time for many centuries it was attended by the Queen Mother. The two little Princesses were also a novel sight in their miniature robes and coronets.

Within a few years the country was plunged into the Second World War. The example of the King and Queen, who refused to leave London throughout the bombing or to send their children to a safe area, did more for public morale than any other single thing. Buckingham Palace received a stick of six bombs in September 1940 and the royal couple had a narrow escape. 'I'm glad we've been bombed', said the Queen. 'Now I can look the East Enders in the face.'

The years succeeding the war were busy ones, including a strenuous tour of South Africa and the Festival of Britain in 1951. King George's never very robust health began to give cause for anxiety, and some months after he and the Queen celebrated their silver wedding in 1948 he underwent an operation for a circulatory obstruction in the leg arteries. Three years later he fell ill again, and in September 1951 part of his left lung was removed and found to be cancerous. He made a partial recovery and in January 1952 felt so much better that his daughter Princess Elizabeth, the heiress-presumptive, was able to set off on a projected world tour without any qualms. On 5 February 1952 the King spent a happy day out shooting on the Sandringham estate, but some time after midnight that night he died peacefully in his sleep.

Few monarchs have been as greatly loved as King George VI, a shy, retiring man who never wanted to be king but who shouldered the burdens of sovereignty with characteristic courage and dignity.

Elizabeth Bowes-Lyon

Born: London 4 August 1900
Married: Westminster Abbey 26 April 1923
Crowned: Westminster Abbey 12 May 1937

If few kings have been as greatly loved as King George VI, no Queen has been as much loved as his consort, now Queen Elizabeth the Queen Mother.

The Hon. Elizabeth Bowes-Lyon was born in London on 4 August 1900. The precise locality of her birth is unknown and her father, Lord Glamis, as he then was, registered the event later as having taken place at St Paul's Walden Bury, his Hertfordshire seat. Nearly four years later the death of Elizabeth's grandfather, the 13th Earl of Strathmore, brought about a change in her status and she became Lady Elizabeth Bowes-Lyon, the style she was to retain until her marriage in 1923, when she became HRH the Duchess of York. The marriage of the Duke and Duchess of York was supremely happy and undoubtedly it was her support and encouragement alone which enabled him to take on the burdens of kingship thrust upon him by the abdication of his elder brother.

As Queen, and even more as Queen Mother, Queen Elizabeth has earned and continues to command the love and respect of all her countrymen and women. May she long continue so to do!

Queen Elizabeth II's first State Opening of Parliament on 4 November 1952. The Queen wears her parliamentary robe and the diadem of George IV (not having yet been crowned) as she processes through the Royal Gallery preceded by Earl Alexander of Tunis bearing the Sword of State. She is followed by her Mistress of the Robes, Mary, Duchess of Devonshire, and other ladies in waiting. This was the first photograph ever taken inside the Palace of Westminster during a State Opening.

ELIZABETH II   1952–

Born:	17 Bruton Street, London W1
	21 April 1926
Acceded:	6 February 1952
Crowned:	Westminster Abbey 2 June 1953
Married:	Westminster Abbey 20 November 1947,
	HRH Prince Philip, Duke of Edinburgh,
	formerly Prince of Greece and Denmark
	(*b.* Mon Repos, Corfu 10 June 1921)
Children:	(1) Charles Philip Arthur George, Prince of Wales: *b.* Buckingham Palace 14 November 1948; *m.* St Paul's Cathedral, London 29 July 1981, Lady Diana Frances Spencer (*b.* Park House, Sandringham, Norfolk 1 July 1961), youngest daughter of Edward John Spencer, 8th Earl Spencer, and his first wife, Hon. Frances Ruth Burke Roche
	Children: (a) William Arthur Philip Louis: *b.* St Mary's Hospital, Paddington 21 June 1982

(b) Henry Charles Albert David: *b.* St Mary's Hospital, Paddington 15 September 1984

(2) Anne Elizabeth Alice Louise: *b.* Clarence House, St James's 15 August 1950; *m.* Westminster Abbey 14 November 1973, Captain Mark Anthony Peter Phillips; has issue

(3) Andrew Albert Christian Edward: *b.* Buckingham Palace 19 February 1960; *m.* Westminster Abbey 23 July 1986, Sarah Margaret (*b.* 27 Welbech Street, London 15 October 1959), daughter of Major Ronald Ivor Ferguson, The Life Guards, and his first wife, Susan Mary Wright.

(4) Edward Anthony Richard Louis: *b.* Buckingham Palace 10 March 1964

The coronation of Queen Elizabeth II on 2 June 1953. The Queen is clad in the cloth-of-gold coronation vestments and wears St Edward's Crown. She holds the royal sceptre and the sceptre with the dove and has just been placed on her throne to receive the homage of the Lords spiritual and temporal.

The first child of the Duke and Duchess of York was born by caesarean section at 2.40 a.m. on 21 April 1926 at the London house of the Duchess's parents, the Earl and Countess of Strathmore. King George V and Queen Mary drove up from Windsor to see their first granddaughter that afternoon and were delighted with her. As she grew older, the little Lilibet (as she called herself in her first childish attempts to say Elizabeth, and has remained ever since in the intimate circle of the royal family) became a firm favourite with her gruff old grandfather who, disgruntled by the behaviour of his eldest son, was to write: 'I pray to God that he [David] may never marry and that nothing may come between Bertie and Lilibet and the throne.' The old King's wish was to be fulfilled and well within a year of his death Bertie was king and Lilibet heiress-presumptive.

Princess Elizabeth was educated privately and spent the greater part of the war years at Windsor Castle with her sister Princess Margaret. After the war the two Princesses accompanied the King and Queen on their South African tour in 1947. Princess Elizabeth celebrated her twenty-first birthday at Cape Town on 21 April, when she made her moving broadcast to the Commonwealth, pledging her whole life to its service.

Soon after the royal family's return to England, the Princess's engagement to Lieutenant Philip Mountbatten, RN, was announced. He had been born HRH Prince Philip of Greece and Denmark, but had spent almost all his life in England under the guardianship of his maternal uncles, the 2nd Marquess of Milford Haven and Lord Louis Mountbatten (later Earl Mountbatten of Burma). On naturalization as a British subject he had chosen to take their surname, which their father had adopted in 1917 as an anglicization of the German Battenberg. The young couple were third cousins, both being great-great-grandchildren of Queen Victoria, and their wedding at Westminster Abbey on 20 November 1947 was the first occasion which saw a relaxation of the wartime austerity which still prevailed. The bridegroom received the title of Duke of Edinburgh on his wedding day and the qualification of Royal Highness, which he had relinquished on his naturalization.

King George VI marked the 600th anniversary of the founding of the Order of the Garter on St George's Day 23 April 1948 by conferring it on his elder daughter, who thus joined her mother and grandmother, and Queen Wilhelmina of the Netherlands, as a Lady of the Order, an honour unprecedented since the Middle Ages when robes of the Order used to be provided for most of the ladies of the royal family.

Princess Elizabeth was recalled from Kenya, where she was about to start a world tour, in February 1952, when the death of her father brought her to the throne as Queen Elizabeth II. Since that day she has gone from strength to strength. She has now reigned for well over

The Investiture of the Prince of Wales at Caernarvon Castle on 1 July 1969. Prince Charles is here seen rendering homage to his mother the Queen. Those peers who attended the ceremony in an official capacity wore their parliamentary robes and the late Duke of Norfolk can be discerned at the bottom right hand corner.

thirty years and is the model of all a twentieth-century monarch should be. As Head of the Commonwealth she undertakes strenuous tours all over the world with unflagging enthusiasm. She is probably one of the most politically astute persons in the country and Lord Wilson of Rievaulx has put on record how much he appreciated and benefited from the Queen's sound advice when he was Prime Minister. In this, as in all else, Queen Elizabeth II fulfils the sovereign's functions admirably. The occasion of the Queen's Silver Jubilee in 1977 saw many spontaneous demonstrations of loyalty and affection from all classes and ages, which were apparent to anyone who was on the streets of London that day, lining the processional route from Buckingham Palace to St Paul's Cathedral. Similar enthusiasm was to mark the celebration of her 60th birthday in April 1986.

The Queen and Prince Philip have brought up their four children in the simple way of life first adopted by King George III and Queen Charlotte over two hundred years ago, and it is largely because of this that every family in the land is able to identify with the royal family and share in its joys and sorrows.

Group at Buckingham Palace after the wedding of the Prince and Princess of Wales on 29 July 1981.

The Prince and Princess of Wales with the Queen and Prince Philip on the balcony of Buckingham Palace after their wedding.

From time to time there is speculation as to whether the Queen will abdicate or, as the popular press puts it, 'hand over' to Prince Charles. There is no such tradition in this country, where the position of sovereign is considered a job for life. The Queen's own dedication, made in South Africa on her twenty-first birthday and renewed on the occasion of her Silver Jubilee, should be enough to banish any such idea. In the event of her incapacity, for any reason, it would be far more likely for a regency to be set up as it was for George III.

APPENDIX A:
GEOFFREY OF MONMOUTH'S
KINGS OF BRITAIN
APPENDIX B:
GENEALOGICAL TABLES

Appendix A

GEOFFREY OF MONMOUTH'S KINGS OF BRITAIN

BRUTUS	Reigned 23 years
LOCRINUS	Son of Brutus; reigned 10 years
GWENDOLEN	Widow of Locrinus; reigned 15 years
MADDAN	Son of Locrinus and Gwendolen; reigned 40 years
MEMPRICIUS	Son of Maddan; reigned 20 years
EBRAUCUS	Son of Mempricius; reigned 39 years; had 20 wives, 20 sons and 30 daughters
BRUTUS GREENSHIELD	Son of Ebraucus; reigned 12 years; contemporary of Solomon
LEIL	Son of Brutus Greenshield; reigned 25 years; founded Carlisle
RUD HUD HUDIBRAS	Son of Leil; reigned 39 years; founded Canterbury, Winchester and Shaftesbury
BLADUD	Son of Rud Hud Hudibras; reigned 20 years; founded Bath and learnt to fly
LEIR	Son of Bladud; reigned 60 years; founded Leicester; Shakespeare's King Lear
CORDELIA	Daughter of Leir; reigned 5 years
MARGANUS I and CUNEDAGIUS	Sons respectively of Goneril and Regan, Leir's elder daughters; rebelled against their aunt and reigned together, dividing the kingdom, for two years. Cunedagius drove Marganus out and reigned alone for 33 years. Rome was founded during his reign
RIVALLO	Son of Cunedagius
GURGUSTIUS	Son of Rivallo
SISILLIUS I	Relationship to predecessor not stated
JAGO	Nephew of Gurgustius
KIMARCUS	Son of Sisillius
GORBODUC	Relationship to predecessor not stated. His sons Ferrex and Porrex quarrelled as to which should succeed and the former was killed by the latter, who in his turn was killed by their mother Judon
FIVE UNNAMED KINGS	A period of civil war
DUNVALLO MOLMUTIUS	Son of Cloten, King of Cornwall; reigned 40 years; established the Molmutine Laws
BELINUS	Son of Dunvallo Molmutius; fought with his brother Brennius
GURGUIT BARBTRUC	Son of Belinus
GUITHELIN	Relationship to predecessor not stated
MARCIA	Widow of Guithelin; author of the *Lex Martiana*
SISILLIUS II	Son of Guithelin and Marcia
KINARIUS	Son of Sisillius II
DANIUS	Brother of Kinarius
MORVIDUS	Illegitimate son of Danius
GORBONIANUS	Eldest son of Morvidus
ELIDURUS	Deposed by his two youngest brothers
INGENIUS and PEREDURUS	Reigned together 7 years until Ingenius died; Peredurus then reigned alone until his death when
ELIDURUS	Reigned a third time until his death
AN UNNAMED KING	Son of Gorbonianus
MARGANUS II	Son of Archgallo
ENNIAUNUS	Brother of Marganus II; deposed in the sixth year of his reign
IDVALLO	Son of Ingenius
RUNO	Son of Peredurus
GERENNUS	Son of Elidurus
CATELLUS	Son of Gerennus
MILLUS	Relationship to predecessor not stated
PORREX	Relationship to predecessor not stated
CHERIN	Relationship to predecessor not stated
FULGENIUS	Son of Cherin
EDADUS	Brother of Fulgenius
ANDRAGIUS	Brother of Edadus
URIANUS	Son of Andragius
ELIUD	
CLEDAUCUS	
CLOTENUS	
GURGINTIUS	
MERIANUS	Nothing recorded of these ten kings
BLEDUDO	
CAP	
OENUS	
SISILLIUS III	
BELDGABRED	

ARCHMAIL	Brother of Beldgabred
ELDOL	
REDON	
REDECHIUS	
SAMUIL	Nothing recorded of these seven kings
PENESSIL	
PIR	
CAPOIR	
DIGUEILLIS	Son of Capoir
HELI	Son of Digueillis; reigned 40 years
LUD	Son of Heli; founded London
CASSIVELAUNUS	Brother of Lud; the historical Cassivelaunus (Caswallon), who fought with Caesar in 55 and 54 BC
ARCHGALLO	Brother of Gorbonianus; deposed
ELIDURUS	Brother of Archgallo; reigned 5 years and then restored the crown to
ARCHGALLO	Reigned 10 years; died and was again succeeded by
LUCIUS	Son of Coilus; converted to Christianity and d. AD 156
Interregnum of about 150 years	
ASCLEPIODOTUS	Duke of Cornwall; elected king by the people
COEL	Duke of Kaelcolim (Colchester); killed Asclepiodotus and usurped the throne; the 'Old King Cole' of the nursery rhyme; can be equated with the historical Coel Hen Godhebog
CONSTANTIUS	Married Coel's daughter Helen; equated with the Roman Emperor Constantius I
CONSTANTINE I	Son of Constantius; the Roman Emperor Constantine the Great
OCTAVIUS	Duke of the Gewissei; seized power while Constantine was in Rome; driven out by
TRAHERN	Brother of Coel; later killed by
OCTAVIUS	who regained the throne
MAXIMIANUS	Son of Ioelinus, brother of Coel; married the daughter of Octavius
GRACIANUS	A freedman; seized power on the death of Maximianus
CONSTANTINE II	Brother of Aldroenus, King of Brittany; invited to Britain and chosen King

TENVANTIUS	Son of Lud; can be equated with the historical Tasciovanus
CYMBELINE	Son of Tenvantius; reigned over 10 years; can be equated with the historical Cunobelinus
GUIDERIUS	Son of Cymbeline
ARVIRARGUS	Brother of Guiderius
MARIUS	Son of Arvirargus
COILUS	Son of Marius
CONSTANS	Son of Constantine II
VORTIGERN	Usurped the throne; a historical figure
VORTIMER	Son of Vortigern, whom he deposed; poisoned by his stepmother
VORTIGERN	Restored
AURELIUS AMBROSIUS	Son of Constantine II; deposed Vortigern
UTHERPENDRAGON	Brother of Aurelius Ambrosius
ARTHUR	Son of Utherpendragon; the mighty King Arthur of legend; died 542
CONSTANTINE III	Son of Cador, Duke of Cornwall and cousin of Arthur
AURELIUS CONANUS	Nephew of Constantine III; died in the third year of his reign
VORTIPORIUS	
MALGO	The historical Maelgwn Gwynedd, King of Gwynedd, who died about 550
KEREDIC	
THREE UNNAMED KINGS	
CADVAN	The historical King of Gwynedd, Cadfan ab Iago, who reigned 616–ca 625
CADWALLO	The historical Cadwallon, son of Cadfan; reigned ca 625–633, although Geoffrey makes him reign 48 years
CADWALLADER	The historical Cadwaladr Fendigaid, son of Cadwallon; reigned 654–664. Geoffrey makes him die at Rome in 689, confusing him with Caedwalla, King of Wessex

Here Geoffrey ends his History.

Appendix B

1 THE DESCENDANTS OF WODEN

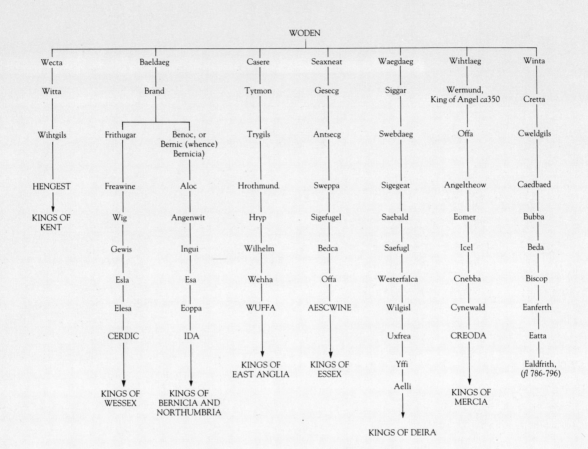

The above table is compiled from a synthesis of the traditional pedigrees recorded in the *Anglo-Saxon Chronicle*, and by Bede, Florence of Worcester and other early historians. Although it probably embodies much genuine material it must be accepted and used with great caution. In some cases names have obviously been omitted, while in others they have been duplicated and, in the case of Wessex in particular, interpolated to bring together two distinct traditions.

2 The Kings of Kent

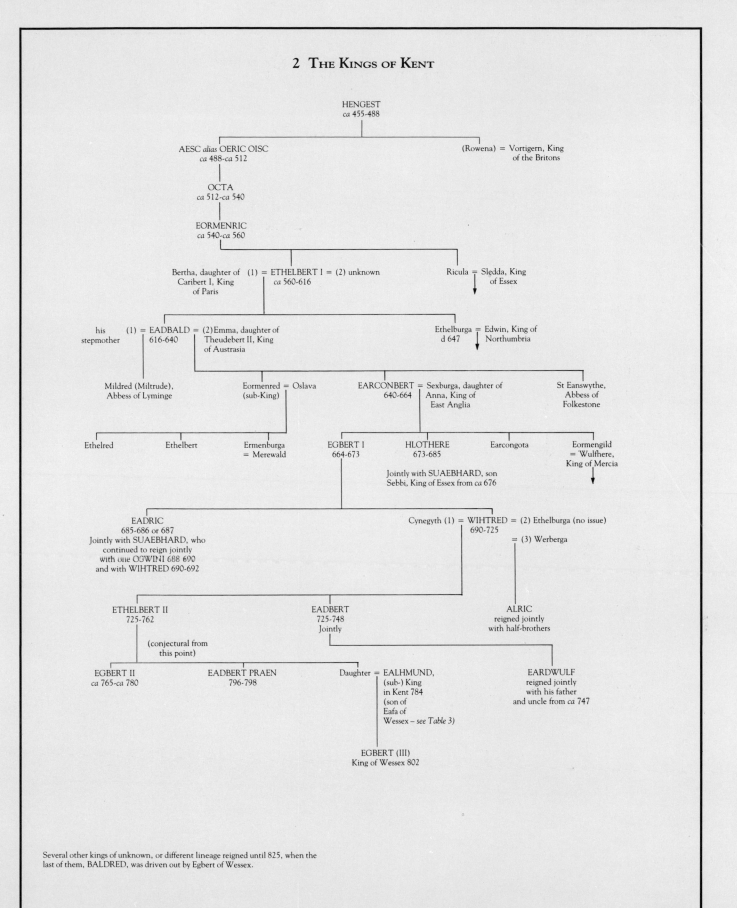

Several other kings of unknown, or different lineage reigned until 825, when the last of them, BALDRED, was driven out by Egbert of Wessex.

3 THE KINGS OF WESSEX FROM CERDIC TO EGBERT

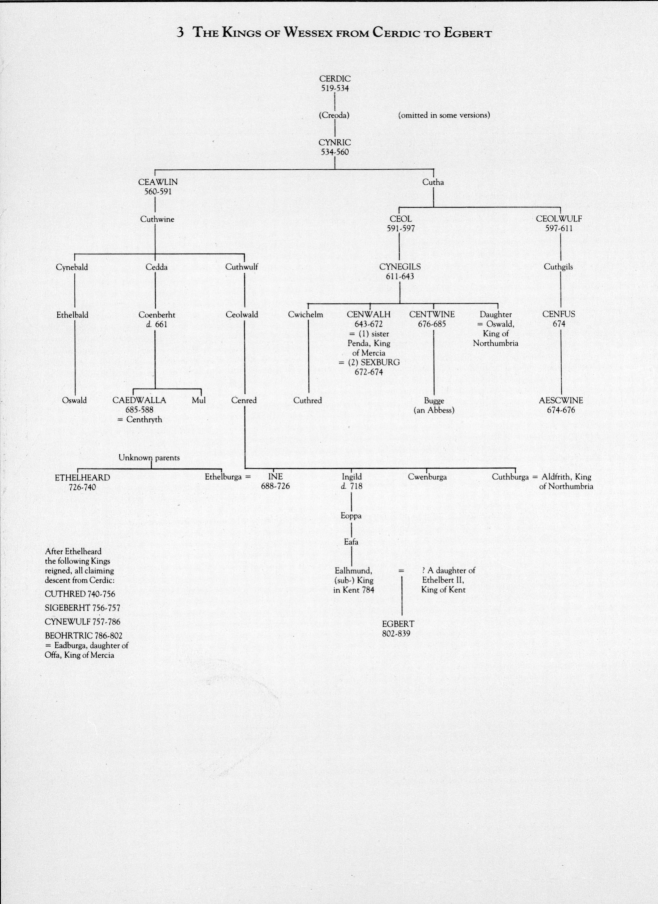

CERDIC
519-534

(Creoda)   (omitted in some versions)

CYNRIC
534-560

CEAWLIN
560-591

Cutha

Cuthwine

CEOL
591-597

CEOLWULF
597-611

Cynebald   Cedda   Cuthwulf

CYNEGILS
611-643

Cuthgils

Ethelbald   Coenberht
d. 661

Ceolwald

Cwichelm

CENWALH
643-672
= (1) sister
Penda, King
of Mercia
= (2) SEXBURG
672-674

CENTWINE
676-685

Daughter
= Oswald,
King of
Northumbria

CENFUS
674

Oswald   CAEDWALLA   Mul
685-588
= Centhryth

Cenred

Cuthred

Bugge
(an Abbess)

AESCWINE
674-676

Unknown parents

ETHELHEARD
726-740

Ethelburga = INE
688-726

Ingild
d. 718

Cwenburga

Cuthburga = Aldfrith, King
of Northumbria

Eoppa

Eafa

After Ethelheard
the following Kings
reigned, all claiming
descent from Cerdic:

CUTHRED 740-756

SIGEBERHT 756-757

CYNEWULF 757-786

BEOHRTRIC 786-802
= Eadburga, daughter of
Offa, King of Mercia

Ealhmund,
(sub-) King
in Kent 784

=

? A daughter of
Ethelbert II,
King of Kent

EGBERT
802-839

4 The Kings of Bernicia and Northumbria

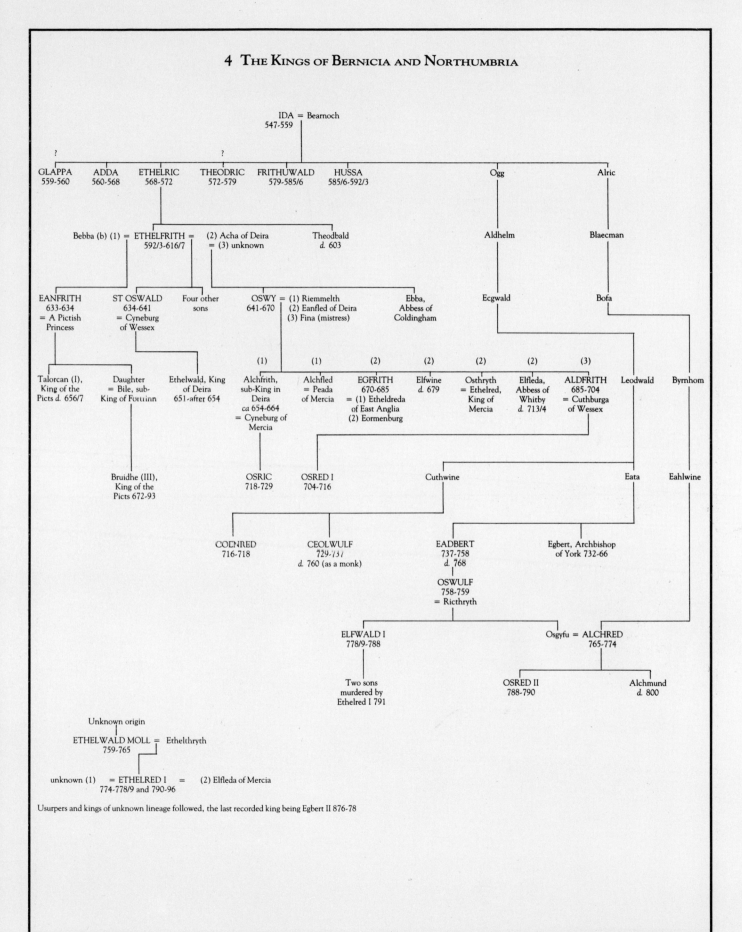

IDA = Bearnoch
547-559

GLAPPA 559-560   ADDA 560-568   ETHELRIC 568-572   THEODRIC 572-579   FRITHUWALD 579-585/6   HUSSA 585/6-592/3   Ogg   Alric

Aldhelm   Blaecman

Bebba (b) (1) = ETHELFRITH = (2) Acha of Deira = (3) unknown 592/3-616/7   Theodbald d. 603

Ecgwald   Bofa

EANFRITH 633-634 = A Pictish Princess   ST OSWALD 634-641 = Cyneburg of Wessex   Four other sons   OSWY 641-670 = (1) Riemmelth (2) Eanfled of Deira (3) Fina (mistress)   Ebba, Abbess of Coldingham

Leodwald   Byrnhom

(1)   (1)   (2)   (2)   (2)   (2)   (3)

Talorcan (I), King of the Picts d. 656/7   Daughter = Bile, sub-King of Fortrinn   Ethelwald, King of Deira 651-after 654   Alchfrith, sub-King in Deira ca 654-664 = Cyneburg of Mercia   Alchfled = Peada of Mercia   EGFRITH 670-685 = (1) Etheldreda of East Anglia (2) Eormenburg   Elfwine d. 679   Osthryth = Ethelred, King of Mercia   Elfleda, Abbess of Whitby d. 713/4   ALDFRITH 685-704 = Cuthburga of Wessex   Eahlwine

Bruidhe (III), King of the Picts 672-93   OSRIC 718-729   OSRED I 704-716   Cuthwine   Eata   Eahlwine

COENRED 716-718   CEOLWULF 729-737 d. 760 (as a monk)   EADBERT 737-758 d. 768   Egbert, Archbishop of York 732-66

OSWULF 758-759 = Ricthryth

ELFWALD I 778/9-788   Osgyfu = ALCHRED 765-774

Two sons murdered by Ethelred I 791   OSRED II 788-790   Alchmund d. 800

Unknown origin

ETHELWALD MOLL = Ethelthryth
759-765

unknown (1)   = ETHELRED I = (2) Elfleda of Mercia
774-778/9 and 790-96

Usurpers and kings of unknown lineage followed, the last recorded king being Egbert II 876-78

5 KINGS OF EAST ANGLIA

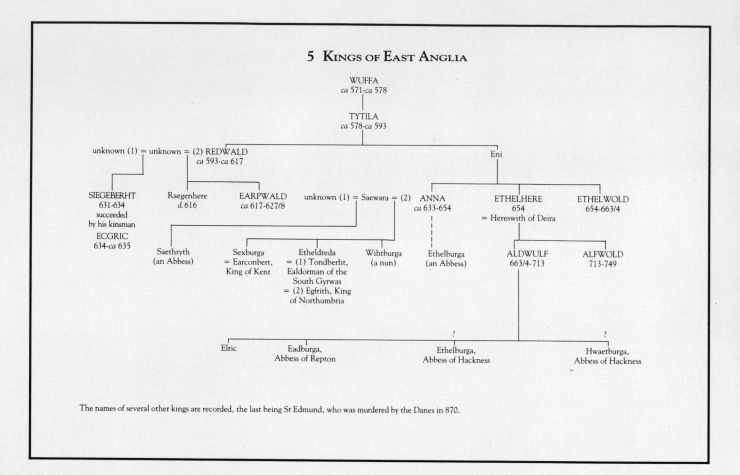

The names of several other kings are recorded, the last being St Edmund, who was murdered by the Danes in 870.

6 KINGS OF ESSEX

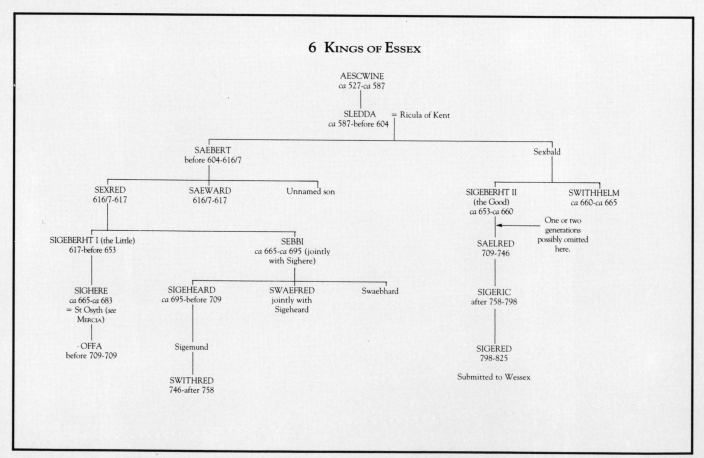

7 KINGS OF DEIRA

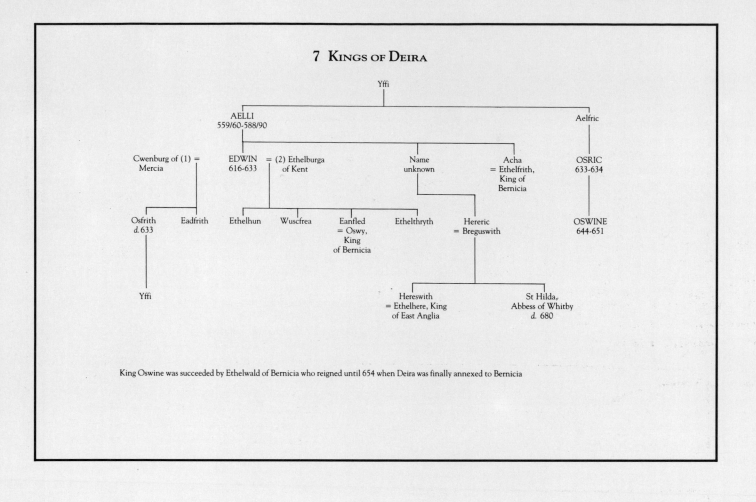

King Oswine was succeeded by Ethelwald of Bernicia who reigned until 654 when Deira was finally annexed to Bernicia

8 Kings of Mercia

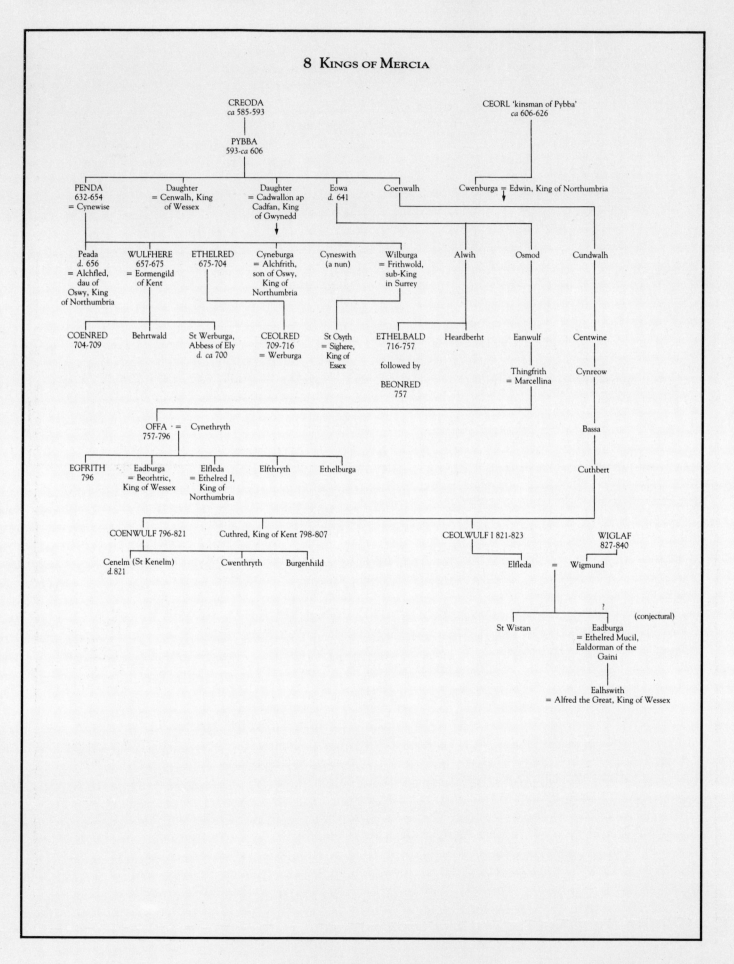

9 KINGS OF WESSEX AND ALL ENGLAND

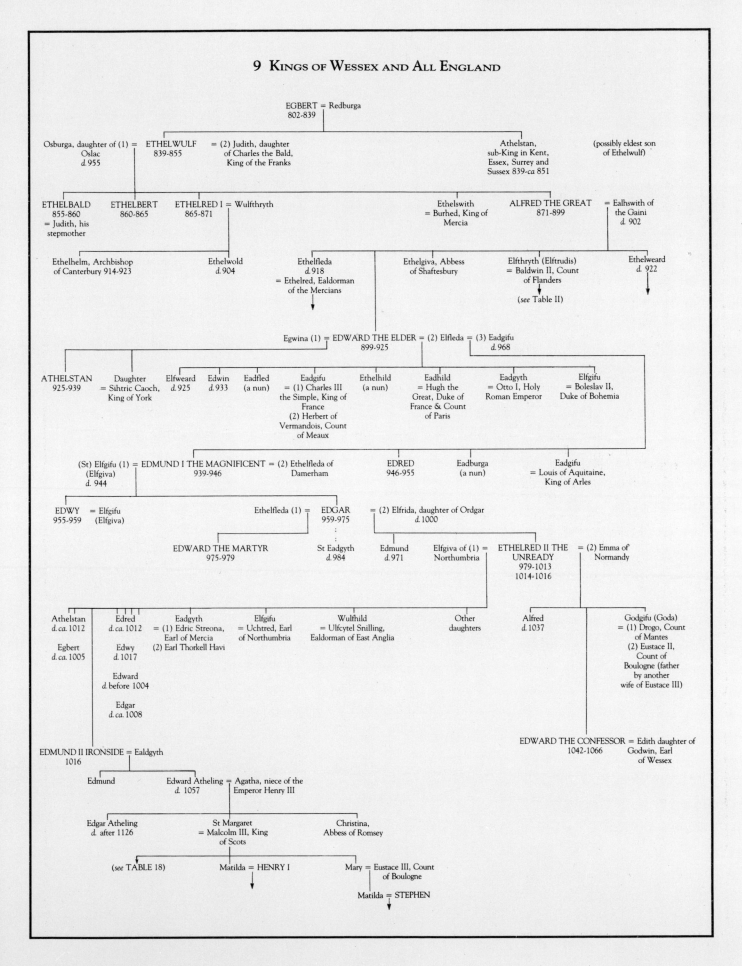

10 THE ANGLO-DANISH KINGS

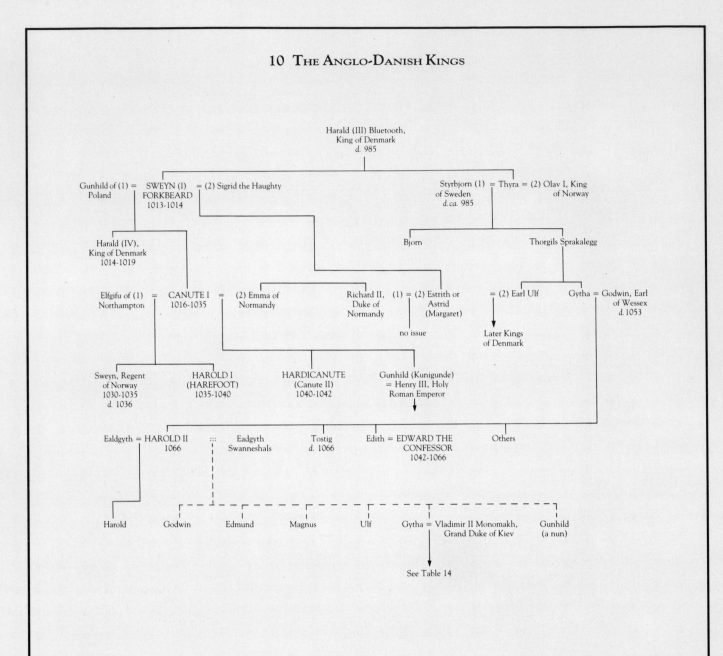

11 THE SAXON/NORMAN SUCCESSION

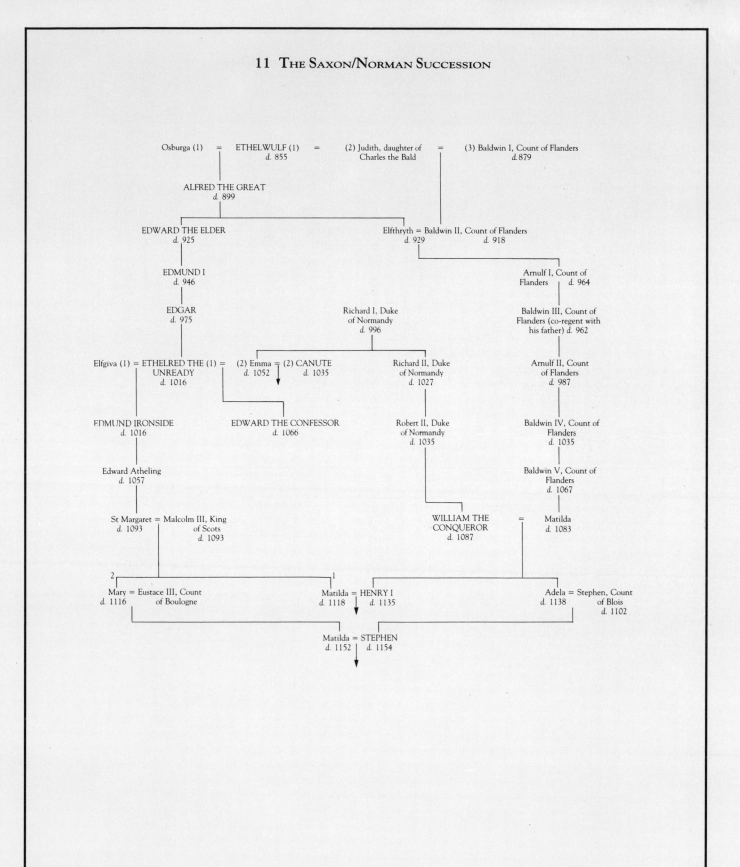

12 THE HOUSES OF NORMANDY AND BLOIS

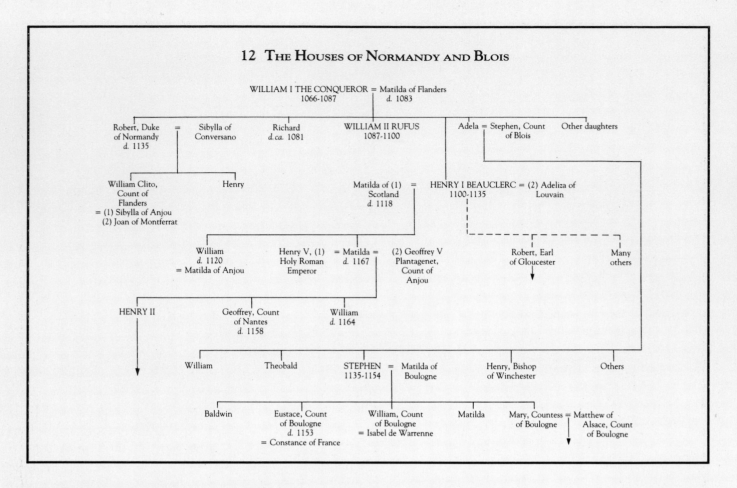

13 THE HOUSE OF ANJOU (PLANTAGENET)

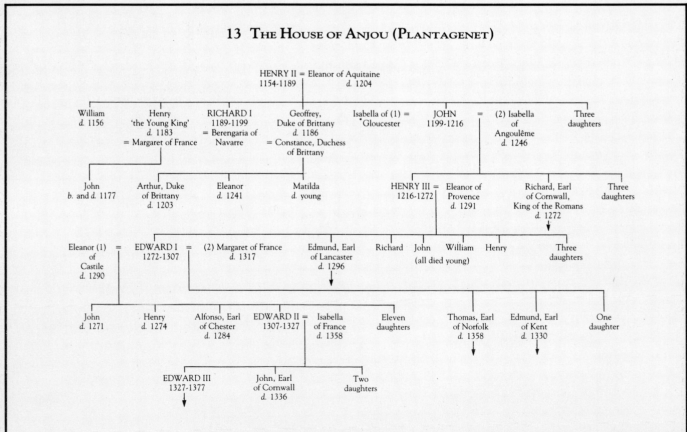

14 THE BLOOD OF HAROLD II RETURNS TO ENGLAND

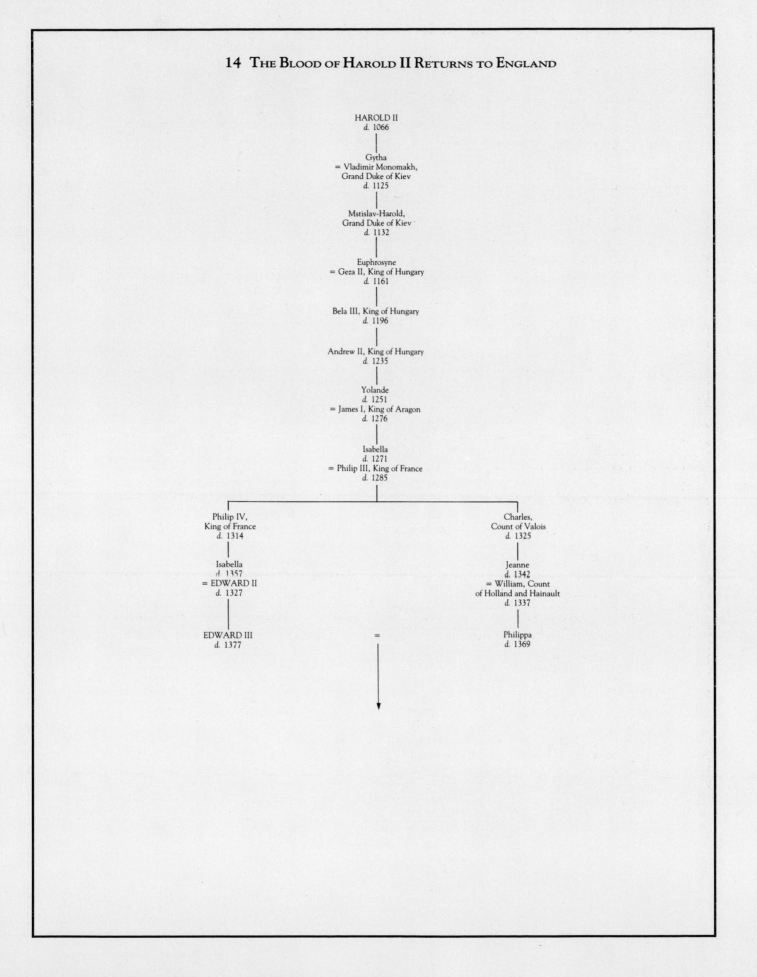

HAROLD II
d. 1066

Gytha
= Vladimir Monomakh,
Grand Duke of Kiev
d. 1125

Mstislav-Harold,
Grand Duke of Kiev
d. 1132

Euphrosyne
= Geza II, King of Hungary
d. 1161

Bela III, King of Hungary
d. 1196

Andrew II, King of Hungary
d. 1235

Yolande
d. 1251
= James I, King of Aragon
d. 1276

Isabella
d. 1271
= Philip III, King of France
d. 1285

| Philip IV, King of France *d.* 1314 | | Charles, Count of Valois *d.* 1325 |

Philip IV,
King of France
d. 1314

Charles,
Count of Valois
d. 1325

Isabella
d. 1357
= EDWARD II
d. 1327

Jeanne
d. 1342
= William, Count
of Holland and Hainault
d. 1337

EDWARD III
d. 1377

=

Philippa
d. 1369

15 Edward III to Henry VII

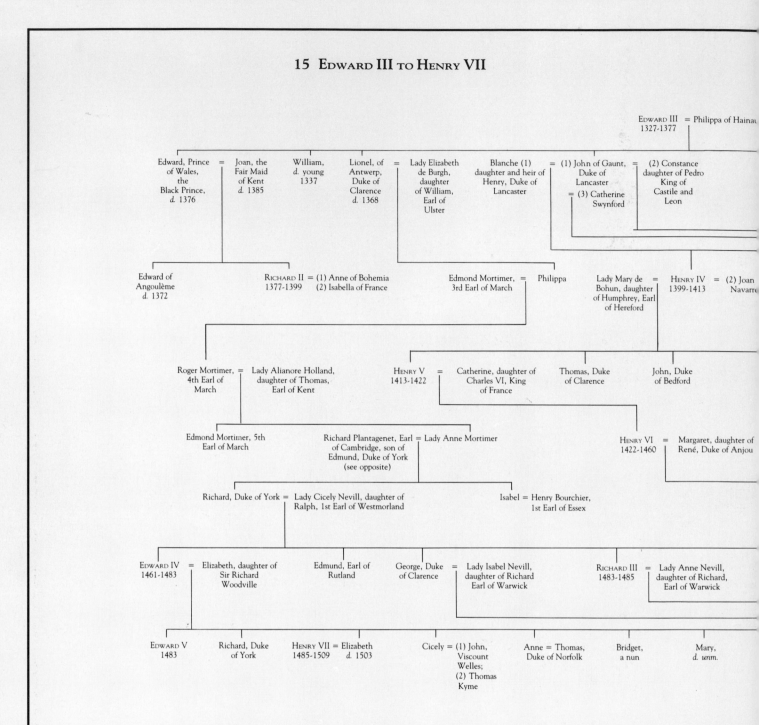

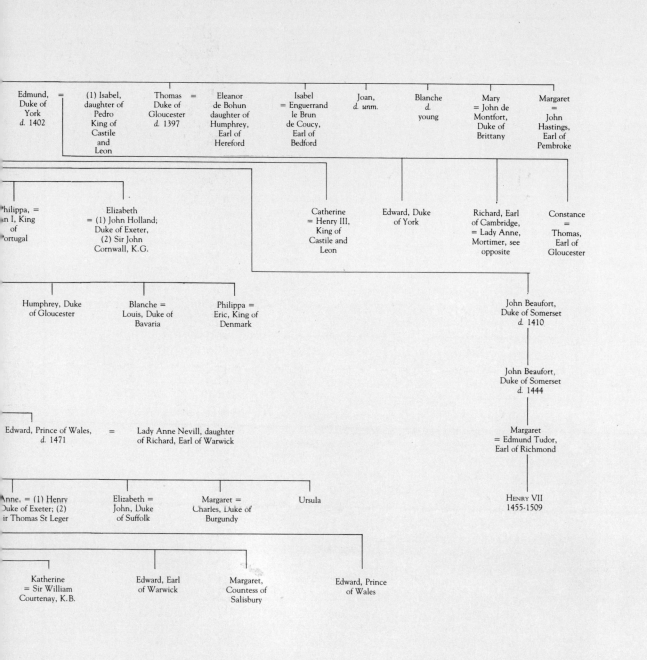

16 THE WELSH ANCESTRY OF KING HENRY VII (This table was compiled by the late P.W. Montague-Smith and appeared in the 1968 edition of Debrett's Peerage)

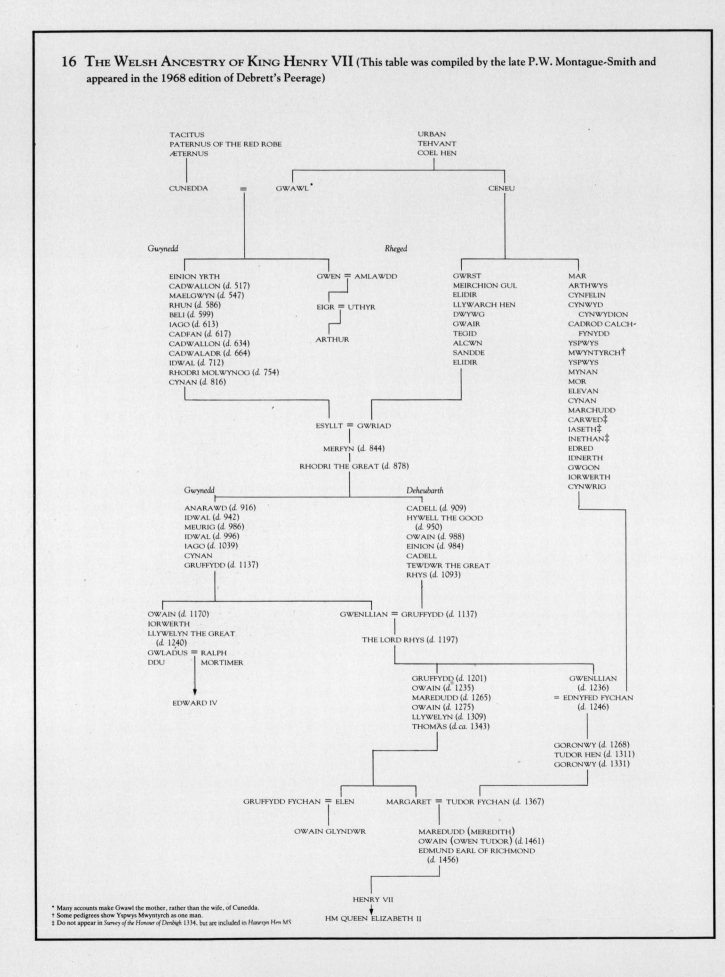

TACITUS
PATERNUS OF THE RED ROBE
ÆTERNUS

URBAN
TEHVANT
COEL HEN

CUNEDDA = GWAWL*   CENEU

Gwynedd   *Rheged*

EINION YRTH
CADWALLON (d. 517)
MAELGWYN (d. 547)
RHUN (d. 586)
BELI (d. 599)
IAGO (d. 613)
CADFAN (d. 617)
CADWALLON (d. 634)
CADWALADR (d. 664)
IDWAL (d. 712)
RHODRI MOLWYNOG (d. 754)
CYNAN (d. 816)

GWEN = AMLAWDD

EIGR = UTHYR

ARTHUR

GWRST
MEIRCHION GUL
ELIDIR
LLYWARCH HEN
DWYWG
GWAIR
TEGID
ALCWN
SANDDE
ELIDIR

MAR
ARTHWYS
CYNFELIN
CYNWYD
    CYNWYDION
CADROD CALCH-
    FYNYDD
YSPWYS
MWYNTYRCH†
YSPWYS
MYNAN
MOR
ELEVAN
CYNAN
MARCHUDD
CARWED‡
IASETH‡
INETHAN‡
EDRED
IDNERTH
GWGON
IORWERTH
CYNWRIG

ESYLLT = GWRIAD

MERFYN (d. 844)

RHODRI THE GREAT (d. 878)

Gwynedd   *Deheubarth*

ANARAWD (d. 916)
IDWAL (d. 942)
MEURIG (d. 986)
IDWAL (d. 996)
IAGO (d. 1039)
CYNAN
GRUFFYDD (d. 1137)

CADELL (d. 909)
HYWELL THE GOOD
    (d. 950)
OWAIN (d. 988)
EINION (d. 984)
CADELL
TEWDWR THE GREAT
RHYS (d. 1093)

OWAIN (d. 1170)
IORWERTH
LLYWELYN THE GREAT
    (d. 1240)
GWLADUS = RALPH
DDU   MORTIMER

GWENLLIAN = GRUFFYDD (d. 1137)

THE LORD RHYS (d. 1197)

EDWARD IV

GRUFFYDD (d. 1201)
OWAIN (d. 1235)
MAREDUDD (d. 1265)
OWAIN (d. 1275)
LLYWELYN (d. 1309)
THOMAS (d.ca. 1343)

GWENLLIAN
    (d. 1236)
= EDNYFED FYCHAN
    (d. 1246)

GORONWY (d. 1268)
TUDOR HEN (d. 1311)
GORONWY (d. 1331)

GRUFFYDD FYCHAN = ELEN   MARGARET = TUDOR FYCHAN (d. 1367)

OWAIN GLYNDWR

MAREDUDD (MEREDITH)
OWAIN (OWEN TUDOR) (d.1461)
EDMUND EARL OF RICHMOND
    (d. 1456)

HENRY VII
HM QUEEN ELIZABETH II

* Many accounts make Gwawl the mother, rather than the wife, of Cunedda.
† Some pedigrees show Yspwys Mwyntyrch as one man.
‡ Do not appear in *Survey of the Honour of Denbigh 1334*, but are included in *Hanesyn Hen* MS

17 The House of Tudor

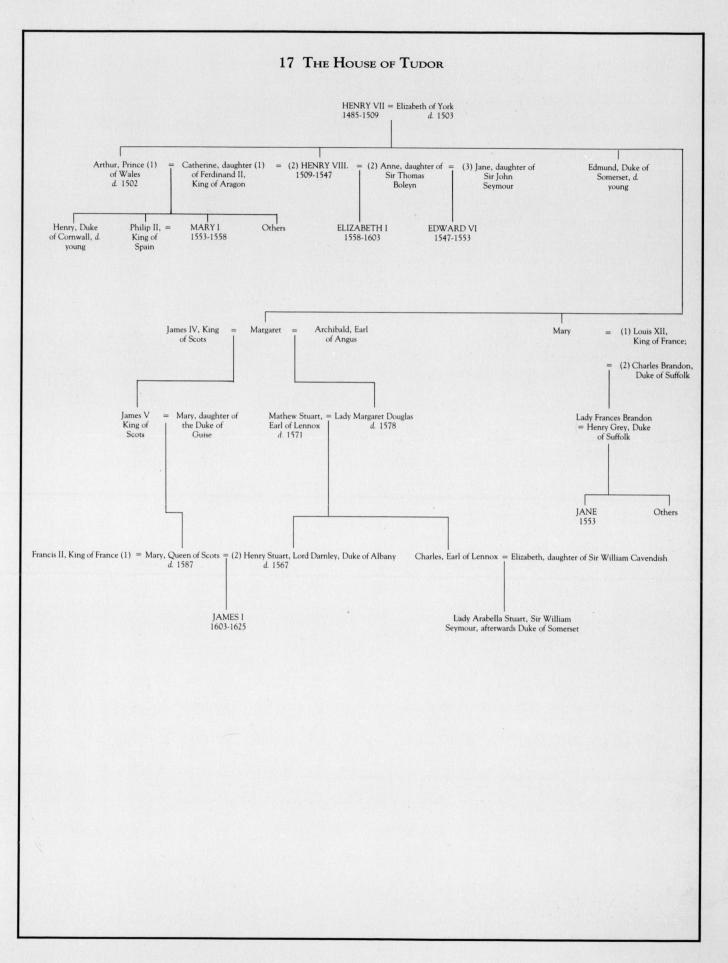

HENRY VII = Elizabeth of York
1485-1509   d. 1503

Arthur, Prince (1) = Catherine, daughter (1) = (2) HENRY VIII. = (2) Anne, daughter of = (3) Jane, daughter of   Edmund, Duke of
of Wales   of Ferdinand II,   1509-1547   Sir Thomas   Sir John   Somerset, d.
d. 1502   King of Aragon   Boleyn   Seymour   young

Henry, Duke   Philip II, = MARY I   Others   ELIZABETH I   EDWARD VI
of Cornwall, d.   King of   1553-1558   1558-1603   1547-1553
young   Spain

James IV, King = Margaret = Archibald, Earl   Mary   = (1) Louis XII,
of Scots   of Angus   King of France;

                                                                                            = (2) Charles Brandon,
                                                                                               Duke of Suffolk

James V = Mary, daughter of   Mathew Stuart, = Lady Margaret Douglas   Lady Frances Brandon
King of   the Duke of   Earl of Lennox   d. 1578   = Henry Grey, Duke
Scots   Guise   d. 1571   of Suffolk

                                                                               JANE   Others
                                                                               1553

Francis II, King of France (1) = Mary, Queen of Scots = (2) Henry Stuart, Lord Darnley, Duke of Albany   Charles, Earl of Lennox = Elizabeth, daughter of Sir William Cavendish
                                 d. 1587   d. 1567

                              JAMES I   Lady Arabella Stuart, Sir William
                              1603-1625   Seymour, afterwards Duke of Somerset

18 THE ROYAL HOUSE OF SCOTLAND

(adapted from *Royal Scotland* by Jean Goodman)

Ancient Britons of Strathclyde

CERETIC (Coroticus) the Gwledig, 5th century
King of Strathclyde, reproached by St Patrick

DYFNWAL Hen 'the Old', King of Strathclyde, 5th century

British princess = BRYCHAN,   CINBELIN
prince in Manau

INGENACH or LLEIAN   King CLINOG Eitin
(possibly of Edinburgh)

Gaels of Argyll

FERGUS Mor Mac Erc, King of Scots of Dalriada *c.* 490
(straddling Irish Channel from Antrim to Argyll), killed 501

DOMANGART, King of Scots of Dalriada (Argyll or 'Frontier of the Gael') *d. ca.* 506

GABHRAN, King of Scots of Argyll (killed by his nephew *ca.* 559)   ═══════

AIDAN, King of Scots of Argyll, consecrated King by his cousin St Columba *ca* 574, killed *ca* 608

EOCHAIDH Buidhe, King of Scots of Argyll, perhaps also maternally King of the Picts, *d. ca.* 629

DOMNALL Brecc 'the Speckled', King of Scots of Argyll, slain in battle against the Britons *ca.* 643

DOMANGART II, King of Scots of Argyll, killed *ca.* 673

EOCHAIDH 'Crook-Nose', King of Scots of Argyll, killed 697

EOCHAIDH III, King of Scots of Argyll (last also to reign in Irish Dalriada), *d.* 733

AEDH Find 'The White', King of Scots of Argyll, at war with Picts, killed 778

Picts of Caledonia

Matrilinear Pictish PRINCESSES ROYAL of Fortrinn (Verturiones) from
at least *ca.* 250, whose brothers reigned as High Kings of Alba (Albany)
by 5th century, probably in pagan times with throne-name of Bruide

Pictish PRINCESS ROYAL

Pictish PRINCESS ROYAL   CONSTANTINE, King of Picts   UNUIST, King of Picts
(?UNUISTICC)   789-820   820-34

EOCHAID 'the Venomous', King of Scots of Argyll (*ca.* 780)   ═══════

ALPIN, King of Kintyre, killed in battle *ca.* 834, possibly claiming Pictish throne

KENNETH mac Alpin, King of the Picts & Scots of all Alba, united both nations through his Pictish royal blood, *d.* 860

CONSTANTINE I, King of the Picts & Scots of all Alba, with his royal city at Scone, killed in battle against the Norsemen 877

DOMNALL II, King of Alba (united Pictland & Argyll), slain 900, buried on Iona

MALCOLM I, King of the Alba (Albany, modern Scotland north of the Forth & Clyde), slain by the Moray men 954

KENNETH II, King of Alba, killed on behalf of his Moray cousin & successor 995

MALCOLM II, King of Alba, mortally wounded by rival branches of royal house 1034, conquered Lothian 1018

Kindred of St Columba

BETHOC,   =   CRINAN, Hereditary Abbot of Dunkeld,
heiress of kingdom   killed in battle 1045
at Scone

DUNCAN I, King of Scots, killed by his successor Macbeth 1040

MALCOLM Canmore (Ceann-Mor), King of Scots, slew Macbeth 1057, (killed, invading England, 1093)   =   (2) SAINT MARGARET (*see* Table 9)

DAVID I 'the Saint', King of Scots (united Alba with Strathclyde), youngest son *d.* 1153   ALEXANDER I, King of Scots, elder brother, *d.* 1124

HENRY, King Designate of Scots, Earl of Northumberland & Huntingdon, predeceased his father 1152

DAVID, Earl of Huntingdon, youngest son, *d.* 1219   MALCOLM IV 'the Maiden', King of Scots, *d.* 1165   WILLIAM 'the Lyon', King of Scots, *d.* 1214

ALEXANDER II, King of Scots, *d.* 1249

ALEXANDER III, King of Scots, *d.* 1286

MARGARET, = ERIC, King of Norway

MARGARET, the 'Maid of Norway' *d.* 1290

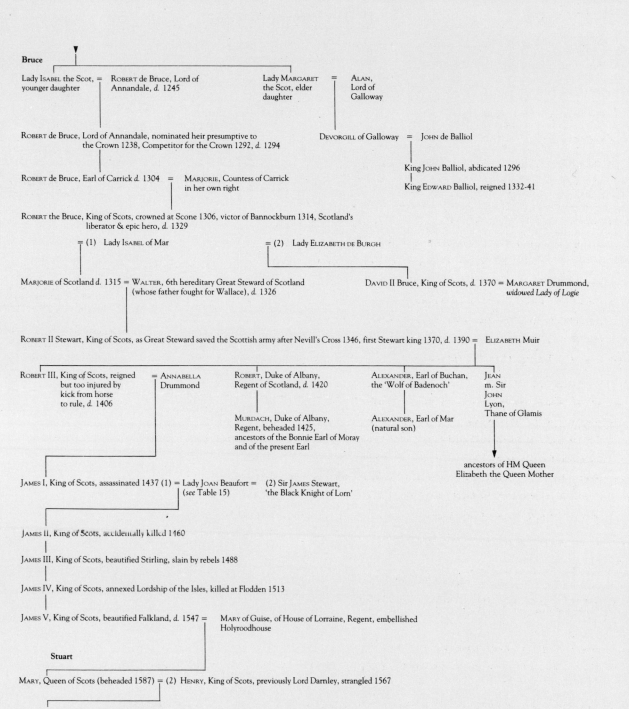

Bruce

Lady ISABEL the Scot, = ROBERT de BRUCE, Lord of   Lady MARGARET   =   ALAN,
younger daughter   Annandale, d. 1245   the Scot, elder   Lord of
                                                          daughter   Galloway

ROBERT de BRUCE, Lord of Annandale, nominated heir presumptive to   DEVORGILL of Galloway = JOHN de BALLIOL
    the Crown 1238, Competitor for the Crown 1292, d. 1294

                                                                                     King JOHN Balliol, abdicated 1296

ROBERT de BRUCE, Earl of Carrick d. 1304 = MARJORIE, Countess of Carrick   King EDWARD Balliol, reigned 1332-41
                                              in her own right

ROBERT the Bruce, King of Scots, crowned at Scone 1306, victor of Bannockburn 1314, Scotland's
    liberator & epic hero, d. 1329

        = (1)   Lady ISABEL of Mar   = (2)   Lady ELIZABETH DE BURGH

MARJORIE of Scotland d. 1315 = WALTER, 6th hereditary Great Steward of Scotland   DAVID II Bruce, King of Scots, d. 1370 = MARGARET Drummond,
                               (whose father fought for Wallace), d. 1326   *widowed Lady of Logie*

ROBERT II Stewart, King of Scots, as Great Steward saved the Scottish army after Nevill's Cross 1346, first Stewart king 1370, d. 1390 = ELIZABETH Muir

ROBERT III, King of Scots, reigned   = ANNABELLA   ROBERT, Duke of Albany,   ALEXANDER, Earl of Buchan,   JEAN
    but too injured by   Drummond   Regent of Scotland, d. 1420   the 'Wolf of Badenoch'   m. Sir
    kick from horse   JOHN
    to rule, d. 1406   Lyon,
                                                     MURDACH, Duke of Albany,   Thane of Glamis
                                                      Regent, beheaded 1425,   ALEXANDER, Earl of Mar
                                                      ancestors of the Bonnie Earl of Moray   (natural son)
                                                      and of the present Earl

                                                                                                                    ancestors of HM Queen
                                                                                                                    Elizabeth the Queen Mother

JAMES I, King of Scots, assassinated 1437 (1) = Lady JOAN Beaufort =   (2) Sir JAMES Stewart,
                                                (*see* Table 15)   'the Black Knight of Lorn'

JAMES II, King of Scots, accidentally killed 1460

JAMES III, King of Scots, beautified Stirling, slain by rebels 1488

JAMES IV, King of Scots, annexed Lordship of the Isles, killed at Flodden 1513

JAMES V, King of Scots, beautified Falkland, d. 1547 =   MARY of Guise, of House of Lorraine, Regent, embellished
                                                          Holyroodhouse

        Stuart

MARY, Queen of Scots (beheaded 1587) = (2) HENRY, King of Scots, previously Lord Darnley, strangled 1567

JAMES VI, King of Scots (James I, King of England), united the Crowns but not the countries, d. 1625

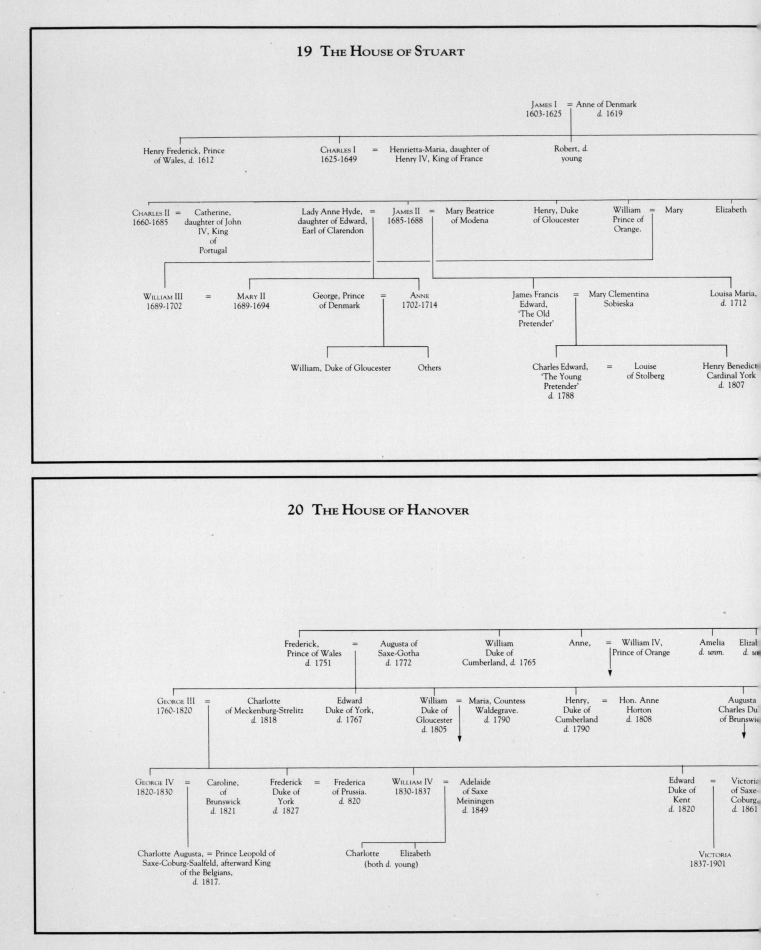

19 THE HOUSE OF STUART

JAMES I = Anne of Denmark
1603-1625   d. 1619

Henry Frederick, Prince
of Wales, d. 1612

CHARLES I = Henrietta-Maria, daughter of
1625-1649   Henry IV, King of France

Robert, d.
young

CHARLES II = Catherine,
1660-1685   daughter of John
IV, King
of
Portugal

Lady Anne Hyde, = JAMES II = Mary Beatrice
daughter of Edward,   1685-1688   of Modena
Earl of Clarendon

Henry, Duke
of Gloucester

William = Mary
Prince of
Orange.

Elizabeth

WILLIAM III = MARY II
1689-1702   1689-1694

George, Prince = ANNE
of Denmark   1702-1714

James Francis = Mary Clementina
Edward,   Sobieska
'The Old
Pretender'

Louisa Maria,
d. 1712

William, Duke of Gloucester   Others

Charles Edward, = Louise
'The Young   of Stolberg
Pretender'
d. 1788

Henry Benedict
Cardinal York
d. 1807

20 THE HOUSE OF HANOVER

Frederick, = Augusta of
Prince of Wales   Saxe-Gotha
d. 1751   d. 1772

William
Duke of
Cumberland, d. 1765

Anne, = William IV,
Prince of Orange

Amelia
d. unm.

Elizab
d. u

GEORGE III = Charlotte
1760-1820   of Meckenburg-Strelitz
d. 1818

Edward
Duke of York,
d. 1767

William = Maria, Countess
Duke of   Waldegrave.
Gloucester   d. 1790
d. 1805

Henry, = Hon. Anne
Duke of   Horton
Cumberland d. 1808
d. 1790

Augusta
Charles Du
of Brunswic

GEORGE IV = Caroline,
1820-1830   of
Brunswick
d. 1821

Frederick = Frederica
Duke of   of Prussia.
York   d. 820
d. 1827

WILLIAM IV = Adelaide
1830-1837   of Saxe
Meiningen
d. 1849

Edward = Victoria
Duke of   of Saxe-
Kent   Coburg,
d. 1820   d. 1861

Charlotte Augusta, = Prince Leopold of
Saxe-Coburg-Saalfeld, afterward King
of the Belgians,
d. 1817.

Charlotte   Elizabeth
(both d. young)

VICTORIA
1837-1901

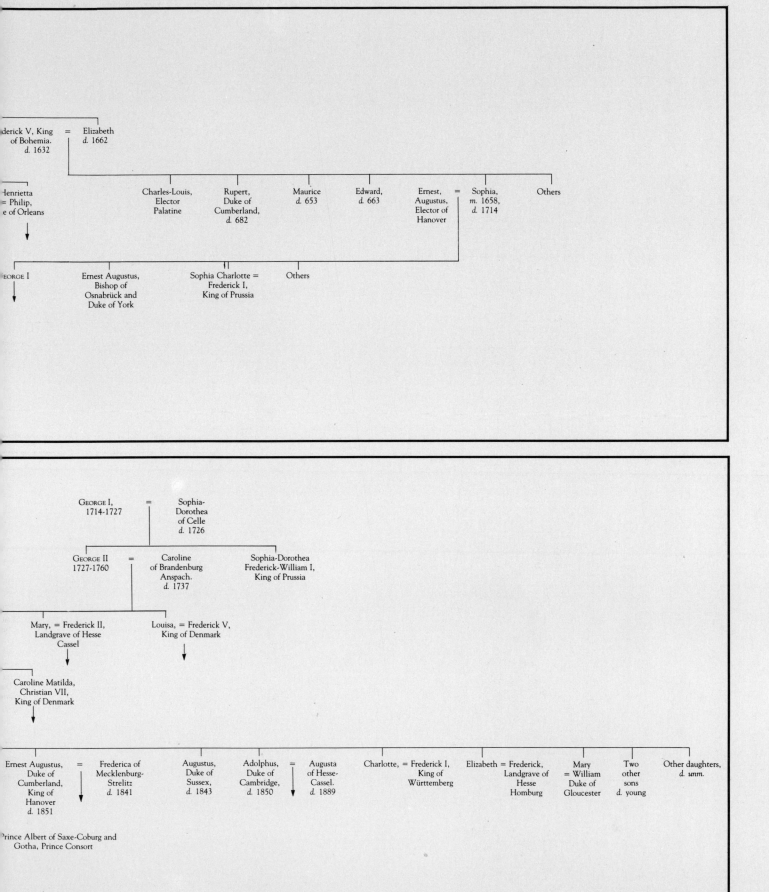

...derick V, King
of Bohemia.
d. 1632
= Elizabeth
d. 1662

...Henrietta
= Philip,
...e of Orleans

Charles-Louis,
Elector
Palatine

Rupert,
Duke of
Cumberland,
d. 682

Maurice
d. 653

Edward,
d. 663

Ernest,
Augustus,
Elector of
Hanover
= Sophia,
m. 1658,
d. 1714

Others

...EORGE I

Ernest Augustus,
Bishop of
Osnabrück and
Duke of York

Sophia Charlotte =
Frederick I,
King of Prussia

Others

GEORGE I,
1714-1727
= Sophia-
Dorothea
of Celle
d. 1726

GEORGE II
1727-1760
= Caroline
of Brandenburg
Anspach.
d. 1737

Sophia-Dorothea
Frederick-William I,
King of Prussia

Mary, = Frederick II,
Landgrave of Hesse
Cassel

Louisa, = Frederick V,
King of Denmark

Caroline Matilda,
Christian VII,
King of Denmark

Ernest Augustus,
Duke of
Cumberland,
King of
Hanover
d. 1851
= Frederica of
Mecklenburg-
Strelitz
d. 1841

Augustus,
Duke of
Sussex,
d. 1843

Adolphus,
Duke of
Cambridge,
d. 1850
= Augusta
of Hesse-
Cassel.
d. 1889

Charlotte, = Frederick I,
King of
Württemberg

Elizabeth = Frederick,
Landgrave of
Hesse
Homburg

Mary
= William
Duke of
Gloucester

Two
other
sons
d. young

Other daughters,
d. unm.

...Prince Albert of Saxe-Coburg and
Gotha, Prince Consort

21 FROM HANOVER TO WINDSOR

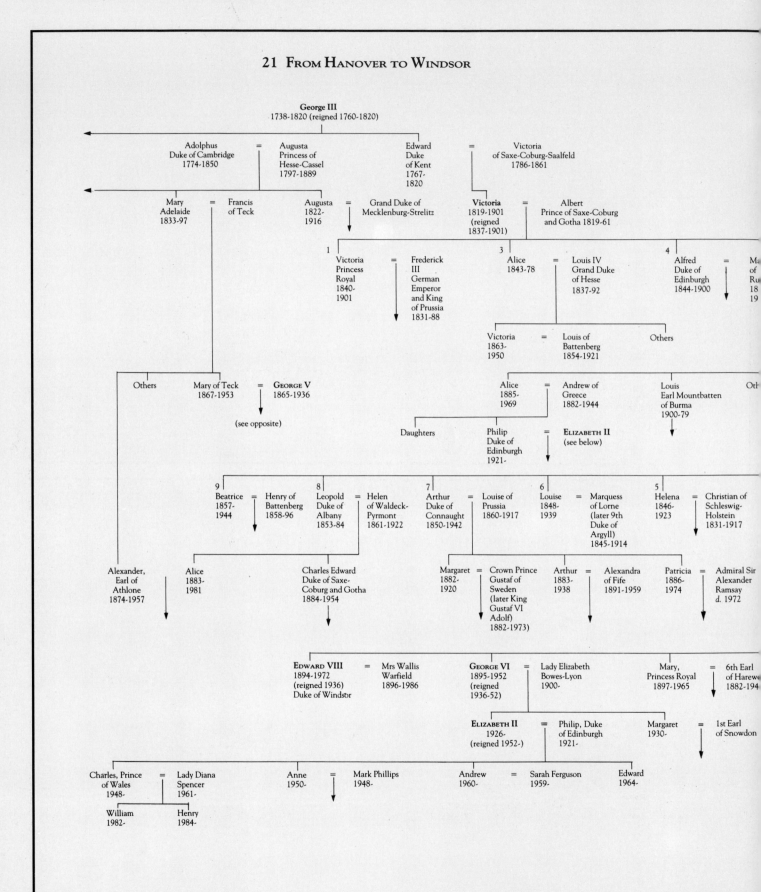

George III
1738-1820 (reigned 1760-1820)

Adolphus
Duke of Cambridge
1774-1850
= Augusta
Princess of
Hesse-Cassel
1797-1889

Edward
Duke
of Kent
1767-
1820
= Victoria
of Saxe-Coburg-Saalfeld
1786-1861

Mary
Adelaide
1833-97
= Francis
of Teck

Augusta
1822-
1916
= Grand Duke of
Mecklenburg-Strelitz

Victoria
1819-1901
(reigned
1837-1901)
= Albert
Prince of Saxe-Coburg
and Gotha 1819-61

1 Victoria
Princess
Royal
1840-
1901
= Frederick
III
German
Emperor
and King
of Prussia
1831-88

3 Alice
1843-78
= Louis IV
Grand Duke
of Hesse
1837-92

4 Alfred
Duke of
Edinburgh
1844-1900
= Ma
of
Ru
18
19

Victoria
1863-
1950
= Louis of
Battenberg
1854-1921

Others

Others

Mary of Teck
1867-1953
= GEORGE V
1865-1936

Alice
1885-
1969
= Andrew of
Greece
1882-1944

Louis
Earl Mountbatten
of Burma
1900-79

Oth

(see opposite)

Daughters

Philip
Duke of
Edinburgh
1921-
= ELIZABETH II
(see below)

9 Beatrice
1857-
1944
= Henry of
Battenberg
1858-96

8 Leopold
Duke of
Albany
1853-84
= Helen
of Waldeck-
Pyrmont
1861-1922

7 Arthur
Duke of
Connaught
1850-1942
= Louise of
Prussia
1860-1917

6 Louise
1848-
1939
= Marquess
of Lorne
(later 9th
Duke of
Argyll)
1845-1914

5 Helena
1846-
1923
= Christian of
Schleswig-
Holstein
1831-1917

Alexander,
Earl of
Athlone
1874-1957

Alice
1883-
1981

Charles Edward
Duke of Saxe-
Coburg and Gotha
1884-1954

Margaret
1882-
1920
= Crown Prince
Gustaf of
Sweden
(later King
Gustaf VI
Adolf)
1882-1973)

Arthur
1883-
1938
= Alexandra
of Fife
1891-1959

Patricia
1886-
1974
= Admiral Sir
Alexander
Ramsay
d. 1972

EDWARD VIII
1894-1972
(reigned 1936)
Duke of Windsor
= Mrs Wallis
Warfield
1896-1986

GEORGE VI
1895-1952
(reigned
1936-52)
= Lady Elizabeth
Bowes-Lyon
1900-

Mary,
Princess Royal
1897-1965
= 6th Earl
of Harew
1882-194

ELIZABETH II
1926-
(reigned 1952-)
= Philip, Duke
of Edinburgh
1921-

Margaret
1930-
= 1st Earl
of Snowdon

Charles, Prince
of Wales
1948-
= Lady Diana
Spencer
1961-

Anne
1950-
= Mark Phillips
1948-

Andrew
1960-
= Sarah Ferguson
1959-

Edward
1964-

William
1982-

Henry
1984-

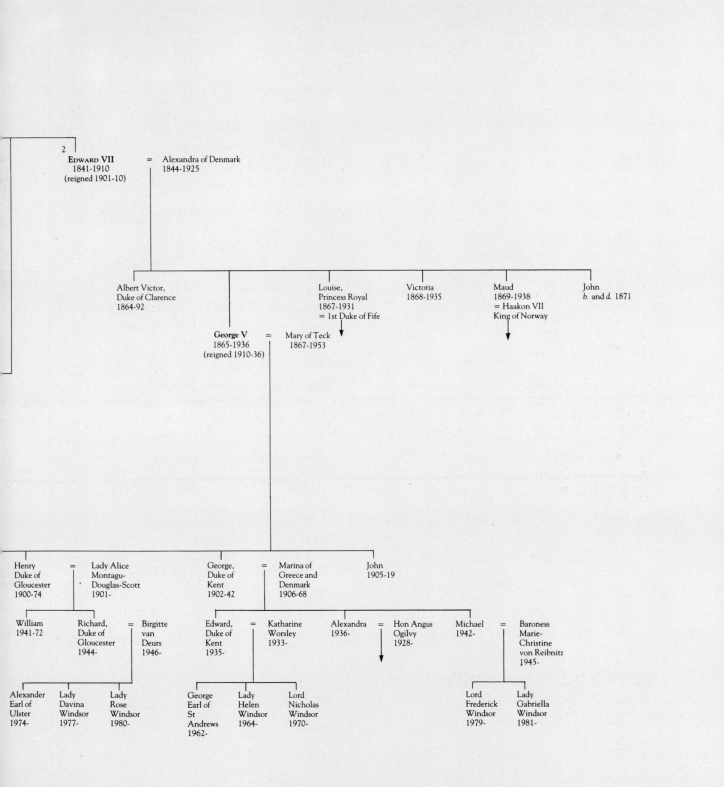

2

EDWARD VII = Alexandra of Denmark
1841-1910   1844-1925
(reigned 1901-10)

Albert Victor,   Louise,   Victoria   Maud   John
Duke of Clarence   Princess Royal   1868-1935   1869-1938   b. and d. 1871
1864-92   1867-1931   = Haakon VII
                                  = 1st Duke of Fife   King of Norway

George V   =   Mary of Teck
1865-1936   1867-1953
(reigned 1910-36)

Henry   =   Lady Alice   George,   =   Marina of   John
Duke of   Montagu-   Duke of   Greece and   1905-19
Gloucester   Douglas-Scott   Kent   Denmark
1900-74   1901-   1902-42   1906-68

William   Richard,   = Birgitte   Edward,   = Katharine   Alexandra   =   Hon Angus   Michael   =   Baroness
1941-72   Duke of   van   Duke of   Worsley   1936-   Ogilvy   1942-   Marie-
                Gloucester   Deurs   Kent   1933-   1928-   Christine
                1944-   1946-   1935-   von Reibnitz
                                                                                                                          1945-

Alexander   Lady   Lady   George   Lady   Lord   Lord   Lady
Earl of   Davina   Rose   Earl of   Helen   Nicholas   Frederick   Gabriella
Ulster   Windsor   Windsor   St   Windsor   Windsor   Windsor   Windsor
1974-   1977-   1980-   Andrews   1964-   1970-   1979-   1981-
                                    1962-

22 THE DESCENT OF THE ROYAL FAMILY FROM IRISH KINGS

Ireland was divided into five main kingdoms, Ulster, Munster, Leinster, Connaught and Meath, each of which was again sub-divided into many petty kingdoms. A High King, or Supreme Monarch of Ireland, was elected from among the main kingdoms and inaugurated in an ancient ceremony on the hill of Tara. Brian Boru, King of Munster, became one of Ireland's greatest High Kings and was killed after the battle of Clontarf, in which he won a great victory over the Danes, in 1014. His descendants continued to reign as Kings of Munster until 1120 and thereafter as Kings of Thomond (North Munster) until they submitted to Henry VIII and were created Earls of Thomond and Barons of Inchiquin. King Henry II invaded Ireland in 1172 and was acknowledged as liege lord by the last native High King, Rory O'Connor, in 1175. The Kings of England then assumed the title of Lord of Ireland, which they bore until 1542, when Henry VIII changed the style to King by Act of Parliament.

BRIAN BORU, High King of Ireland, 1002-1014

TEIGE (TERENCE) (d. 1023)   DONNCHAD, King of Munster 1023-64

DEARBFORGAIL (d. 1080) = DERMOT MacMAILNAMO, King of Leinster, and High King of Ireland (d. 1072)

TURLOUGH, King of Munster 1064-1086, and High King of Ireland 1072-1086

MURCHAD, King of Leinster (d. 1090)

DERMOT, King of Munster 1116-1120

DONCHAD, King of Leinster (d. 1115)

ENNA, King of Leinster (d. 1126)

TURLOUGH, King of Thomond 1142-1167

DERMOT MacMURROUGH, King of Leinster (d. 1171)

DONNELL MORE, King of Thomond (d. 1194) = URLACHAN

AOIFE (EVA) = RICHARD (STRONGBOW), Earl of Pembroke

DONOUGH CAIRBREACH, King of Thomond 1239-1242

ISABEL = WILLIAM MARSHAL Earl of Pembroke

CONOR NA SUIDANE, King of Thomond 1242-1258

EVA = WILLIAM DE BRAOSE

TEIGE CAELUISCE, King of Thomond 1258-1259

MAUD = ROGER MORTIMER

TURLOUGH, King of Thomond (d. 1306)

EDMUND MORTIMER 1st Lord Mortimer

MORTOGH, King of Thomond 1307-1343

ROGER MORTIMER 1st Earl of March

MAHON MOINMOY, King of Thomond 1343-1369

Sir EDMUND MORTIMER

BRIAN CATHA AN EANAIGH, King of Thomond 1370-1399

ROGER MORTIMER 2nd Earl of March

TURLOUGH BOG (The Soft), King of Thomond 1446-1459

EDMUND MORTIMER 3rd Earl of March (d. 1382)

TEIGE AN CHOMARD, King of Thomond 1461-1466

ROGER MORTIMER 4th Earl of March (d. 1398)

TURLOUGH DON, King of Thomond 1499-1528

Lady ANNE MORTIMER = RICHARD, Earl of Cambridge

MURROUGH, last King of Thomond 1540-1543, 1st Earl of Thomond and Lord Inchiquin (d. 1551)

RICHARD, Duke of York

DERMOD O'BRIEN, 2nd Lord Inchiquin (d. 1557)

EDWARD IV

MURROUGH O'BRIEN, 3rd Lord Inchiquin (d. 1573)

ELIZABETH of York = HENRY VII

MURROUGH O'BRIEN, 4th Lord Inchiquin (d. 1597)

MARGARET = JAMES IV, King of Scots

DERMOT O'BRIEN, 5th Lord Inchiquin (d. 1624)

JAMES V

MARY (sister of 1st Earl of Inchiquin) = Dr. MICHAEL BOYLE, Archbishop of Armagh

MARY, Queen of Scots = HENRY, Lord Darnley

JAMES VI and I

ELEANOR BOYLE = WILLIAM HILL

ELIZABETH = FREDERICK, King of Bohemia

MICHAEL HILL of Hillsborough

SOPHIA = ERNEST AUGUSTUS, Elector of Hanover

ARTHUR HILL, 1st Viscount Dungannon

GEORGE I

Hon. ANNE HILL (d. 1831) = GARRET WELLESLEY, 1st Earl of Mornington

GEORGE II

RICHARD WELLESLEY, Marquess Wellesley (d. 1842)   ARTHUR WELLESLEY, 1st Duke of Wellington

FREDERICK, Prince of Wales

ANNE WELLESLEY = Lord WILLIAM CHARLES AUGUSTUS CAVENDISH-BENTINCK (d. 1826)

GEORGE III

Rev. CHARLES WILLIAM FREDERICK CAVENDISH-BENTINCK (d. 1865)

EDWARD, Duke of Kent

Queen VICTORIA = ALBERT of Saxe-Coburg and Gotha (Prince Consort)

NINA CECILIA CAVENDISH-BENTINCK = CLAUDE GEORGE BOWES-LYON 14th Earl of Strathmore and Kinghorne

EDWARD VII

GEORGE V

Lady ELIZABETH BOWES-LYON = H.M. King GEORGE VI

H.M. Queen ELIZABETH II

BIBLIOGRAPHY

ADDINGTON, A.C. *The Royal House of Stuart* 3 vols (1969-76)

ALICE, H.R.H. PRINCESS, COUNTESS OF ATHLONE *For My Grandchildren* (1966)

ALLEN, D.F. *The Belgic Dynasties of Britain and their Coins* (1944)

APPLEBY, JOHN T. *The Troubled Reign of King Stephen* (1969)

ASHLEY, MAURICE *James II* (1977)

BARLOW, FRANK *William I and the Norman Conquest* (1965); *Edward the Confessor* (1970); *William Rufus* (1983)

BATTISCOMBE, GEORGINA *Queen Alexandra* (1969)

BEDE *A History of the English Church and People* (translated by Leo Sherley-Price, revised by R.E. Latham) (1968)

BINGHAM, CAROLINE *James I of England* (1982)

BLAND, OLIVIA *The Royal Way of Death* (1986)

BOLITHO, HECTOR *The Prince Consort and His Brother* (1933)

BROOKE, CHRISTOPHER *The Saxon and Norman Kings* (1963)

BROOKE, JOHN *King George III* (1972)

Burke's Guide to the Royal Family (1973)

Burke's Royal Families of the World Vol I (1977)

CHAPMAN, HESTER W. *Queen Anne's Son – A Memoir of William Henry, Duke of Gloucester 1689-1700* (1954)

CHENEY, C.R. *Handbook of Dates for Students of English History* (1945)

CONNELL, NEVILLE *Anne* (1937)

COWLES, VIRGINIA *Edward VII and his Circle* (1956)

CRESTON, DORMER *The Regent and his Daughter* (1932)

DAVIS, R.H.C. *King Stephen* (1967)

Dictionary of National Biography (1882-)

Dictionary of Welsh Biography (1959)

DONALDSON, FRANCES *Edward VIII* (1974)

DOUGLAS, DAVID C. *William the Conqueror* (1964)

ELLIS, PETER BERESFORD *Caesar's Invasion of Britain* (1978)

FRASER, ANTONIA *Mary, Queen of Scots* (1969); *King James VI of Scotland, I of England* (1974); *King Charles II* (1979)

FULFORD, ROGER *Royal Dukes* (1933); *George IV* (1935); *The Prince Consort* (1949); *Queen Victoria* (1951); *Hanover to Windsor* (1960); *Dearest Child* (1964); *Dearest Mama* (1968); *Your Dear Letter* (1971); *Darling Child* (1976); *The Trial of Queen Caroline* (1967)

GARMONSWAY, G.N. (translator) *The Anglo-Saxon Chronicle* (1953)

G.E.C. (George Edward Cokayne) *The Complete Peerage* (1910-1959)

GEOFFREY OF MONMOUTH *The History of the Kings of Britain* (translated by Lewis Thorpe) (1966)

GREEN, DAVID *Queen Anne* (1970)

GREENWOOD, ALICE *Lives of the Hanoverian Queens of England* 2 vols (1909-11)

HAMPDEN, J. *Crusader King* (1956)

HARVEY, JOHN *The Plantagenets* (1948, revised edn 1959)

HATTON, RAGNHILD *George I – Elector and King* (1978)

HEDLEY, OLWEN *Queen Charlotte* (1975)

HENDERSON, P. *Richard Coeur-de-Lion* (1958)

HIBBERT, CHRISTOPHER *Charles I* (1968); *George, Prince of Wales* (1972); *George IV, Regent and King* (1973)

HOBHOUSE, HERMIONE *Prince Albert – His Life and Work* (1983)

HOLM, THEA *Caroline – A Biography of Caroline of Brunswick* (1979)

HOPKIRK, MARY *Queen Adelaide* (1946)

ILLUSTRATED LONDON NEWS *Record of the Coronation Service and Ceremony – King Edward VII and Queen Alexandra* (1902)

KENDALL, PAUL MURRAY *Richard the Third* (1955)

KEYNES, SIMON and LAPIDGE, MICHAEL (translators) *Alfred the Great – Asser's Life of King Alfred and other contemporary sources* (1983)

LANE, H.M. *The Royal Daughters of England* 2 vols (1910)

LESLIE, SHANE *Mrs Fitzherbert* 2 vols (1939)

LLOYD, SIR JOHN EDWARD *A History of Wales* (1930)

LOFTS, NORAH *Anne Boleyn* (1979)

LONGFORD, ELIZABETH *Victoria R.I.* (1964)

McNAUGHTON, ARNOLD *The Book of Kings, A Royal Genealogy* (1973)

MAGNUS, PHILIP *King Edward the Seventh* (1964)

MARIE LOUISE, H.H. PRINCESS *My Memories of Six Reigns* (1956)

MONTAGUE-SMITH, PATRICK W. *Queen Elizabeth The Queen Mother* (1985)

MORRIS, JOHN *The Age of Arthur* (1973); *Londinivm: London in the Roman Empire* (1982)

NICOLSON, HAROLD *King George V – His Life and Reign* (1952)

OMAN, CAROLA *Mary of Modena* (1962)

ONSLOW, EARL OF *The Empress Maud* (1939)

PANTER, HELEN *King Edgar* (1971)

PARRY, SIR EDWARD *Queen Caroline* (1970)

PEPYS, SAMUEL *The Diary of Samuel Pepys* (edited by R.C. Latham and W. Matthews) (1972)

POPE-HENNESSY, JAMES *Queen Mary* (1959)

POWICKE, F.M. *Handbook of British Chronology* (1939)

QUENNELL, PETER *Caroline of England* (1939)

RAISTRICK, ARTHUR *The Romans in Yorkshire* (1965)

ROSE, KENNETH *King George V* (1983)

The Royal Mausoleum, Frogmore Guide Book (1964)

SALZMAN, L.F. *Edward I* (1968)

SCARISBRICK, J.J. *Henry VIII* (1968)

SISAM, KENNETH *Anglo-Saxon Royal Genealogies* (Proceedings of the British Academy, Vol XXXIX)

SMITH, L.B. *A Tudor Tragedy – The Life and Times of Catherine Howard* (1961)

STALEY, EDGCUMBE *King René d'Anjou and his Seven Queens* (1912)

STRICKLAND, AGNES *Lives of the Queens of England* (1840-48, revised edition 1869)

STUART, DOROTHY MARGARET *The Daughters of George III* (1939); *The Mother of Victoria* (1942); *Daughter of England* (1951)

THORPE, LEWIS *The Bayeux Tapestry and the Norman Invasion* (1973)

TURNER, F.C. *James II* (1948)

VICTORIA, H.M. QUEEN *Letters*, edited by A.C. Benson and Viscount Esher (1907)

WARREN, W.L. *King John* (1961)

WEDGWOOD, C.V. *The Trial of Charles I* (1964)

WHEELER-BENNETT, J.W. *King George VI* (1958)

WINDSOR, H.R.H. THE DUKE OF *A King's Story* (1951)

WOODHAM-SMITH, CECIL *Queen Victoria – Her Life and Times* Vol I 1819-1861 (all published) (1972)

YEARSLEY, MACLEOD *Le Roy est Mort! An account of the deaths of the rulers of England* (1935)

ZIEGLER, PHILIP *William IV* (1971)

ACKNOWLEDGEMENTS

The publishers would like to thank the following for supplying illustrations:

Black and white

Ashmolean Museum   105
James Austin   45
Bristol Cathedral   78
British Library   16, 18, 26, 28, 29, 31 (left), 195
British Museum   20, 54, 80, 84, 92 (right), 108
British Tourist Authority   23
Burghley House Collection by kind permission of the Trustees   133
Central Press   198, 199, 200, 204
E.T. Archive   14 (above), 23, 82, 99, 105, 132, 135, 140, 179
Fox Photos   203, 205
Clive Hiche   22, 27, 32
J. Allan Cash   9, 12, 14 (below)
Keystone   189, 195, 201, 206, 208
Mansell Collection   11, 13, 15
National Maritime Museum   130
National Portrait Gallery   31 (right), 83, 87, 89, 92 (left), 97, 103, 104, 106, 107, 110, 121, 122, 124, 126, 127, 129, 132, 136, 145, 147, 148, 154, 158, 160, 161, 166, 178, 187
Her Majesty the Queen   109, 111, 135, 137, 139, 142, 143, 151, 163, 165, 167, 181, 184, 191, 193, 194
Rijksmuseum   149
Society of Antiquities   99
Warburg Institute   68, 74, 75, 77

Colour

Allan Cash   33 (above)
Ashmolean Museum   37 (below)
British Library   59 (above), 113 (left), 115 (above), 116 (above left)
British Museum   58 (below), 59 (below), 63 (below), 116 (below left)
E. T. Archive   63 (above), 169
Guildhall Library   60
Clive Hicks   37, 38
Michael Holford   34 (below), 35, 36, 40, 57 (above), 62, 64 (above), 113 (right)
A. F. Kersting   39 (below), 61
Keystone   172, 173, 174, 175
National Maritime Museum   119 (top)
National Portrait Gallery   115 (below), 119 (above)
The Royal Collection   117 (above), 119 (below), 169 (left)
Royal Naval College, Greenwich   120 (above)
Victoria and Albert Museum   117 (below)
Andy Williams   33 (below), 34 (above), 39 (above), 64 (below), 113 (below), 114, 116 (right), 120 (below), 170, 171

Index